Organizational Semiotics

This edited volume brings together two largely separate fields – organization studies and multimodal social semiotics – to develop an integrated research agenda for the novel interdisciplinary field of 'organizational semiotics'.

Organizations, whether for profit, non-profit, or governmental, dominate much of everyday life, and multimodal communication is not only an output of organizations but is also constitutive of them. This volume argues in particular for the importance of organization studies for social semioticians – not just as a site of application but also as a critical contemporary context that requires novel and expanded methods of analysis and critique and new practices of partnership. The volume addresses a range of institutions and sectors, from civil to retail to medical, from corporations to universities, and reveals how a deep engagement with their meaning-making practices produces insights not just about communication but also about the broader contemporary cultural context in which organizations play such a significant role. Fundamentally, it reveals that the rich analytical and theoretical resources of multimodal perspectives on organizations studies can – and should – make a fundamental contribution to our understanding of organizations in social life.

This volume is relevant to social semioticians and organizational researchers as well as to practitioners and decision-makers in organizations.

Louise Ravelli is Professor of Communication in the School of Arts and Media at UNSW Sydney. Her research explores how multimodality works in specific communication contexts, such as museums. She has published widely with monographs, edited volumes and articles, and is joint Chief Editor of the journal *Visual Communication*.

Theo van Leeuwen is Professor of Language and Communication at the University of Southern Denmark. He has published widely in the areas of visual communication, multimodality, and critical discourse analysis. His latest books are the third revised edition of *Reading Images – The Grammar of Visual Design* (with Gunther Kress) and *Multimodality and Identity*.

Markus A. Höllerer is Professor of Organization and Management at UNSW Sydney. His scholarly work currently focuses on social change, novel forms of organization and governance, and institutions as multimodal accomplishments. He has been widely published in leading academic outlets and is currently Editor-in-Chief of *Organization Theory*.

Dennis Jancsary is Assistant Professor at the Institute for Organization Studies at WU (Vienna University of Economics and Business). He is particularly interested in the role of language and multimodal communication at the interface of organizations and institutions. His work further includes methodological contributions to visual and multimodal analysis.

Routledge Studies in Multimodality
Edited by Kay L. O'Halloran, University of Liverpool

Titles include:

Genres and Intersemiotic Relations in Digital Science Communication
Carmen Pérez-Llantada and María José Luzón

Southernizing Sociolinguistics
Colonialism, Racism, and Patriarchy in Language in the Global South
Edited by Bassey E. Antia and Sinfree Makoni

Discourses, Modes, Media, and Meaning in an Era of Pandemic
A Multimodal Discourse Analysis Approach
Edited by Sabine Tan and Marissa K. L. E

Designing Learning for Multimodal Literacy
Teaching, Viewing, and Representing
Fei Victor Lim and Lydia Tan-Chia

Multilingualism from Manuscript to 3D
Intersections of Modalities from Medieval to Modern Times
Edited by Matylda Włodarczyk, Elżbieta Adamczyk, and Jukka Tyrkkö

Multimodal Experiences Across Cultures, Spaces, and Identities
Ayelet Kohn and Rachel Weissbrod

A Multimodal Stylistic Approach to Screen Adaptations of the Work of Alice Munro
Sabrina Francesconi

Multimodal Chinese Discourse
Understanding Communication and Society in Contemporary China
Dezheng (William) Feng

Organizational Semiotics
Multimodal Perspectives on Organization Studies
Edited by Louise Ravelli, Theo van Leeuwen, Markus A. Höllerer, and Dennis Jancsary

For more information about this series, please visit: https://www.routledge.com/Routledge-Studies-in-Multimodality/book-series/RSMM

Organizational Semiotics
Multimodal Perspectives on Organization Studies

Edited by Louise Ravelli,
Theo van Leeuwen, Markus A. Höllerer,
Dennis Jancsary

NEW YORK AND LONDON

First published 2023
by Routledge
605 Third Avenue, New York, NY 10158

and by Routledge
4 Park Square, Milton Park, Abingdon, Oxon, OX14 4RN

Routledge is an imprint of the Taylor & Francis Group, an informa business

© 2023 Taylor & Francis

The right of Louise Ravelli, Theo van Leeuwen, Markus A. Höllerer, and Dennis Jancsary to be identified as the authors of the editorial material, and of the authors for their individual chapters, has been asserted in accordance with sections 77 and 78 of the Copyright, Designs and Patents Act 1988.

All rights reserved. No part of this book may be reprinted or reproduced or utilised in any form or by any electronic, mechanical, or other means, now known or hereafter invented, including photocopying and recording, or in any information storage or retrieval system, without permission in writing from the publishers.

Trademark notice: Product or corporate names may be trademarks or registered trademarks, and are used only for identification and explanation without intent to infringe.

Library of Congress Cataloging-in-Publication Data
Title: Organizational semiotics : multimodal perspectives on organization studies / edited by Louise Ravelli, Theo Van Leeuwen, Markus A. Höllerer, Dennis Jancsary.
Description: New York, NY : Routledge, 2023. | Series: Routledge studies in multimodality | Includes bibliographical references and index. |
Identifiers: LCCN 2022052106 (print) | LCCN 2022052107 (ebook) |
Subjects: LCSH: Organizational sociology. | Semiotics–Social aspects. | Modality (Linguistics)
Classification: LCC HM711 .O7276 2023 (print) | LCC HM711 (ebook) | DDC 302.3/5–dc23/eng/20230130
LC record available at https://lccn.loc.gov/2022052106
LC ebook record available at https://lccn.loc.gov/2022052107

ISBN: 9780367504557 (hbk)
ISBN: 9781032469720 (pbk)
ISBN: 9781003049920 (ebk)

DOI: 10.4324/9781003049920

Typeset in Sabon
by Deanta Global Publishing Services, Chennai, India

Contents

List of Figures vii
List of Tables ix
Author biographies x

1 'Organizational semiotics': Toward an integrated research agenda 1
LOUISE RAVELLI, THEO VAN LEEUWEN, MARKUS A. HÖLLERER, AND DENNIS JANCSARY

2 Social semiotics and organization studies: Building an effective bridge 25
DENNIS JANCSARY, MARKUS A. HÖLLERER, LOUISE RAVELLI, AND THEO VAN LEEUWEN

3 The resemiotisation of health information in a family planning organization 54
THEO VAN LEEUWEN AND NIKOLINA ZONJIC

4 Organizational identity design: The evolution of a university web homepage 73
NATALIIA LABA

5 The emotional civil servant: On the multimodal construction of affect in 'platform of values' texts of Swedish public authorities 99
ANDERS BJÖRKVALL

6 Communicating in space: Relating the physical and the social in open-plan offices 122
KEN TANN AND OLUREMI B. AYOKO

7 Redesigning organizations through the built environment: Changes at a university campus 143
LOUISE RAVELLI

8 How multimodal structures constitute organization: The meaning of structure in offline and online shopping environments 166
MORTEN BOERIIS

9 'It's not just getting a biopsy': Transposing 'take-home' messages from the operating theatre to a proforma 190
ARPAN TAHIM AND JEFF BEZEMER

10 Texture and texturization in organizational identity design and legitimacy work 212
GIORGIA AIELLO

Afterword 231
THEO VAN LEEUWEN AND RENATE E. MEYER

Index 240

Figures

3.1	Screen shots from the *Know Your Health: Cervical Screening Test* videos (With permission, FPNSW 2019)	61
3.2	Cover of *Yarning about Girls Business* (With permission, FPNSW 2019)	64
3.3	Pages 1 and 2 of *The Low Down* (With permission, FPNSW 2019)	65
4.1	Organizational identity communication as a social semiotic practice	77
4.2	Early 'designs' of the UNSW web homepage: (left) V1, (right) V2. *Note.* Above the dotted line is the viewport (the part of the webpage visible on-screen, i.e., without scrolling)	80
4.3	V3 of the UNSW web homepage	81
4.4	Overt taxonomies in the viewport of V1	88
4.5	Overt and covert taxonomies in the viewport of V2	89
4.6	Key representational structures of V3	90
5.1	Platform of values from the Swedish National Road and Transport Research Institute (VTI)	107
5.2	Platform of values from the Riksbank (Sweden's central bank)	111
5.3	Handbook for the strategy process for leaders 2023–2027 from the Swedish Board of Agriculture (extract)	112
5.4	Platform of values from the Swedish Geotechnical Institute (SGI)	113
6.1	SSC office layout and reporting line	125
6.2	Relationship between spatial design and social practice (adapted from Martin and Rose 2007)	126
6.3	The SSC open-plan employee workspace	129
7.1	Campus map, with Quadrangle highlighted	152
7.2	Overview of the Quad (left) and walkways prior to renovation (middle and right) (Photograph by the author)	153

7.3	UNSW walkways in the Quad following renovation (Photograph by the author)	153
7.4	Self-binding (left); collaboration (right) (Photograph by the author)	156
8.1	Fixating the sign	175
8.2	TS1 search by salience (circles = fixations; lines = saccades)	177
8.3	Traversal hindered by other people	178
8.4	Alphabetical search	178
8.5	Leaflet search and employee-assisted search	179
8.6	Online searching	181
9.1	The surgical trainee's (T1) completed WBA form	195
9.2	Operating theatre environment in which this WBA occurred	199
9.3	Multimodal plot diagram transcribing this clinical activity with colour key	200
9.4	First excerpt showing how trainee and supervisor begin to visualise the tumour	202
9.5	Further attempts to visualise the tumour	202
9.6	The trainee (T1) takes an appropriate biopsy. Key for Figure 9.6a: A = metal tubing of scope; B = vocal cord; C = forceps; D = lesion (partially obscured by metal); E = space under vocal cords leading to windpipe	203
9.7	The supervisor highlights the purpose of the procedure that the trainee (T1) is about to perform	206
9.8	The trainee and supervisor explore the surgical field and begin to explore the implications for future surgical management	207
9.9	Supervisor uses the image on the screen to demonstrate where cuts might be made in a future procedure	207
10.1	A community table made from wood planks from an old boat in the 15th Avenue East Starbucks store in Seattle (Photograph by the author)	219
10.2	A full-length black and white photograph of burlap sacks on the side of the Starbucks store on the corner of Mortimer Street and Regent Street in London (Photograph by the author)	220
10.3	Blown up Starbucks logo on store window by the Old Street tube station in London (Photograph by the author)	221
10.4	Texturisation in stock images: (left) 'Transvestite Asian senior man dancing'; (right) 'Woman breaking the rules of gender' (With permission, Getty Images)	224

Tables

4.1	Historical versions of the UNSW homepage	79
4.2	Consistencies (in white) and absences (in grey) of the menu items	83
7.1	Metafunctional terminology across language, image, and the built environment	145
7.2	Key analytical questions for each metafunction (relevant to current analysis)	146
7.3	Relational meanings of the walkways in the Quad, pre-, and post- design changes	160
7.4	Contrasting positive and negative evaluations of the Quad	161
8.1	Contrast forms relevant for analysing salience in web texts and spatial texts (from Boeriis 2009, 237)	169
8.2	Salience types	171
8.3	Rank	173

Author biographies

Giorgia Aiello is Professor of Culture and Communication at the University of Leeds and Associate Professor of Sociology of Culture and Communication and the University of Bologna. Her books include *Communication, Espace, Image* (2022, Les Presses du Réel) and *Visual Communication: Understanding Images in Media Culture* (with Katy Parry, 2020, SAGE).

Oluremi (Remi) Ayoko is Associate Professor of Management in the UQ Business School at the University of Queensland, Australia. Her main research interest is the physical/virtual workspaces. Remi is the Editor-in-Chief of the *Journal of Management and Organization*. She has co-edited several books and published in high-quality journals.

Jeff Bezemer is Professor of Communication at the University College London Institute of Education. His research is focused on clinical communication and education and health care delivery and aimed at developing an account of the semiotics of health care and tools to support frontline staff. Central to this approach are theoretical advances in social semiotics, applied linguistics, and ethnography and the in-depth analysis of video recordings of professional activity.

Anders Björkvall has a PhD in Scandinavian Languages from Stockholm University and is Professor of Swedish at Örebro University, Sweden. His interests include organizational discourse, critical genre analysis, and semiotic change in urban landscapes. Recent publications have appeared in *The Cambridge Handbook of Discourse Studies*, *Discourse & Communication*, and *Visual Communication*.

Morten Boeriis has a PhD in multimodality and moving images. He is Associate Professor in Visual Communication at University of Southern Denmark, specialising in multimodality and business communication, and teaches undergraduate, post-graduate and doctoral courses on visual communication at Business Communication and Film and Media studies at University of Southern Denmark.

Author biographies xi

Markus A. Höllerer is Professor of Organization and Management at UNSW Sydney. His scholarly work currently focuses on social change, novel forms of organization and governance, and institutions as multimodal accomplishments. He has been widely published in leading academic outlets and is currently Editor-in-Chief of *Organization Theory*.

Dennis Jancsary is Assistant Professor at the Institute for Organization Studies at WU (Vienna University of Economics and Business). He is particularly interested in the role of language and multimodal communication at the interface of organizations and institutions. His work further includes methodological contributions to visual and multimodal analysis.

Nataliia Laba is a PhD Candidate in Media Studies at UNSW Sydney. Her research focuses on organizational identities communicated on university websites from a multimodal social semiotic perspective.

Renate E. Meyer is Professor of Organization Studies at WU (Vienna University of Economics and Business), Head of the Institute for Organization Studies, and Co-Director of the Research Institute for Urban Management & Governance. She holds visiting positions at Saïd Business School (Oxford University), Copenhagen Business School, the University of Alberta, and the University of Liverpool.

Louise Ravelli is Professor of Communication in the School of Arts and Media at UNSW Sydney. Her research explores how multimodality works in specific communication contexts, such as museums. She has published widely with monographs, edited volumes and articles, and is joint Chief Editor of the journal *Visual Communication*.

Arpan Tahim is a specialty trainee in Oral and Maxillofacial Surgery with an interest in medical education. His research focuses on workplace learning in health care environments, where he uses ethnographic techniques and in-depth video analysis to better understand how workplace learning practices unfold and impact learners.

Ken Tann is Lecturer in Communication Management at UQ Business School, University of Queensland, Australia. His research applies linguistics and sociological methods to management, organizational, and marketing communication and to educational contexts. He has published on communication in business and non-governmental partnership, institutional policy, industry media representation, and open-plan office design.

Theo van Leeuwen is Professor of Language and Communication at the University of Southern Denmark. He has published widely in the areas of visual communication, multimodality, and critical discourse analysis. His latest books are the third revised edition of *Reading Images – The Grammar of Visual Design* (with Gunther Kress) and *Multimodality and Identity*.

Nikolina Zonjic is a public health professional working in Sydney, Australia. While working as the Health Promotion Manager at Family Planning NSW, she oversaw health promotion programs aimed at improving sexual health for priority populations, including culturally diverse communities, Indigenous Australians, people with disability, and young people.

1 'Organizational semiotics'
Toward an integrated research agenda

Louise Ravelli, Theo van Leeuwen, Markus A. Höllerer, and Dennis Jancsary

Introduction

Modern society is a society of organizations, with practices of organization and organising regulating, enhancing, frustrating, and enabling all spheres of life. Organizations are, therefore, socially critical sites of study.

But what do we mean by *organization*? An organization may be formal or informal, large or small, for-profit or not-for-profit, or commercial, governmental, or social. An organization may be housed in a building, but it is not a physical entity, even if the nature of the building and how that building is used may well contribute to the organization's identity and purpose. An organization must necessarily consist of people, but it is more than a group of individuals. An organization may produce specific documents, but it is more than a collection of textual outputs. It may have its own logo, website, or corporate uniform, but it is more than its visual branding.

In this volume, we wish to argue that organizations are, in fact, complexes of meaning-making practices. They communicate meanings that are multiple, multifaceted, multimodal, social, and contextual. These meaning-making practices enact relationships – hierarchies, departmental divisions, teams, roles, and responsibilities as well as external relations. At the same time, such meaning-making practices legitimate the very nature and purpose of an organization – for example, through the strategic documents, mission and vision statements, performance appraisals, and annual reports that play such a large role in creating and maintaining organizational cultures. In the words of Meyer (2017, n.p.), organizations are 'inherently semiotic entities'.

Semiotics – the study of meaning-making – is, thus, an essential framework for a scholarly understanding of organizations. Semiotics is a way of documenting semiotic resources, investigating their use, and contributing to new resources and practices (van Leeuwen 2005, 3; see also van Leeuwen 2008, 2011, 2021). Crucially, the meanings made in and by organizations are always socially contextualised, whether that be in the micro-moments of interaction between individuals or the macro-moments of large-scale institutional operations. Society and culture routinely shape the processes and products of meaning-making, and such processes and products, in turn, shape society and culture.

Thus, our approach to semiotics is that of *social semiotics* – a way of studying meaning that foregrounds the intertwined nature of social context and specific meaning-making practices. Boxenbaum and her colleagues, in their editorial for a special issue on the *Material and Visual Turn in Organization Studies*, refer to this intertwining as 'the constitutive relationships that exist between the material realm and the social realm' (Boxenbaum et al. 2018, 601). They refer to Paul M. Leonardi's 2012 chapter, 'Materiality, Sociomateriality, and Socio-Technical Systems: what Do These Terms Mean? How Are They Related? Do We Need Them?', which states: 'All materiality ... is social in that it was created through social processes and it is interpreted and used in social contexts, and ... all social action is possible because of some materiality' (Leonardi 2012, 32, quoted in Boxenbaum et al. 2018, 601). Yet they also note a lack of knowledge about 'detailing how the social realm and the material realm become intertwined, and what effect these processes have on organizational practice' (Boxenbaum et al. 2018, 601). Social semiotics aims to identify the different strands of this complex intertwining between the social and the material and to find ways to use the material as explicit evidence for claims about the social.

Importantly, the 'material' of organizations is necessarily *multimodal* (Höllerer et al. 2019). A face-to-face interaction such as an interview, a performance appraisal, or a meeting comes not only with talk in a specific setting but also with intonation, facial expression, gesture, posture, and self-presentation by means of dress and grooming. When such interactions move online, all these elements might be materialised slightly differently, and other elements may be added, such as the framing of the speaker, the presence of icons to indicate particular meeting functions (e.g., the 'raise hand' function), or a break-out room to enable parallel communication. Similarly, the written textual products of an organization make meaning not only with words but also with images, layout, colour, and typography; and if such written products are online, then perhaps also with hyperlinks and audio-visual components. All these semiotic practices take place in environments that have been designed or arranged to facilitate them, drawing on a range of meaning-making resources – spatial arrangements, texture, colour, and, at times, even scent and aroma. Additionally, multimodality is a constitutive element of the 'sociality' of organizations. The hierarchy of an organization can be materialised in multiple ways: who gets the corner office, and who sits at a cubicle alongside many others; who gets to speak first in a meeting, and who has to wait; who gets to sign off on a document, and who creates it; who abides by the implicit dress code, and who joins in for 'casual Friday'.

Thus, any understanding of the semiotic nature of organizations must account for both multimodality and sociality. We argue that organizations cannot be fully understood without accounting for their multimodal and socially contextualised communicative practices and that multimodal social semiotic studies need to account for the semiotic nature of organizations as socially critical sites of our contemporary world. We come to this project from both sides: van Leeuwen and Ravelli from social semiotics and Höllerer and Jancsary from organization and management studies. Through aspects of our individual and shared work (e.g., Höllerer, Daudigeos, and Jancsary 2018; Höllerer et al. 2019; Jancsary, Höllerer, and Meyer 2016; Meyer et al. 2013), we see the enormous potential of this agenda and the frustrations of it being insufficiently realised. The primary aim of this volume, then, is to bring organization studies and multimodal, social semiotic research together in an integrated framework that we label *organizational semiotics*. More than simply using organizations as a site of application, organizational semiotics aims to effectively bridge the theories and methodologies of both organization studies and multimodal social semiotics in ways that allow the reach of both to be extended and nuanced. To elaborate this agenda, we now turn to some of the foundational 'building blocks' and concepts of this approach. We will unpack organizational semiotics in more detail in Chapter 2.

A social semiotic perspective on multimodality

Multimodal communication

We understand communication, in the broad sense of the term, as comprising all externalisations of social meaning, whether purpose-driven or incidental, in any mode or medium. This includes face-to-face communication as much as corporate slogans and guidelines but also dress codes and office layout, among other instances. From such a perspective, communication holds organizations together and is even constitutive of them (e.g., Ashcraft, Kuhn, and Cooren 2009; Cooren et al. 2014; Schoeneborn 2011). Streams of communication organise, coordinate, classify, and animate interactions between people, practices, and artefacts within and across organizations; communication also interweaves organizations and their cultural and institutional environments (e.g., Cornelissen et al. 2015; Meyer and Vaara 2020). Communicative acts and artefacts exert environmental pressures on organizations and legitimate those that conform to these expectations; organizations, in turn, design communicative practices and artefacts to protect their 'license to operate', increase their reputation, and project certain identities. Communication also creates, establishes, and sustains broader discourses in the societal environment of organizations (e.g., Phillips, Lawrence, and Hardy 2004), resulting in specific understandings of organizational roles and societal expectations. Accordingly, communication shapes meanings and interactions within organizations, across organizations, and between organizations and their broader environments.

As noted earlier, communication is necessarily multimodal. This is not a new phenomenon, but it is a relatively new observation. Until recently, communication theories have largely overlooked what we might call 'implicit' multimodality: the co-presence of multiple semiotic resources that are so integrated as to not be noticed. Thus, in terms of written language, the focus has largely been on lexical, grammatical, and discoursal patterns as the conveyors of meaning, with little attention being given to its material and visual aspects. These, however, are intrinsic to the overall meanings being communicated (e.g., Johannessen and van Leeuwen 2018; Nørgaard 2018). More recently, the digital age has further highlighted what we might call 'explicit' multimodality: the evident co-presence of multiple semiotic resources, as in a webpage that combines images, layout, and writing as a single communicative text. Such development has forced communication theorists to take greater account of multimodality and to broaden the scope of what counts as 'communication' (e.g., Bateman, Wildfeuer, and Hiipala 2017; Kress and van Leeuwen 2021). In this volume, we attend to communication in many forms, from the design of a brochure for a public health campaign to the placement of furniture in a university learning environment. The focus shifts from the details of semiotic artefacts such as logos and websites to the details of semiotic practices such as wayfinding in a bookstore and surgical training, in which small gestures can be infused with distinct meanings.

From semiotics to social semiotics

While communication theories have insufficiently attended to multimodality as a phenomenon, the broad field of semiotics has certainly had some significant engagement with it. Throughout the twentieth century, different branches of semiotics developed conceptual and methodological resources for understanding various multimodal semiotic practices. Prague School semioticians focused on the arts in the 1930s and 1940s, a period when avant-garde artists were foreshadowing the rise of multimodality. Paris School semiotics focused on popular culture and the mass media in the 1960s, when television began to make its impact. Social semiotics, from the late 1980s onward, focused on newly emerging digital forms of communication as well as on multimodality more generally.

At least one area of organizational communication practice has also been a consistent focus for semiotic studies: advertising. As early as 1932, the Prague School semiotician Jan Mukařovský commented on the use of 'poetic language' in advertising, in which 'euphonic sequences' and 'unusual patterns' serve to 'attract attention first to the wording, and then to the thing advertised' (1964 [1932], 39), and Roland Barthes's (1977) analysis of the use of words and pictures in an advertisement for Panzani pasta has become a classic in semiotic literature. The first International Conference in Semiotics and Marketing was held in 1986, co-organised by Indiana University's Research Centre for Language and Semiotic Studies and the

J.L. Kellogg Graduate School of Management in Evanston, Illinois, which resulted in a seminal anthology titled *Marketing and Semiotics – New Directions in the Study of Signs for Sale* (Umiker-Sebeok 1987). As Umiker-Sebeok aptly noted in her introduction, semioticians and marketing scholars discovered that they were 'all studying the same thing – message production and consumption' and that their 'different research traditions are complementary' (1987, xi). As a result, marketing and consumer research began to recognise the importance of product meanings and their cultural contexts. And while in the United States, studies of this kind would remain methodologically eclectic, in Europe, they became a branch of structuralist semiotics, focusing, for the most part, on the 'message' as 'the point of passage which supports the social circulation of significations' (Véron, quoted in Umiker-Sebeok 1987, x). This also led to commercial applications of semiotics, whether as a form of 'diagnosis' of marketing strategies (Magariños de Morentin 1987) or as a tool for 'organizing and focusing meaning associated with the brand, the consumer and culture in order to achieve strategic goals', as formulated in *Marketing Semiotics* (Oswald 2012, 1), a key text in the field. Oswald emphasised the structuralist concept of 'codes' as articulating 'the inchoate mass of phenomena we call reality into cultural categories and meanings' (11), and hence as a key to understanding how marketing can rely on 'collective perceptions and behaviours in the market place' (19).

Social semiotics, however, departed from structuralist semiotics due to its pronounced emphasis on the social. As Hodge and Kress wrote in the introduction of their pioneering book:

> Mainstream semiotics' emphasizes structures and codes at the expense of functions and social uses of semiotic systems [...]. It stresses systems and codes rather than speakers and writers or other participants in semiotic activity as connected and interacting in a variety of ways in concrete social contexts. It attributes power to meaning instead of meaning to power. It dissolves boundaries within the field of semiotics, but tacitly accepts an impenetrable wall cutting off semiotics from society and from social and political thought.
>
> (Hodge and Kress 1988, 1–2)

It is this wall that social semiotics seeks to penetrate, and for that reason, it does not trace its origins to Saussure, as do structuralist semioticians, but to Malinowski (1923, 1935) who introduced two concepts that became crucial in social semiotics: 'Context of situation' and 'context of culture'. Malinowski saw language as inextricably intertwined with situational contexts with practical activities, such as fishing or gardening as well as with narrative and ritual practices, and he broadened his definition of language to include 'not only spoken words, but also facial expression, gesture, bodily activities, the whole group of people present during an exchange of utterances, and the environment in which these people are engaged' (1935, 22), recommending the use of sound film, then a new medium, to study 'fully contextualized utterances' (2).

Social semiotics, therefore, foregrounds *practices* rather than *structures*. While many linguists and semioticians have described language as a layered structure ('stratification'), Kress and van Leeuwen (2001), inspired by Goffman (1981), focus not on 'language' but on embodied and material linguistic practices – speech and writing – describing them as sequences of practices, such as designing, producing, disseminating, recording etc., which may be integrated in some contexts but organised via specific divisions of labour in others. Thus, an individual may plan (design) and deliver (produce) a speech at a meeting; or the speech may be written by one person and delivered by another, to be recorded by a third and then edited by a fourth for further dissemination. Each aspect of 'the' speech is a specific social practice.

Particularly important is Malinowski's emphasis on recontextualisation. In his appendix to Ogden and Richards's *The Meaning of Meaning* (Malinowski 1923), Malinowski described how fishing, as practiced by the Trobriand islanders, whose culture he studied, was recontextualised in stories *about* fishing, enacted in the different context of storytelling, which introduced a different purpose: 'Justifying the social order' and 'regulating conduct in relation to hunger, sex, economic values' (Malinowski 1935, 7). These stories, in turn, were recontextualised in what he called 'the language of ritual and magic' – verbal acts that 'exercise a powerful influence on social organizing' (9), perhaps not entirely unlike today's vision and mission statements.

Finally, equally important is Malinowski's concept of 'context of culture', which Halliday (1985) summarised as 'the whole cultural history behind the kind of practices [people] are engaging in, determining their significance for the culture, whether practical or ritual' (6). To study the context of culture, social semiotics must connect with social theory and with social, cultural, and political history – i.e., with resources that can explain *why* semiotic practices and products are the way they are. In Saussure, society had remained an 'inscrutably powerful collective being' (Hodge and Kress 1988, 22). And, though Peirce (1982) emphasised the process of semiosis and had a dialogic conception of language, he presented this as 'a fact of personal psychology, without explicit roots in the social process' (Hodge and Kress 1988, 20). With its emphasis on social practices, social semiotics chose a different path. Nevertheless, it also retained much that was valuable in the theoretical concepts and analytical practices of earlier semiotics, especially its emphasis on developing 'ways of semiotically describing and explaining the processes and structures through which meaning is constituted' (Hodge and Kress 1988, 2).

One other fundamental innovation of social semiotics was its adoption of Halliday's 'metafunctions' – overarching clusters of meaning that serve different communicative functions (Halliday 1978; Halliday and Matthiessen 2014). For Halliday, meaning is not of one type but of several different types all co-existing in mutually informing layers. Halliday calls these the *interpersonal*, *ideational*, and *textual* metafunctions, synonymous with 'meanings'. Respectively, these metafunctions *enact* social relations, *construe* human experience, and *enable* communication, and they do so by drawing on different and distinct linguistic resources. Resources for interpersonal meaning-making, for instance, include forms of address (e.g., personal pronouns), speech acts (e.g., mood choices, such as declarative, interrogative, and imperative), and much more. This approach was subsequently applied to other semiotic modes, such as visual communication (Kress and van Leeuwen 2021), illuminating the specific resources of images that enable interpersonal meanings, such as gaze; and it has been applied to the built environment (Ravelli and McMurtrie 2016), in which resources such as height on the vertical plane can construe interpersonal meanings. As a result, social semiotics has built up a set of analytical frameworks that allow claims about meaning to be grounded in material evidence. While social semiotics is itself not a singular or monolithic theory, many of the chapters in this volume make use of a metafunctional approach to meaning, exploring either one aspect in depth and detail or analysing all three functions simultaneously.

Largely as a result of Halliday's influence, one of the main attributes of a social semiotic approach to communication is that it is seen as 'appliable' (Mahboob and Knight 2012; Martin 2016) – that is, relevant to and revealing of actual communicative texts, processes, and practices, be they historical or contemporary, as opposed to idealised forms of communication or complex theorisations that bear little relation to actual communication. As van Leeuwen (2005, 1) remarks, social semiotics 'only comes into its own when it is applied to specific instances and specific problems, and it always requires immersing oneself not just in semiotic concepts and methods as such but also in some other field'. One of the key areas of interest and application for social semioticians has been that of education. Much work has been devoted to the written and spoken texts of education – those of students, teachers, and educational resources – but also to education in its multimodal dimensions, including its visual resources in print and digital forms, classroom designs, the embodied nature of teaching and learning, and the discipline-specific attributes of pedagogical resources across age groups (see Doran 2018; Jewitt 2009; Kress, Jewitt, and Ogborn 2001; Lim 2019; Myskow 2018; Painter, Martin, and Unsworth 2013; Unsworth and Thomas 2014, to cite some indicative examples).

As with structuralist semioticians, another area of application for social semioticians has been that of advertising (e.g., Baldry and Thibault 2006; Molnar 2019; Roderick 2013; van Leeuwen et al. 2016). But, inspired by Fairclough (1993), who forcefully argued that marketing discourse is gradually 'colonising' other forms of discourse, they have also begun to study the multimodal semiotic practices of organizations, such as office, shop, and museum design (Aiello and Dickinson 2014; Ravelli 2006; Roderick 2016; van Leeuwen 2005), the use of diagrams in organizational strategies (Ledin and Machin 2016) as well as the nature of company logos (Johannessen 2017), the reorganization of academic work on sites such as ResearchGate (Djonov and van Leeuwen 2018), and the use of music in fashion stores (Graakjær 2012) to mention just a few examples. In such work, these scholars have tentatively begun to do what Umiker-Sebeok propagated more than 30 years ago when she argued that marketers and semioticians should begin to 'question their "received" research techniques and theory' and to 'delve into each other's literatures' (1987, x). This volume at hand intends to represent a moment in that development.

However, what has largely been missing in social semiotic 'applications', at least beyond the domain of education, is an appreciation of just what it is that multimodal social semiotics can bring *to* organizations, or put another way, what it can reveal *about* organizations (as well as processes of organising and those being organised). From our point of view, the potential for multimodal social semiotics engaging with organization and management is substantial – but the full potential of this is, as yet, untapped.

Organizations, organising, and the organised

In the spirit of van Leeuwen's (2005) call for social semioticians to immerse themselves in the fields in which semiotic processes are applied, we wish to provide a brief discussion of organization(s) as well as specific instances and problems of organization that lend themselves to a deeper social semiotic engagement.

Delineating organization(s)

While a precise and exhaustive definition of 'organization' is difficult and nigh impossible considering the plethora of different organizational forms and phenomena that populate the contemporary social world, there are a number of commonly agreed definitions that might serve as excellent starting points for our endeavour.

An 'institutional' definition sees organizations as a specific type of social collective and form of association that can be usefully distinguished from other collectives, such as families, professions, social movements, or informal groups. These social collectives are characterised by associative membership and perceived as some kind of 'entity' with relatively identifiable boundaries to the outside world (e.g., Santos and Eisenhardt 2005). Such collectives are goal-directed; that is, they are founded and maintained in pursuit of an overarching goal (e.g., Daft 2015; Tolbert and Hall 2015). Organizations are, furthermore, designed in the form of deliberately structured and coordinated systems of activities. Such coordination relies on formal structure, systems and processes, routines, cultural norms, and formal as well as informal rules. Finally, organizations are embedded in an 'environment' that they interact with regularly and often in systematic ways (e.g., contracts, partnerships, public relations). Such a definition means that organizations are captured as distinct social entities with relatively clear boundaries and prolonged duration. It allows an understanding of organizations as distinct types of social actors and imbues them with legal rights and obligations.

An alternative definition is an 'instrumental' one, which focuses on activities and processes of organising. From this perspective, organization means both the managerial task to structure and guide activities in a way that ensures the achievement of goals and the configuration of certain elements or parameters of organizational design. These elements include structure, culture, goals, processes/activities, technology, organizational members(hip), and organizational forms. The institutional definition of organization suggests that 'formal' organizations are a distinct type of association that needs to be distinguished from others; the instrumental definition, on the other hand, suggests that organization, as a principle and an activity, happens in a variety of types of social collectives. Both definitions also highlight 'the organised' – that is, the people subjected to organization(s) – which includes organizational members but also people outside the formal framework of a distinct organization.

Some researchers (e.g., Ahrne and Brunsson 2011, 2019) have, therefore, suggested that there is 'organization outside of organizations'. They argue that organizational analysis can also be usefully applied to social collectives that do not satisfy the criteria of 'formal' organizations. These criteria, they claim, are formal membership, a defined hierarchy, and clear rules as well as practices of monitoring rule-following and practices of sanctioning deviant behaviour. In formal organizations, all these elements are deliberately designed; however, 'partial' organizations do exist with some of these elements being designed, while others are constantly emerging. This is true, for instance, for different types of network organizations (e.g., open source software communities; see, for instance, Barberio et al. 2018; O'Mahony and Ferraro 2007), social movements (e.g., the 'Anonymous' collective; see, for instance, Dobusch and Schoeneborn 2015), and platform organizations (e.g., in the sharing economy or as crowd-funding initiatives; see, for instance, Vith et al. 2019; Logue and Grimes 2022), in which membership may be fluid rather than formalised and hierarchies minimal. Often, these partial organizations are held together by a shared identity rather than a legal and/or contractual framework. The trend toward partial organizations coincides with a global trend of rationalisation and formalisation, in which organizations increasingly have become the dominant mode of association in a globalised society (e.g., Bromley and Meyer 2015; Meyer and Bromley 2013) and that subjects ever more spheres of life (such as education, art, family, religion, etc.) to formal organization.

The chapters in this volume all relate to the 'institutional' perspective on organizations, in that they identify them, for instance, as Swedish public authorities, hospitals in the United Kingdom, or Australian universities. But all the chapters also provide insights that are potentially relevant to instrumental understandings of organization, for example, in terms of multiple ways in which 'identity' and 'affect' may be construed in the members of an organization or how the arrangement of furniture can contribute to specific social relations. It is our hope that, individually and collectively, these chapters will inspire considerable further research in a wide variety of organizational domains.

Multimodal aspects of organizational instances

Organizations are genuinely multimodal phenomena and, therefore, conducive to multimodal analysis. While Chapter 2 will discuss in greater detail how various aspects of organization(s) need to be understood from a multimodal social semiotic perspective, the general arguments can already be sketched here. From its very beginning, the study of organizations has existed in a generative tension between the macro- and the micro-level of analysis: cultural legitimacy and technical efficiency as well as stability and dynamism (e.g., Hinings and Meyer 2018). Far from being narrowly focused on organizational efficiency and financial profit, organizational issues and problems emerge in a variety of forms and arenas, from micro-level interactions of individuals to the cultural and institutional macro-environments within which organizations operate. Within the more micro-level and instrumentally focused perspective, there have been attempts to identify 'universal' problems of organising, such as, for instance, task allocation and task division (i.e., division of labour) or the provision of rewards and information (i.e., integration of effort) (Puranam, Alexy, and Reitzig 2014). While the universality of these problems may well be debatable, they provide an excellent starting point to engage with organization as a managerial task. From a more macro-level, institutional perspective, relationships between organizations as distinct societal actors and their (cultural) environments come to the fore. This raises questions of conformity with societal expectations (e.g., Meyer and Rowan 1977) or the sweeping adoption of 'novel' and 'rational' organizational practices and structures (e.g., DiMaggio and Powell 1983).

Shared across these two perspectives is the insight that organizations are *sites* of communication as well as *products* of communication (e.g., Meyer and Vaara 2020; Schoeneborn 2011). What is important from a social semiotic perspective is that organizations come with specific sets of multimodal semiotic resources and artefacts. Formal structures that address the tension between division of labour and integration of effort, for instance, manifest in elaborate charts or in spatial and material designs. Organizational hierarchies can be expressed in the aesthetics of office design, dress codes, and architectural layout (e.g., the 'corner office'). Activities and processes, likewise, are visually designed in charts and diagrams and materially instantiated in architecture, both physically and virtually. Organizational culture as an alternative mechanism of integration manifests in logos, slogans, visual imagery, office decoration, the design of meeting rooms, and a variety of other artefacts. This means that organizations are multimodally constituted but, at the same time, create and adapt their own specific practices and artefacts of multimodal communication.

Pioneering research in organization theory – including our own – has studied, for instance, how the visual and the verbal provide different affordances for the institutionalisation and diffusion of novel organizational ideas and practices (Meyer et al. 2018), how the news media combine visual and verbal resources to make sense of broader socio-economic phenomena (e.g., Höllerer, Jancsary, and Grafström 2018; Klein and Amis 2021), or how organizations mobilise combinations of visual and verbal text to claim the legitimacy or illegitimacy of certain practices (e.g., Höllerer et al. 2013; Lefsrud, Graves, and Phillips 2018). While these studies consider the benefit of observing the interaction of individual modes, they are still mainly restricted to combinations of visual and verbal text. Additional modes that have been considered in the context of organization studies – but mostly in isolation – are, for instance, materiality (e.g., Jarzabkowski, Spee, and Smets 2013; Jones and Massa 2013; Leonardi and Barley 2010; de Vaujany et al. 2019), space (e.g., Beyes and Steyaert 2012; Kingma, Dale, and Wasserman 2018; Wasserman and Frenkel 2015), and scent (e.g., Gümüsay, Höllerer, and Meyer 2018; Islam, Endrissat, and Noppeney 2016; Riach and Warren 2015).

Although substantial progress in organization studies has been made in moving from a purely verbal understanding of communication toward a more genuinely multimodal research agenda (e.g., Höllerer et al. 2019; Zilber 2018), several issues and challenges remain. Most generally, no shared understanding of multimodality exists, as of yet, within organization studies. Akin to the biblical story about the 'Tower of Babel', organizational researchers have drawn inspiration from a variety of disciplines and created different theoretical and methodological approaches toward multimodality. While this is certainly not a problem in itself and has led to substantial creativity and innovation, it complicates communication across different communities of scholars, as the same terminology often means very different things and refers to quite different theoretical traditions. Additionally, some of these approaches tend to 'ascribe essential qualities' to individual modes (van Leeuwen 2018, 239); for instance, the verbal is seen as the language of enlightenment, education, and knowledge, while the visual stands for emotion and affect. Finally, facing a lack of established multimodal 'tools' and procedures for organizational analysis, organizational researchers are mostly creating idiosyncratic methodologies from scratch. This presents certain challenges, for instance, regarding the varying degrees of explicitness and accessibility of different modes in terms of how they convey social meanings and how to combine meanings from quite different modes into a single analysis (e.g., Forgues and May 2018). Incorporating a social semiotic approach within organization studies has the potential to provide detailed tools for analysis (e.g., Jancsary, Höllerer, and Meyer 2016) and an enhanced understanding of meaning.

The chapters in this volume aim to build on the prior work of both the traditions of social semiotics and organization studies to highlight what a genuine, deep study of multimodal communication in organizations might be able to reveal. However, beyond demonstrating the potential for social and multimodal accounts of communication in organizations, we also wish to develop an approach that integrates the disciplinarity of both multimodal social semiotics and organization studies. The next section elaborates this point.

Toward an integrated theory of organizational semiotics

The cornerstones of organizational semiotics

We have introduced *organizational semiotics* here as a novel interdisciplinary research program that integrates a systematic social semiotic approach to multimodal communication with established insights from organizational research. The term itself, however, is not entirely new and has been used since at least the late 1990s in relation to the use of semiotic approaches in the development of business information systems; there, it refers to 'the semiotic nature of information systems in organizational contexts' (Clarke 2001, 76; see also Cooren 1999; Jorna 2009; Liu et al. 2002; Liu and Li 2014). While information systems are evidently a key meaning-making resource of organizations and organizational processes, our approach conceives of organizations and their meaning-making resources far more broadly. In fact, we use the term organizational semiotics (based on social semiotic theory) as an umbrella term for an approach that sees multimodal communication as being not just an output of organizations but also a fundamental constituent of them that is both shaped by and shaping organizational structures, processes, practices, and relations. Accordingly, organizations are not just 'physical' but also meaning-making entities – with meanings being tri-functional (i.e., representational, interactional, compositional) and constituted multimodally in materiality, structures, and processes.

At the core of our approach to organizational semiotics is an understanding of organizations as managed complexes of semiotic practices, united by an overall purpose, structure, and a set of cultural values. For the research agenda of organizational semiotics, this implies a focus on (a) the semiotic resources used in organizational practices, their functional potential, and their potential for expressing and enacting meanings and values as well as their histories; (b) the roles of these resources in specific (complexes of) organizational practices, including how their use is understood, maintained, legitimated, critiqued, and changed; and (c) the ways in which new semiotic resources and new roles of existing semiotic resources can be developed with the objectives of improving and innovating organizational and/or management practices.

With this purpose and these foci in mind, our approach to organizational semiotics builds on four core assumptions.

- Organizational elements (e.g., structure, culture, goals, processes/activities, technology, organizational membership, organizational forms, etc.) are meaningful; that is, they are imbued with social meanings that influence how these aspects are evaluated, adopted, and managed.
- Organizational-level systems of meanings are influenced and influence broader societal meaning structures: organizations and their cultural and institutional environments co-constitute each other. To study organizations is to study society, and to study society is, in turn, to study organizations.
- Organizational-level meanings are socially constructed; that is, they are constantly (re)negotiated in organizational, field-level, and broader societal contexts and develop in historically and locally distinct trajectories. Organizational semiotics is, therefore, also interested in the processes and very practices through which these meanings (as well as the semiotic resources by which these meanings are evoked) emerge, stabilise, and change.
- Organizational-level meanings manifest textually (in the broadest sense) in tangible instantiations of multimodal sign systems (i.e., documents, images, spaces, buildings, etc.). These textual cues are constantly 'read', 'interpreted', and 'manipulated' in practice. A good manager, therefore, to some degree, needs to be a social semiotician (see Chapter 2).

These core assumptions further imply that organizational semiotics needs to be more than just a methodological approach to organizational phenomena but a conceptual and theoretical complement to organization theory. It draws on, but also advances, existing conceptual and theoretical achievements of organizational theory and relates to core organizational themes such as organizational design and capabilities, legitimacy, or environmental fit from a social semiotic perspective. In other words, organizational semiotics highlights and advances the semiotic aspects of organizational realities without ignoring or replacing existing insights in organization theory. Conversely, a more nuanced and contextually grounded understanding of multimodality is also enabled. From an organizational semiotics perspective, multimodality is instantiated in complex intersections of structures, processes, practices, and relations. It is through multimodal practices that issues and phenomena of organization and management become accessible for conceptual and empirical research.

Finally, our aim to use intersections of organization studies and social semiotics as a platform for fundamental implications in both will hopefully allow researchers to move beyond the relative autonomy of disciplines that characterises much interdisciplinary research. Novotny (1997) has referred to such an autonomous approach as 'pluri-disciplinarity', characterised by co-operation and collaboration between disciplines on shared interests, without fundamental change in the originating disciplines. In contrast, our editorial team brings together scholars from organization studies, who have substantially engaged with social semiotics and multimodality, and social semioticians, who have substantially engaged with organizations. Our shared research agenda builds on common interests in materiality, innovation, and meaning design. At the same time, it also seeks to fundamentally reorient the focus and methods of each originating discipline: organization studies toward deep engagement with communicative texts, using rigorous analytical frameworks and social semiotics toward deep engagement with the specific contexts of organizations, its practitioners, and the explanatory concepts used in organizational research. Organizational semiotics should be something new, for both. Given that organizations are a dominant model of association and a dominant source of values across literally all spheres of modern societies, organizational semiotics is well positioned to contribute significant insights to our understanding of contemporary social and cultural life.

Implications for both social semioticians and organizational researchers

There are multiple ways in which organization studies might change social semiotics and social semiotics change organization studies. One of the key areas that stands out in this regard is the conceptualisation of 'context'. As already discussed in this chapter, context is a fundamental concept in social semiotics. In a social semiotic approach, language is not to be studied as an autonomous system but in relation to the contexts in which it is used. As Halliday has said: 'We attempt to relate language primarily to one particular aspect of human experience, namely that of social structure' (1985, 4), and the words we exchange 'get their meaning from activities in which they are embedded, which again are social activities with social agencies' (5). Equally important is the broader 'context of culture'. We cannot understand social communication without 'the total cultural background', without taking into account not only 'the immediate sights and sounds surrounding an event but also the whole cultural history behind the participants, and behind the kind of practices they are engaging in, determining their significance for the culture, whether practical or ritual' (6). All this applies in equal measure to the multimodal extensions of Halliday's theory.

However, while social semiotics has developed detailed frameworks for the analysis of linguistic and multimodal texts, detailed frameworks of this kind have not been developed for the analysis of contexts. Although Halliday's concepts of field (the activities taking place), tenor (the relationships involved), and mode (the communicative resources used) are useful, their application in contextual analyses has often been impressionistic rather than based on methodical and well-documented social inquiry. Even less detailed attention has been paid to the cultural context and to the historical considerations that should be an integral part of it. Van Leeuwen (2005, 3) has argued that history is fundamental to an understanding of semiotic resources, whether these histories cover a relatively short time span, as in Iedema's (2001, 2003a) study of resemiotisation, in which semiotic resources and meanings are reshaped from one social practice, such as a planning meeting, to another, such as a blueprint for a design, or whether they cover a longer time span, as in the same author's history of organizational discourse from early Mesopotamian writing to Fordism and the recent 'post-bureaucratic' turn (Iedema 2003b, ch 1). In organization studies, on the other hand, the importance of history is, by now, well recognised (e.g., Clark and Rowlinson 2004; Kieser 1994; Maclean, Harvey, and Clegg 2016; Wadhwani et al. 2018). Cartel, Colombero, and Boxenbaum (2018), for instance, in a fascinating study of the 'theorisation' of reinforced concrete, show how such 'theories' initially focused on technical functionality, then moved to the expression of the values associated with this new building material, before, finally, in the mid-1970s, beginning to de-legitimise the 'brutalist' architecture to which it had given rise.

Although social semioticians have drawn on sociological literature to strengthen descriptions of the cultural context (for instance in Hasan's linguistic accounts of mother–child interaction, which draw on Bernstein's (1971) account of social class), there is, in this respect, much to learn from organization studies and its detailed and sociologically grounded accounts of the meaning-making activities of organizations, such as managing, innovating, controlling, or marketing and of the relations between its participants – its hierarchies, leadership models, team dynamics, etc. Organization studies is, therefore, well placed to reconnect social semiotics with 'the functions and uses of semiotic systems' and with 'social and political thought', to once more quote Hodge and Kress's foundational social semiotics text (1988, 1–2).

An integrated research agenda would then see the strengths of the two disciplines lined up. As it is, many social semiotic studies of multimodal communication start with a text or a body of texts (or other multimodal phenomena) and then apply analytical frameworks in order to find patterns and explain these patterns in ways that may or may not be informed by organization and management theory. Work in organization studies often starts with a theoretical exploration of a particular issue before engaging in data analysis. Here, social semiotics can learn from organization studies by engaging, at the outset, with social theory to give direction, coherence, and meaning to research before assessing which multimodal phenomena and which modes of analysing them are best placed to investigate the social issues thus established. Organization studies, on the other hand, might pay greater attention to actual communicative practices and draw on social semiotics for detailed analyses of multiple semiotic resources: writing and speech, images, spatial design, and more.

One example of an integrated approach can be seen in the work of Jancsary et al. (2018) who examined Austrian Corporate Social Responsibility (CSR) reports. Jancsary and colleagues started from theoretical insights on institutions and institutional domains, conceptually integrating these ideas with the theoretical notion of register. Then, through systematic multimodal analysis, they found in the illustrations of the reports a pattern of three 'gazes' aimed at (and thus constructing) different types of viewers – the 'scrutinising gaze' toward ecological impact, the 'partner-like' gaze toward management, and the 'benevolent gaze' toward the human 'other', so closing the loop between organization theory ('context') and analysis ('text') and adding new insights to institutional theory as well as to social semiotics' understanding of the meaning potential of the gaze – and doing so through a novel way of clustering the analyses of individual aspects of the images in a large data set.

There is finally one other way in which social semiotics can learn from organization studies – the link between research and practice and, more specifically, its practitioners. Organization and management research of necessity usually involves working with practitioners – not just gathering 'their texts' but also engaging deeply with their practices, needs, and insights. Social semioticians have done so less often, although there are notable exceptions, for instance, Bezemer's work with health professionals (Bezemer and Tahim in this volume; see also Iedema and Carroll 2010), and social semiotic work on education, which has had a significant impact on educational curricula. It may be the case that, in some areas, practitioners do not feel a need for analytical research about their own practices; perhaps because they are secure in their traditional ways of doing things or fear it might interfere with creativity. But where innovation is needed, and where traditional practices are in crisis, strong engagement with practice, and hence with practitioners, can open up options that may not have been evident to either researchers or practitioners prior to such engagement.

These are, of necessity, only brief and somewhat eclectic glimpses into the implications of an organizational semiotics approach. A more elaborate and detailed discussion of the envisioned potential for cross-fertilisation and integration that organizational semiotics offers, as well as with the research-practical implications, will be provided in Chapter 2. In the final section of this introduction, we wish to sketch the various contributions to this volume and venture a look into a possible future.

Outlook: The chapters featured in this volume

This volume aims to demonstrate that organization studies is a natural 'conversation partner' and source of inspiration for the social semiotic analysis of contemporary multimodal communication in organizational and business settings. As socially critical sites, organizations merit much more – and much more thorough – attention from social semiotics than has hitherto been the case. The chapters in this volume demonstrate what such attention can reveal, across diverse types of organizations, across a broad range of communicative practices, and in relation to a range of organizational issues. The chapters progress from the more familiar, in terms of domains of multimodality, to aspects of communication that might seem to be more novel as an object of study.

Following Chapter 2 (Jancsary, Höllerer, Ravelli, and van Leeuwen), which further unpacks organizational semiotics, a first set of empirical chapters addresses aspects of visual and written communication in both printed and online media. Van Leeuwen and Zonjic, in an analysis of the use of visuals in online and offline information about sexual and reproductive health, show how presentations of the 'same' material for different audiences can change critical aspects of the medical knowledge being conveyed and how this can result from the way the production of these resources is organised. Laba presents a historical analysis of the online projection of a university's identity in the light of universities' increasingly consumer-oriented approach, which may exclude or marginalise other stakeholders, while Björkvall shows how corporate documents, such as the visions and values statements of Swedish public authorities, aim at instilling affective engagement and enthusiasm in civil servants rather than seeking to control them by means of rules and regulations.

The next chapters turn to the materiality of the working environment and show the role of spatial design in organising work and its attendant relations and interactions, with Tann and Ayoko focusing on the interactions and hierarchies in an office, and Ravelli on the reorganization and informalisation of learning spaces in a university.

The last chapters closely observe meaning-making *practices* rather than semiotic artefacts and environments, with Boeriis focusing on wayfinding in offline and online bookshops and Tahim and Bezemer on face-to-face apprenticeship practices in surgical training and the way these are recontextualised in formalised assessment practices. Finally, Aiello links two case studies of corporate rebranding to the semiotic resource of 'texturisation' and its affordances for conveying authenticity and diversity. In an afterword, van Leeuwen and Meyer assess the degree to which the aims we have set out for this volume have been achieved.

We hope that, collectively, these chapters will elucidate the scope, potential, and challenges of understanding multimodal communication in organizations (see also Höllerer et al. 2019), demonstrating the centrality of multimodality to organizations and the impact of diverse forms of multimodal communication on organizational members within, across, and around organizations. Social reality is a multimodal reality, and multimodality needs to be placed center-stage in managerial considerations. But it is not yet part of the standard body of knowledge that managers share, as similarities in managerial training lead to the convergence of organizational structures and practices – a kind of 'normative isomorphism' (e.g.,

18 *Louise Ravelli et al.*

DiMaggio and Powell 1983). Today, management is as much a semiotic practice as it is any other, and managers more than ever need to be, among other things, 'organizational semioticians'. Social semiotic perspectives on multimodality and meaning have substantial benefits for managers in terms of raising awareness for the crucial role of multimodality in organizations, in enabling a critical assessment and reflection on taken-for-granted organizational processes, and in broadening the communicative toolbox and putting it center-stage in organizational design and communication.

Even more importantly, organizations across all sectors of the economy need to be a priority for social semiotic scholarship. Whether from an institutional, instrumental, or social perspective, organizations play a crucial and powerful role in societies. Working in partnership with organizations, and addressing their specific contexts and histories, social semioticians can provide the critical tools necessary for a deeper understanding of multimodal communication, across all media, and in relation to a wide range of meanings and impacts.

A research model that integrates social semiotics, multimodality, and organization studies, and that draws on the strengths of each, will provide practical, methodological, and theoretical benefits. Practically, it is a new domain of application for social semioticians and a new knowledge framework for organizations. Methodologically, social semioticians need to embed partnerships with organizations more effectively into their analytical processes, and organizational scholars need to learn to make use of detailed and complex communication analysis. Theoretically, social semioticians need to re-evaluate received explanations of context, engage with established concepts for the explanation of organizational realities, and acknowledge the intrinsic role of history and practice on communication. Organizational scholars, as well as practitioners, need to greatly enhance their conceptualisations of meaning – what it is and how it is made – and recognise that meanings are embedded in every facet of practice. Organizational semiotics poses a challenging agenda for both originating disciplines, and as editors, we trust that this volume advances this agenda in critical ways. Organizational decision makers may be able to become better organizational semioticians, and social semioticians may be able to contribute in important ways to another facet of the world in which we live. A more detailed discussion of what such integration and mutual learning could look like, as well as a brief engagement with the practical challenges and possible best practices of doing so, will be presented in the next chapter.

References

Ahrne, G., and N. Brunsson. (2011). "Organization outside organizations: The significance of partial organization." *Organization* 18(1): 83–104.

Ahrne, G., and N. Brunsson (Eds.). (2019). *Organization Outside Organizations: The Abundance of Partial Organization in Social Life*. Cambridge University Press.

Aiello, G., and G. Dickinson. (2014). "Beyond authenticity: A visual-material analysis of locality in the global redesign of Starbucks stores." *Visual Communication* 13(3): 303–321.

Ashcraft, K.L., T.R. Kuhn, and F. Cooren. (2009). "Constitutional amendments: 'Materializing' organizational communication." *Academy of Management Annals* 3(1): 1–64.

Baldry A., and P.J. Thibault. (2006). *Multimodal Transcription and Text Analysis.* London: Equinox.

Barberio, V., M.A. Höllerer, R.E. Meyer, and D. Jancsary. (2018). "Organizational boundaries in fluid forms of production: The case of Apache open-source software." In L. Ringel, P. Hiller, and C. Zietsma (Eds.), *Toward Permeable Boundaries of Organizations? (Research in the Sociology of Organizations Vol. 57).* Bingley, UK: Emerald Publishing Limited, 139–168.

Barthes, R. (1977). *Image, Music, Text.* London: Fontana.

Bateman, J., J. Wildfeuer, and T. Hiippala. (2017). *Multimodality: Foundations, Research and Analysis. A problem-oriented Introduction.* Berlin: De Gruyter.

Bernstein, B. (1971). *Class, Codes and Control, Vol. I.* London: Routledge and Kegan Paul.

Beyes, T., and C. Steyaert. (2012). "Spacing organization: Non-representational theory and performing organizational space." *Organization* 19(1): 45–61.

Boxenbaum, E., C. Jones, R. Meyer, and S. Svejenova. (2018). "Towards an articulation of the material and visual turn in organization studies." *Organization Studies* 39(5–6): 597–616.

Bromley, P., and J.W. Meyer. (2015). *Hyper-organization: Global Organizational Expansion.* Oxford: Oxford University Press.

Cartel, M., S. Colombero, and E. Boxenbaum. (2018). "Towards a multimodal model of theorization processes." In M.A. Höllerer, T. Daudigeos, and D. Jancsary (Eds.), *Multimodality, Meaning, and Institutions. (Research in the Sociology of Organizations, Vol. 54A).* Bingley: Emerald Publishing Limited, 153–183.

Clark, P., and M. Rowlinson. (2004). "The treatment of history in organisation studies: Towards an 'historic turn'?" *Business History* 46(3): 331–352.

Clarke, R. (2001). "Studies in organisational semiotics: An introduction." *Australasian Journal of Information Systems* 8(2): 75–82.

Cooren, F. (1999). "Applying socio-semiotics to organizational communication." *Management Communication Quarterly* 13(2): 294–304.

Cooren, F., E. Vaara, A. Langley, and H. Tsoukas (Eds.). (2014). *Language and Communication at Work: Discourse, Narrativity, and Organizing.* Vol. 4. Oxford: Oxford University Press.

Cornelissen, J.P., R. Durand, P.C. Fiss, J.C. Lammers, and E. Vaara. (2015). "Putting communication front and center in institutional theory and analysis." *Academy of Management Review* 40(1): 10–27.

Daft, R.L. (2015). *Organization Theory and Design.* Boston, MA: Cengage Learning.

DiMaggio, P.J., and W.W. Powell. (1983). "The iron cage revisited: Institutional isomorphism and collective rationality in organizational fields." *American Sociological Review* 48(2): 147–160.

Djonov, E., and T. van Leeuwen. (2018). "Social media as semiotic technology and social practice: The case of ResearchGate's design and its potential to transform social practice." *Social Semiotics* 28(5): 641–664.

Dobusch, L., & Schoeneborn, D. (2015). Fluidity, identity, and organizationality: The communicative constitution of Anonymous. *Journal of Management Studies* 52(8): 1005–1035.

Doran, Y.J. (2018). The *Discourse of Physics: Building Knowledge through Language, Mathematics and Image*. London: Routledge.

Fairclough, N. (1993). "Critical discourse analysis and the marketization of public discourse." *Discourse & Society* 4(2): 133–168.

Forgues, B., and T. May. (2018). "Message in a bottle: Multiple modes and multiple media in market identity claims." In M.A. Höllerer, T. Daudigeos, and D. Jancsary (Eds.), *Multimodality, Meaning, and Institutions. (Research in the Sociology of Organizations, Vol. 54B)*. Bingley, UK: Emerald Publishing, 179–202.

Goffman, E. (1981). *Forms of Talk*. Oxford: Blackwell.

Graakjær, N.J. (2012). "Dance in the store: On the use and production of music in Abercrombie and Fitch." *Critical Discourse Studies* 9(4): 393–406.

Gümüsay, A.A., M.A. Höllerer, and R.E. Meyer. (2018). "Organizational scent." *M@n@gement* 21(4): 1424–1428.

Halliday, M.A.K. (1978). *Language as Social Semiotic: Aspects of Language in a Social-semiotic Perspective*. London: Arnold.

Halliday, M.A.K. (1985). 'Context of situation.' In Halliday, M.A.K., and R. Hasan (Eds.), *Language, context and text*. Geelong: Deakin University Press, 3–12.

Halliday, M.A.K., and C. Matthiessen. (2014). *Halliday's Introduction to Functional Grammar*. 4th edition. London: Routledge.

Hinings, B., and R.E. Meyer. (2018). *Starting Points: Intellectual and Institutional Foundations of Organization Theory*. Cambridge: Cambridge University Press.

Hodge, R., and G. Kress. (1988). *Social Semiotics*. Cambridge: Polity Press.

Höllerer, M.A., T. Daudigeos, and D. Jancsary. (2018). Multimodality, meaning, and institutions: Editorial. In M.A. Höllerer, T. Daudigeos, and D. Jancsary (Eds.), *Multimodality, Meaning, and Institutions. (Research in the Sociology of Organizations, Vol. 54A)*. Bingley: Emerald Publishing Limited, 1–26.

Höllerer, M.A., D. Jancsary, and M. Grafström. (2018). ""A picture is worth a thousand words": Multimodal sensemaking of the global financial crisis." *Organization Studies* 39(5–6): 617–644.

Höllerer, M.A., D. Jancsary, R.E. Meyer, and O. Vettori. (2013). "Imageries of corporate social responsibility: Visual recontextualization and field-level meaning." In M. Lounsbury, and E. Boxenbaum (Eds.), *Institutional Logics in Action, Part B*. Emerald Group Publishing Limited, 139–174.

Höllerer, M.A., T. van Leeuwen, D. Jancsary, R.E. Meyer, T.H. Andersen, and E. Vaara. (2019). *Visual and Multimodal Research in Organization and Management Studies*. London: Routledge.

Iedema, R. (2001). "Resemiotization." *Semiotica* 37(1–4): 23–40.

Iedema, R. (2003a). "Multimodality, resemiotization: Extending the analysis of discourse as multi-semiotic practice." *Visual Communication* 2(1): 29–57.

Iedema, R. (2003b). *Discourses of Post-bureaucratic Organization*. Amsterdam: Benjamins.

Iedema, R., and K. Carroll. (2010). "Discourse research that intervenes in the quality and safety of care practices." *Discourse and Communication* 4(1): 680–86.

Islam, G., N. Endrissat, and C. Noppeney. (2016). "Beyond "the eye"of the beholder: Scent innovation through analogical reconfiguration." *Organization Studies* 37(6): 769–795.
Jancsary, D., M.A. Höllerer, and R.E. Meyer. (2016). "Critical analysis of visual and multimodal texts." *Methods of Critical Discourse Studies* 3: 180–204.
Jancsary, D., R.E. Meyer, M.A. Höllerer, and E. Boxenbaum. (2018). "Institutions as multimodal accomplishments: Towards the analysis of visual registers." In M.A. Höllerer, T. Daudigeos, and D. Jancsary (Eds.), *Multimodality, Meaning, and Institutions. (Research in the Sociology of Organizations, Vol. 54A)*. Bingley: Emerald Publishing Limited, 87–118.
Jarzabkowski, P., A.P. Spee, and M. Smets. (2013). "Material artifacts: Practices for doing strategy with 'stuff'." *European Management Journal* 31(1): 41–54.
Jewitt, C. (2009). "Classrooms and the design of pedagogic discourse: A multimodal approach." *Culture & Psychology* 11(3): 309–320.
Johannessen, C.M. (2017). "The challenge of simple graphics for multimodal studies: Articulation and time scales in fuel retail logos." *Visual Communication* 17(2): 163–185.
Johannessen, C.M., and T. van Leeuwen (Eds.). (2018). *The Materiality of Writing: A Trace-Making Perspective*. London: Routledge.
Jones, C., and F.G. Massa. (2013). "From novel practice to consecrated exemplar: Unity Temple as a case of institutional evangelizing." *Organization Studies* 34(8): 1099–1136.
Jorna, R. (2009). "Introduction: Organizational Semiotics and Social Simulation." *Semiotica* 175: 311–316.
Kieser, A. (1994). "Crossroads: Why organization theory needs historical analyses: And how these should be performed." *Organization Science* 5(4): 608–620.
Klein, J., and J.M. Amis. (2021). "The dynamics of framing: Image, emotion, and the European migration crisis." *Academy of Management Journal* 64(5): 1324–1354.
Kress, G., and T. van Leeuwen. (2001). *Multimodal Discourse: The Modes and Media of Contemporary Communication*. London: Arnold.
Kress, G., and Van Leeuwen, T. (2021). *Reading Images: The Grammar of Visual Design*. 3rd edition. London: Routledge.
Kress, G., C. Jewitt, and J. Ogborn. (2001). *Multimodal Teaching and Learning: Rhetorics of the Science Classroom*. London: Bloomsbury.
Kingma, S.F., K. Dale, and V. Wasserman. (2018). *Organizational Space and beyond*. London: Routledge.
Ledin, P., and Machin, D. (2016). "Performance management discourse and the shift to an administrative logic of operation: A multimodal critical discourse analytical approach." *Text and Talk -An Interdisciplinary Journal of Language Discourse Communication Studies* 36(4): 445–467.
Lefsrud, L.M., H. Graves, and N. Phillips. (2018). "Dirty oil or ethical oil? Visual rhetoric in legitimation struggles." In M.A. Höllerer, T. Daudigeos, and D. Jancsary (Eds.), *Multimodality, Meaning, and Institutions. (Research in the Sociology of Organizations, Vol. 54B)*. Bingley: Emerald Publishing Limited, 101–144.
Leonardi, P.M., and S.R. Barley. (2010). "What's under construction here? Social action, materiality, and power in constructivist studies of technology and organizing." *Academy of Management Annals* 4(1): 1–51.

Leonardi, P. M. (2012). "Materiality, sociomateriality, and socio-technical systems: What do these terms mean? How are they different? Do we need them?" In P. M. Leonardi, B. A. Nardi, & J. Kallinikos (Eds.), *Materiality and organizing: Social interaction in a technological world*. Oxford, UK: Oxford University Press, 25–48.

Lim, V.F. (2019). "Investigating intersemiosis: A systemic functional multimodal discourse analysis of the relationship between language and gesture in classroom discourse." *Visual Communication* 20(1): 34–58.

Liu, K., and W. Li. (2014). *Organisational Semiotics for Business Informatics*. London: Routledge.

Liu, K., R.J. Clarke, P.B. Andersen, R.K. Stamper, and E-S. Abou-Zeid. (2002). *Organizational Semiotics*. New York: Springer.

Logue, D., and M. Grimes. (2022). "Platforms for the people: Enabling civic crowdfunding through the cultivation of institutional infrastructure." *Strategic Management Journal* 43(3): 663–693.

Maclean, M., C. Harvey, and S.R. Clegg. (2016). "Conceptualizing historical organization studies." *Academy of Management Review* 41(4): 609–632.

Magariños de Morentin, J.A. (1987). "The semiotic diagnosis of marketing culture." In J. Umiker-Sebeok (Ed.), *Marketing and Semiotics- New Directions in the Study of Signs for Sale*. Berlin: Mouton de Gruyter, 97–517.

Mahboob, A., and N. Knight. (Eds.). (2012). *Applicable Linguistics*. London: Bloomsbury.

Malinowski, B. (1923). "Supplement 1. The problem of meaning in primitive languages." In C.K. Ogden, and I.A. Richards (Eds.), *The Meaning of Meaning: A Study of the Influence of Language upon Thought and of the Science of Symbolism*. London: Routledge and Kegan Paul, 296–336.

Malinowski, B. (1935). *Coral Gardens and Their Magic*. Vol II. London: Allen and Unwin.

Martin, J.R. (2016). "Meaning matters: A short history of systemic functional linguistics." *WORD* 62:1: 35–58.

Meyer, R. (2017). "Communication in and around organizations: An institutional perspective." Symposium on Multimodality, Semiotics and Organization Studies. School of the Arts and Media, University of New South Wales, Sydney, October.

Meyer, J.W., and P. Bromley. (2013). "The worldwide expansion of "organization."" *Sociological Theory* 31(4): 366–389.

Meyer, J.W., and B. Rowan. (1977). "Institutionalized organizations: Formal structure as myth and ceremony." *American Journal of Sociology* 83(2): 340–363.

Meyer, R.E., and E. Vaara. (2020). "Institutions and actorhood as co-constitutive and co-constructed: The argument and areas for future research." *Journal of Management Studies* 57(4): 898–910.

Meyer, R.E., M.A. Höllerer, D. Jancsary, and T. van Leeuwen. (2013). "The visual dimension in organizing, organization, and organization research: Core ideas, current developments, and promising avenues." *Academy of Management Annals* 7(1): 489–555.

Meyer, R.E., D. Jancsary, M.A. Höllerer, and E. Boxenbaum. (2018). "The role of verbal and visual text in the process of institutionalization." *Academy of Management Review* 43(3): 392–418.

Molnar, S. (2019). "The birth of the print ad genre." In A. Brock, J. Pflaeging, and P. Schildhauer (Eds.), *Genre Emergence: Developments in Print, TV and Digital Media*. Berlin: Peter Lang, 29–50.

Mukařovský, J. (1964 [1932]). "Standard language and poetic language." In P.L. Garvin (Ed.), *A Prague School Reader on Esthetics, Literary Structure and Style*. Washington, DC: Georgetown University Press, 17–30.

Myskow, G. (2018). "Calibrating the "right" values: The role of critical inquiry tasks in social studies textbooks." *Visual Communication* 18(1): 31–54.

Nørgaard, N. (2018). *Multimodal Stylistics of the Novel: More than Words*. London: Routledge.

Novotny, H. (1997). "Transdisziplinäre Wissenschaftsproduktion – Eine Antwort auf die Wissensexplosion?" In F.Stadler (Ed.), *Wissenschaft als Kultur. Österreichs Beitrag zur Moderne*. Vienna and New York: Springer, 188–204.

O'Mahony, S., and F. Ferraro. (2007). "The emergence of governance in an open source community." *Academy of Management Journal* 50(5): 1079–1106.

Oswald, L.R. (2012). *Marketing Semiotics: Signs, Strategies and Brand Value*. Oxford: Oxford University Press.

Painter, C., J.R. Martin, and L. Unsworth. (2013). *Reading Visual Narratives: Image Analysis of Children's Picture Books*. London: Equinox.

Peirce, C.S. (1982). *Writings of Charles S. Peirce: A Chronological Edition, Vols I–VIII*. Bloomington/Indianapolis: Indiana University Press.

Phillips, N., T.B. Lawrence, and C. Hardy. (2004). "Discourse and institutions." *Academy of Management Review* 29(4): 635–652.

Puranam, P., O. Alexy, and M. Reitzig. (2014). "What's "new" about new forms of organizing?" *Academy of Management Review* 39(2): 162–180.

Ravelli, L. (2006). *Museum Texts: Communication Frameworks*. London: Routledge.

Ravelli, L., and R. McMurtrie. (2016). *Multimodality in the Built Environment*. London: Routledge.

Riach, K., and S. Warren. (2015). "Smell organization: Bodies and corporeal porosity in office work." *Human Relations* 68(5): 789–809.

Roderick, I. (2013). "Representing robots as living labour in advertisements: The new discourse of worker-employer power relations." *Critical Discourse Studies* 10(4): 392–405.

Roderick, I. (2016). The politics of office design: Translating neoliberalism into furnishing. *Journal of Language and Politics* 15(3): 274–287.

Santos, F.M., and K.M. Eisenhardt. (2005). "Organizational boundaries and theories of organization." *Organization Science* 16 (5): 491–508.

Schoeneborn, D. (2011). "Organization as communication: A Luhmannian perspective." *Management Communication Quarterly* 25(4): 663–689.

Tolbert, P.S., and R.H. Hall. (2015). *Organizations: Structures, Processes and Outcomes*. London: Routledge.

Umiker-Sebeok, J. (Ed.) (1987). *Marketing and Semiotics: New Directions in the Study of Signs for Sale*. Berlin: Mouton de Gruyter.

Unsworth, L., and A. Thomas. (2014). *English Teaching and New Literacies Pedagogy: Interpreting and Authoring Digital Multimedia Narratives*. New York: Peter Lang Publishing.

Van Leeuwen, T. (2005). *Introducing Social Semiotics*. London: Routledge.

Van Leeuwen, T. (2008). *Discourse and Practice: New Tools for Critical Discourse Analysis*. New York: Oxford University Press.

Van Leeuwen, T. (2011). *The Language of Colour: An Introduction*. London: Routledge.

Van Leeuwen, T. (2018). "Multimodality in organization studies: Afterword." In M.A. Höllerer, T. Daudigeos, and D. Jancsary (Eds.), *Multimodality, Meaning, and Institutions. (Research in the Sociology of Organizations, Vol. 54A)*. Bingley, UK: Emerald Publishing, 235–242.

Van Leeuwen, T. (2021). *Multimodality and Identity*. London: Routledge.

Van Leeuwen, T., D.J. Bateson, B. Le Hunte, A. Barratt, K.I. Black, M. Kelly, K. Inoue, A. Rutherford, M. Stewart, and J. Richters. (2016). "Contraceptive advertising: A critical multimodal analysis." *Journal of Applied Linguistics and Professional Practice* 13(1-3): 321–342.

De Vaujany, F-X., A. Adrot, E. Boxenbaum, and B. Leca. (2019). *Materiality in Institutions Spaces, Embodiment and Technology in Management and Organization*. Cham: Springer International Publishing.

Vith, S., A. Oberg, M.A. Höllerer, and R.E. Meyer. (2019). "Envisioning the "sharing city": Governance strategies for the sharing economy." *Journal of Business Ethics* 159(4): 1023–1046.

Wadhwani, R.D., R. Suddaby, M. Mordhorst, and A. Popp. (2018). "History as organizing: Uses of the past in organization studies." *Organization Studies* 39(12): 1663–1683.

Wasserman, V., and M. Frenkel. (2015). "Spatial work in between glass ceilings and glass walls: Gender-class intersectionality and organizational aesthetics." *Organization Studies* 36(11): 1485–1505.

Zilber, T.B. (2018). "A call for "strong" multimodal research in institutional theory." In M.A. Höllerer, T. Daudigeos, and D. Jancsary (Eds.), *Multimodality, Meaning, and Institutions. (Research in the Sociology of Organizations, Vol. 54A)*. Bingley: Emerald Publishing Limited, 63–86.

2 Social semiotics and organization studies
Building an effective bridge

Dennis Jancsary, Markus A. Höllerer, Louise Ravelli, and Theo van Leeuwen

Unpacking 'organizational semiotics'

In this chapter, we wish to further unpack our proposed concept of 'organizational semiotics' (see Chapter 1) and explain in detail how such an approach is conducive to establishing a bridge between social semiotic research on multimodality, on the one hand, and (business) organization research, on the other. Effectively, we wish to provide more detailed arguments and illustrations of how our notion of organizational semiotics, as a strongly integrated research program, benefits both social semioticians and organization researchers, practitioners, and decision makers and what it would entail and mean to do research from a genuinely organizational semiotics approach. While a similar case for integration of social semiotics and organization theory has been elaborated from the perspective of organization scholars (Höllerer, Daudigeos, and Jancsary 2018b; Höllerer et al. 2019), here, we take the perspective of multimodality researchers. Our main aim in this chapter is to outline how a stronger engagement with organizations and organising through a social semiotic lens is a worthwhile endeavour both for social semioticians studying multimodality and for organizational actors.

We kickstart our arguments by highlighting three important areas in which the interests of social semioticians and organization researchers coincide. While there are certainly additional ones, the areas that we discuss constitute foundational and/or timely debates across the two disciplines that illustrate significant potential for cross-fertilisation.

A first area of commonality is the two disciplines' recognition of the way *functional* and *symbolic meaning* are combined in organizations and specifically in organizational communication. Functional meaning is, very loosely, what a material object or social practice 'is' or what it 'does'; symbolic meaning is what that might stand for or 'connote' – what van Leeuwen (2021) refers to as 'identity' design. In a similar manner, organizational institutionalism has long debated the relationship between *technical efficiency* and *cultural legitimacy*; that is, between functionalist and symbolic/cultural perspectives on organization(s) (e.g., Meyer and Rowan 1977; Tolbert and

Zucker 1996). For instance, Boxenbaum, Daudigeos, and colleagues (2018) evoke the notion of 'rational myths' that combine the technical rationality behind certain products or practices with their symbolic meanings, so as to make and spread social meanings and associated institutional effects.

Van Leeuwen (2021) argues that contemporary texts, artefacts, and spaces emphasise a particular balance of functional and identity design and uses spectacles as an example. While in the past, much inventiveness was expended on different functional designs of 'glasses' (lorgnettes, pince-nez, monocles etc.), today, a single basic design is often dominant. But it is realised in a multitude of shapes, colours, and materials – the Italian firm Luxicotta alone produces 27,000 different frames (Knight 2018) – and choosing a frame contributes importantly to expressing how we see ourselves and how we want to be seen by others. Thus, today, functional design tends to become increasingly homogeneous, while identity design becomes increasingly diverse, as it has to be able to express the identities of organizations, lifestyle communities, and individuals (for similar insights in organization research, see, for instance, Eisenman 2013, 2018). Functional design and identity design are then said to be expressed in different ways, the former through *modes* – 'grammatical' principles of construction that can be materially realised in different ways (e.g., a frame that holds lenses, two arms articulated with the frames, a nose bridge etc.) – and the latter through *media* – the materialities that realise functional designs (e.g., plastic, metal, or bamboo; any colour; many shapes for the lenses, etc.).

This principle can also be applied to texts and to technologies for producing texts. In PowerPoint, for instance, a single functional schema for the use of colour plays a crucial role in generating 'themes' for expressing corporate or individual identities. Such technologies also play a key role in spreading multimodal genres of organizational communication to other social spheres. PowerPoint was originally invented at the Bell Laboratories to pitch ideas to management for funding (Gaskins 2012), but its 'heading-plus-bullet points' template is now used in many other contexts, 'turning information into a sales pitch and presenters into marketeers' (Tufte 2006, 4). In a similar way, Kvåle has analysed how Microsoft SmartArt, originally a resource for producing organization charts, has become a model for interpreting many other phenomena, including in education (Kvåle 2016; see also Höllerer et al. 2019, 104–128).

A second, closely related concern, shared by both social semiotics and organization studies, is an emphasis on *materiality*. In organization studies, Zilber (2018, 21) has, for instance, forcefully argued that material objects, spaces, and visuals must be understood in relation to the concrete interactions in and on which they act – 'the web of practices in which they are interwoven' (on materiality in organizational research, see also Jarzabkowski, Spee, and Smets 2013; Jones and Massa 2013; Leonardi and Barley 2010; De Vaujany et al. 2019). Social semiotics has always stressed the importance of analysing multimodal texts, artefacts, spaces, and so on in relation to their context, and in particular, van Leeuwen (2008) has argued for an approach to analysing social practices that conceives of texts and practices as an indivisible whole. This allows the elements of social practices to be linked to specific materialities – actors and their (inter)actions to embodied performances, spaces to architecture and interior design, texts and other semiotic artefacts to the material forms they take, and so on.

Finally, the close connection between *innovation* and *(re)contextualisation* is an important topic both in organization studies and in social semiotics following Malinowski's important early work. To give an example from the field of social semiotics, Iedema's study of what he refers to as the 'resemiotisation' of a health facility (Iedema 2001, 2003a) analyses a process that started with meetings between architect planners, bureaucrats, and future users, which were then transformed into written documents, which were not only more formal and general but also more authoritative and non-negotiable than the spoken discourses they resemiotised. These documents were then further resemiotised into architectural drawings, which were even less negotiable, as by this time, significant resources had been committed, and finally into the bricks and mortar of the new facility. Each of these stages used different material resources – spoken language, non-verbal communication, and the spatial arrangements of the meeting room in the case of the meetings, printing and bureaucratic text layouts in the case of the written documents, and so on. Iedema should, in fact, be considered a forerunner of the kind of 'organizational semiotics' we are proposing here (e.g., Iedema 2003b). In organization theory, similar ideas about the relationship of innovation to tensions between de- and recontextualisation have been presented, for instance, in the literatures on 'translation' and 'editing' (e.g., Czarniawska and Joerges 1996; Meyer 2014; Wedlin and Sahlin 2017) and, in particular, on 'glocalisation' (e.g., Drori, Höllerer, and Walgenbach 2014; Höllerer, Walgenbach, and Drori 2017). Regarding the role of multimodality in these processes, Höllerer et al. (2013), for instance, studied how the concept of 'corporate social responsibility' (CSR) was contextualised visually in Austria. Barry and Meisiek (2010), show how engaging with art in the context of work may enable organizational members to see more and see differently (see also Quattrone et al. 2021). Comi and Whyte (2018) come close to Iedema's idea of 'resemiotisation' when they study how visual artefacts are employed in practices of imagining, testing, stabilising, and reifying, through which abstract imaginings of organizational futures are transformed into palpable courses of action. In this volume, van Leeuwen and Zonjic (Chapter 3), illustrate how resemiotisation facilitates making information more accessible for various organizational audiences in the context of delivering clinical and health promotion services in the area of sexual and reproductive health across the Australian state of New South Wales.

While by no means exhaustive, these three common areas of interest illustrate that there is substantial value in systematically bringing conceptual and methodological insights from social semiotics into contact with conceptual and empirical issues of organization and management. In the subsequent section of this chapter, we further elaborate the potential for cross-fertilisation. The following section provides arguments about why social semioticians should turn to and engage with organization and management as a promising domain of scholarly inquiry. We introduce some of the history of organization theory and discuss how the inner workings of organizations, the interactions between organizations, and the broader relations between organizations and their environments can only be fully understood in the (multimodal) contexts in which they play out. We then explore why, in turn, organizations and businesses should bother with social semiotic approaches to multimodality. We argue that the management of organizations, in large part, can be understood as semiotic practice, and a social semiotic perspective implies that a good manager needs to be an 'organizational semiotician'. Against this backdrop, we elaborate the substantial benefits of a social semiotic perspective for the management of organizations. Finally, we turn toward the practicalities of doing organizational research from a social semiotic and multimodal perspective and outline the complexities of working with actual organizations and the range of sensitivities that needs to be accommodated. We draw from our long-standing experience in working with a wide array of organizations, building a framework for practical and effective engagement, and setting the stage for a fair collaboration that creates sustainable mutual benefits.

The relevance of organization and management for social semioticians

Surveying the land: The case for multimodal organizational research

It is important to provide a brief history and characterisation of organization (and management) theory as a field of research and further elaborate our brief arguments from Chapter 1 by highlighting how the study of multimodal semiotic resources is increasingly taking hold in the collective research agenda. This provides many opportunities for social semioticians to engage with organizational phenomena.

The field of organization theory is vast and diverse, with a rich history (e.g., Adler et al. 2014). Following Hinings and Meyer (2018), we trace its roots back to the early twentieth century and the foundational work of Max Weber and Robert Michels. Especially for Weber, the study of organizations was not yet a distinct field of research but, rather, part of a larger sociological endeavour. He discussed the emerging form of 'organization' as part of a broader trend toward an increasing rationalisation of society. Weber's gaze, accordingly, was a genuinely social scientific one. In contrast, later proponents of organization research, such as Henri Fayol and Frederick Taylor, studied organizations from an engineering point of view. For them, production and its efficient management and administration were paramount, and they, therefore, mainly focused on the rational design of structures and processes. In the subsequent growth phase of the field, organization theory branched out into a variety of different theories and traditions, focusing on different aspects of organizations and introducing a variety of conceptual constructs (for more detailed discussions, see Hinings and Meyer 2018). The different approaches are informed by a variety of neighbouring disciplines, such as sociology, psychology, and economics but also by philosophy, communication studies, and linguistics.

As briefly outlined in Chapter 1, various communities of organizational researchers stress the foundational importance of communication and understanding organizations as *sites* of communication as well as *products* of communication. Indeed, there is a vast body of literature on the crucial role of language, communication, and social meaning in and around organizations, which is sometimes referred to as the 'linguistic and discursive' turn in organization and management research (e.g., Alvesson and Kärreman 2000; Deetz 2003). While the potential relationships between organization and communication are complex and manifold (e.g., Putnam and Boys 2006), we delineate our perspective in this volume from those that see communication as directed flows of information and organizations as mere containers and/or conduits of communication. Instead, in line with social semiotics, we draw from organization theories that understand organising as an inherently communicative activity and practices of communication as constitutive of organizations and organizational meanings (e.g., Cooren et al. 2014; Cornelissen et al. 2015; Meyer and Vaara 2020; Schoeneborn 2011). However, until recently, 'discourse' and 'text' have been restricted to predominantly verbal practices and artefacts. With the turn of the millennium, organizational scholars have become increasingly interested in visual aspects of organization (e.g., Bell, Warren, and Schroeder 2014; Davison, McLean, and Warren 2012; Meyer et al. 2013). Such research has presented strong evidence that organizations are constituted as much through visual as through verbal means. This work has refocused the attention of organization researchers on visual aspects of organizational identities, legitimation strategies, truth claims, intra-organizational coordination, as well as issues of power and conflict, among other topics (for an overview, see Meyer et al. 2013).

Multiple attempts at collecting and systematising multimodal organization research have been made in recent years. Most prominently, Höllerer et al. (2019) suggest a social semiotic perspective to research on multimodality in and around organizations and review existing multimodal research in this area. They provide a number of exemplary cases that illustrate the value of multimodality in the study of organizational structure, organizational identity, the organization–customer interface, and organizational legitimation. In their collection of work on *Multimodality, Meaning, and Institutions*, Höllerer, Daudigeos, and Jancsary (2018a) bring together a variety of articles on how multimodality may enrich institutional organization research.

In this double volume, pre-eminent scholars from institutional organization theory and beyond discuss the value of a 'multimodal agenda', suggest methodological advances, and present empirical multimodal research on topics such as the institutionalisation of innovations, institutional persistence and change, and organizational identities. Additionally, a recent special issue in the journal *Organization Studies* (Boxenbaum et al. 2018) collects articles on the material and visual turn in organization theory. The different articles in this special issue explore the visual, material, and multimodal aspects of sensemaking, organizational actorhood, issue framing, financial decisions, accounting, aesthetic knowledge, and suffering.

In the light of increasing trends toward multimodal organization research, the potential for multimodal social semiotics engaging with organizations and organization theory is substantial. In the following, we wish to elaborate further why and how more thorough and systematic social semiotic analyses of multimodality in and around organizations could benefit both researchers and practitioners.

Staking out the territory: The societal relevance of organizations and organising

Having established the ubiquity and relevance of multimodal artefacts in and around organizations, we outline here a perspective on organizations that we consider to be highly compatible with organizational semiotics. Prominent strands within organization theory have long contended that modern society is a 'society of organizations' (e.g., Perrow 1991). Organizations are omnipresent in everyday life; they have become the dominant form of association. In the Global North, most people are born in organizations (hospitals), live their lives in different relationships to organizations (for instance, as employees, customers, clients, or members), and are confronted with organizations even after death (e.g., funeral homes, churches, law firms, etc.) (e.g., Etzioni 1964). Formal organization has become the rationalised global model for organising societies (e.g., Bromley and Meyer 2015; Meyer and Bromley 2013) and many spheres of life, such as art, education, and even romantic love are becoming increasingly organised. Since organizations, therefore, structure how the majority of ordinary people live their lives, their study cannot be restricted to how (formal) organizations can be optimised and managed efficiently but needs to extend to the broader social and societal issues, of which organizations and organising are central aspects and manifestations.

Such a research program lies well within the boundaries of organization research. Since its very inception, organization and management theory has built on both sociological and technical roots (e.g., Hinings and Meyer 2018). While approaches in the sociological tradition are mostly interested in explaining organization as a social phenomenon and practices of organising as mechanisms of social coordination, approaches building on an engineering perspective focus on optimisation, standardisation, and formalisation for the sake of efficiency. Throughout the history of organization research, repeating 'waves' of managerial ideologies have been diagnosed (e.g., Barley and Kunda 1992), shifting between rational and normative/cultural explanations of organization. This goes to show that organization theory cannot be reduced to a purely managerialist agenda. In order to understand the crucial entanglement of organizations and societies, organizations have to be understood as specific forms of collective activity that are socially constructed and maintained through practices of meaning-making. This idea is one cornerstone of organizational semiotics (see Chapter 1). To study society means to study organizations, and to study organizations means to study a central aspect of modern societies.

Considering such inherent entanglement of organizations and broader society, we locate ourselves in a sociologically oriented perspective on organizations and organising (see also Höllerer et al. 2019). We see particular value in connecting to theoretical frameworks that understand organizations as embedded in institutionalised systems of cultural meanings (e.g., Greenwood et al. 2017; Meyer, Jancsary, and Höllerer 2021; Zilber 2017), which manifest primarily in a communicative manner (e.g., Cornelissen et al. 2015). Organizations cannot be understood adequately without considering the institutionalised norms, values, and meanings that shape organizational structures, forms, and practices. At the same time, organizations do not only create products and services but also meanings. In this way, they engage in the negotiation, stabilisation, and change of the very societal meanings that shape them.

This also means that components of organising can only be properly understood against the backdrop of the specific cultural and institutional context in which they proliferate. Organizational structures, for instance, are not only influenced by the technical requirements of organizational environments as classical contingency theory (e.g., Burns and Stalker 1961; Lawrence and Lorsch 1967) would suggest. They are also driven by legitimacy concerns and societal myths on what is considered 'rational' (e.g., Meyer and Rowan 1977). Activities and practices are subject to broader trends and fashions (e.g., Abrahamson and Fairchild 1999; Kieser 1997), as organizations look for guidance from leading peers. Business school curricula strongly influence understandings of 'good' and 'proper' organization, and cohorts of managers with homogenous educational backgrounds initiate isomorphic adaptation based on prevalent societal norms (e.g., DiMaggio and Powell 1983). Changing societal values manifest in novel organizational forms, for instance in 'sharing' organizations (e.g., Vith et al. 2019) or 'benefit corporations' (e.g., Gehman, Grimes, and Cao 2019).

Summing up, organizations have societal relevance far beyond profit maximisation and efficiency optimisation. Studying organizations from a social scientific perspective is, therefore, highly compatible with a social semiotic research program that understands semiotic resources as societally constituted and, at the same time, constitutive of societal arrangements.

Tilling the field: The multimodality of organizational practices

It is specifically with regard to the multimodal communicative resources that constitute social collectives – such as organizations – and practices that we see a plethora of opportunities for *organizational semiotics*. Communication, understood broadly, comprises all externalisations of social meanings, whether deliberate or unintentional. Streams of communication organise, coordinate, classify, and animate interactions between people, practices, and artefacts within and across organizations. Considering that most contemporary communication is multimodal, multimodality shapes meanings and interactions (a) within organizations, (b) across organizations, and (c) between organizations and their broader environments. Communicative acts and artefacts exert environmental pressures on organizations and legitimise those that conform to these expectations; organizations, in turn, design communicative practices and artefacts to protect their 'license to operate', increase their reputation, and project certain identities. Finally, communication also creates, establishes, and sustains broader discourses in the societal environment of organizations (e.g., Phillips, Lawrence, and Hardy 2004), resulting in specific understandings of organizational roles and societal expectations.

Regarding *intra-organizational* phenomena, organizational semiotics can further illuminate how individuals experience and interpret organizational realities, how they coordinate processes and practices, and/or how they interact in groups. Organizational members create order and predictability in their everyday operations through collective sensemaking (e.g., Weick 1995), drawing on a variety of communicative cues, many of which are multimodal in character (e.g., Höllerer, Daudigeos, and Jancsary 2018b; Höllerer, Jancsary, and Grafström 2018). Bezemer and Tahim (Chapter 9) analyse in great detail how multimodality features in sensemaking, organizational learning, and performance appraisal in the interactions between supervisors and trainees in the surgical theatre and beyond. Additionally, organizational structures and practices are materially instantiated in spatial layout and material architecture, which affords certain ways of relating to each other (e.g., Beyes and Steyaert 2012; Wasserman and Frenkel 2015). The consequences of physical layout for the assignment of member roles are studied in-depth by Ravelli (Chapter 7), who reconstructs the functional and dysfunctional consequences of spatial redesign at a university campus, revealing that such material change has the potential to influence what it means to be a student and where (and how) learning should take place. Visual, spatial, and material resources also strongly influence power relations and enable specific forms of managerial control, for instance, through bureaucracy, culture, architecture, or technology (e.g., Sandner 1990;

Wasserman and Frenkel 2011). Tann and Ayoko (Chapter 6), in their study of open-plan offices, show how space is much more than simply a physical vessel, enabling distinct social practices around the meanings it communicates, thereby manifesting interactions between management discourses and employee voices.

Regarding *inter-organizational* interaction, organizational semiotics can contribute to more and deeper insights into how organizations relate to each other and their stakeholders. Different forms of organizational collaboration such as networks, industry clusters, or meta-organizations (e.g., Ahrne and Brunsson 2008) require coordination and shared understandings and identities. Multimodal resources provide opportunities for coordination and integration of cultures and identities (e.g., Erjansola et al. 2021; Höllerer et al. 2019). In their interactions with competitors, customers, and broader stakeholders, organizations claim membership in specific social categories (e.g., 'upscale shoe store', 'Asian cuisine', or 'investment bank') to achieve cognitive 'fit' with the expectations of their audiences (e.g., Zuckerman 1999). Boeriis (Chapter 8) provides an illustration of how shop layouts become windows to the organization's self-image by showing how customers interact with both material and virtual organizational interfaces in their search for products. This elucidates how the structural logics behind 'textual' layouts reveal how the organization sees itself, its employees, and its customers. Existing research in organization studies has also explored how organizations visually communicate commitment to societal values, such as sustainability and social responsibilities (e.g., Höllerer et al. 2013), how they claim a desirable role in society, and how they use multimodal strategies to enhance their societal legitimacy and that of their products and services more broadly (e.g., Lefsrud, Graves, and Phillips 2020). Van Leeuwen and Zonjic (Chapter 3), for instance, analyse the health promotion practices of a New South Wales based non-profit organization delivering services in the area of sexual health. They demonstrate how health promotion work is a form of stakeholder engagement and that 'resemiotisation' (e.g., Iedema 2003a) is a practical strategy to make organizational communication more relevant and resonant with stakeholder groups.

Regarding the relationships between *organizations and their broader cultural and institutional environments*, organization research studies how meanings emerge, stabilise, and diffuse and what this means for management. Societal discourses influence what it entails to be a 'modern', 'good', and 'proper' – that is, societally legitimate (e.g., Suchman 1995) – organization. When new templates for organizational forms and practices emerge, they either rise and wane as fads and fashions (e.g., Abrahamson and Fairchild 1999; Kieser 1997) or become entrenched in social stocks of knowledge and endure (e.g., Zeitz, Mittal, and McAulay 1999). Organizations participate in the discursive negotiations of what constitutes 'appropriate' organizational goals, forms, and practices (e.g., Meyer and Höllerer 2010; Strang and Meyer 1993). Novel organizational ideas and practices are often adopted in contexts quite different from their origin and by organizations that are also quite different from those that have initially employed them successfully. During such diffusion, these practices are constantly revised, adapted, and thereby 'translated' (e.g., Wedlin and Sahlin 2017) into their new context of use – often by multimodal means. Laba (Chapter 4), for instance, explores how the marketisation of public discourses changes the ways in which universities present themselves to their audiences in order to communicate membership in a legitimate category. She employs metafunctional analysis to better understand the different dimensions of organizational identity on university websites. Björkvall (Chapter 5) starts from the proliferation of 'visions and values' in the public sector and analyses how the 'affect-driven civil servant' diffuses as a novel category on the websites of public authorities in Sweden. Both chapters apply a social semiotic toolkit to the study of how the intrusion of novel societal ideas and values changes the ways in which organizations operate and communicate.

The chapters in this volume constitute a selected sample of studies that showcases how the vast landscape of organizational phenomena that relate to multimodality can be fruitfully analysed with the toolbox of social semiotics – with established theories and conversations in organization theory in mind. Accordingly, organizational semiotics as a research program has the potential to extend the variety of social and discursive phenomena that social semioticians address – and conversely help (re)contextualise the central theoretical constructs of social semiotics. Additionally, these phenomena are highly relevant in everyday organizational life, which brings us to the practical value of organizational semiotics.

Bringing in the harvest: Opportunities for social semioticians to 'matter in the real world'

Social semioticians have had considerable impact on the work of educational organizations. They have been trailblazers in developing the concept of literacy (see for example, Rose and Martin 2012) and have extended this to multimodality (Jewitt and Kress 2003; Kress 2010; Macken-Horarik et al. 2017; New London Group 1996; Painter, Martin, and Unsworth 2013; Unsworth 2008), with significant impact on curricula across the world, and in part by studying the distinct styles of writing and multimodal communication of different school subjects in order to detail the various literacies required to succeed in these subjects. They have drawn attention to the fact that, for instance, learning science or math is, to a large extent, a matter of mastering a particular 'register' of language and multimodal communication (e.g. Doran 2018; Halliday and Martin 1993; Kress et al. 2001; O'Halloran 2005) and that the new curricula of English studies and English language learning also make multimodal demands (Diamantopoulou and Ørevik 2022; Djonov, Teseng, and Lim 2021). But, to a large extent, these studies have not engaged with schools as organizations, though this is now changing, particularly in work on tertiary education (see this volume, Laba, Chapter 4, and Ravelli Chapter 7; also Feng, in press). In addition, social semioticians have worked in the area of health communication (Iedema 2001, 2003a; van Leeuwen and Zonjic, Chapter 3; Bezemer and Tahim, Chapter 9).

A number of social semioticians have linked social semiotics to critical discourse analysis, and their work has displayed an increasing interest in organizational communication, inspired by Fairclough's seminal paper on the 'marketisation of discourse' (1993), which discusses the impact of corporate communication practices on social communication generally. This has led to three kinds of studies – studies of digital semiotics developed by corporations for their own purposes but that, today, are also used in many other contexts, such as PowerPoint (Zhao, Djonov, and van Leeuwen 2014), Microsoft Word (Kvåle 2016), and Getty Images (Machin 2004; see also Aiello, Chapter 10); semiotic resources developed for internal organizational purposes such as organization charts and strategic diagrams (Ledin and Machin 2016; Höllerer et al. 2019); and, more recently, the arrangement of organizational environments, including shopping centres (Ravelli and McMurtrie 2016) and offices (Roderick 2016; Tann and Ayoko, Chapter 6; van Leeuwen 2005) and organizational practices such as online shopping (Boeriis, Chapter 8; van Leeuwen and Rasmussen 2022), analysing how multimodal resources constitute shop design, practices of shopping, and social roles for shoppers. Although some of these studies have included ethnographic observation and interviews with participants, most have remained at a distance from the organizations whose outputs they have studied, using text analysis for purposes of ideological critique. We suggest that this is unfortunate and a missed opportunity. As we have argued, organizational issues are not restricted to efficiency optimisation and profit maximisation. While these may very well be the main objectives driving for-profit organizations (but see below), even these organizations must deal with issues that go beyond such a narrow perspective of what an organization should strive for. Milton Friedman's credo that 'the business of business is business' rings somewhat hollow in a society in which corporate (social) responsibility, sustainability, social inclusion, employee empowerment, and other similar topics rank high on the agenda of both central organizational stakeholders and regulators – not to mention the abundance of organizations in the public and non-profit sector, as well as new 'hybrid' organizational forms at the interstices of societal sectors (e.g., social enterprises, benefit corporations, or the growing market for impact investment). Engaging with organizations is necessary in order to potentially change organizations, and social semiotics has great potential to do this as 'critical friends', thus, complementing critical voices in organization theory and supporting research that matters in, and changes, organizational practices.

Building on the above, it is important to recall that the term 'organization' encompasses a vast variety of social collectives with quite different goals and modes of operation. Organizations exist in all societal sectors: private business, public sector, and civil society. Although they all draw on the central components of formal structure, culture, processes, forms, and activities, their ultimate objectives vary considerably, from the provision of goods and services to the regulation of policy fields, the conservation of natural resources, or the improvement of public health and maximisation of social good, to name just a few. Accordingly, insights from organization research that help organizations better achieve their objectives does not necessarily mean improving financial performance; such insights may also help transform society by leading to better social outcomes, less inequality, and more sustainable business practices. 'Mattering in the world of organization and business' can mean many things, and there is a great need for organizational research from a broad social scientific perspective that understands organizations as a necessary element of fair, sustainable, and inclusive societies.

The relevance of social semiotics for organizations, management, and business

Even if social semioticians can be convinced to engage with organizations more substantially, why should these organizations be interested in social semiotic insights on multimodal aspects of organizational life? One of the central debates in organization research is its ongoing quest for practical and societal relevance (e.g., Astley and Zammuto 1992; Bartunek and Rynes 2014; Miller, Greenwood, and Prakash 2009). On the topic of designing and transforming organizations internally, some feel that organization theory has become too abstract and fails to connect with the everyday experiences of managers and organizational members. Regarding more macro-issues and the role of organizations in the economy and broader society, organization theory consistently seems to 'lose' against economics in terms of convincing and informing policymakers. This is unfortunate, as organization and management theory have a lot to contribute. Here, we see substantial potential for *organizational semiotics* to help align research more closely with the everyday problems and experiences of people in and around organizations. Social reality is a multimodal reality, and organizational members constantly need to deal with issues of creating and interpreting multimodal texts.

Management as semiotic practice

Organizations are shaped and held together by communication; thus managers, decision makers, and organizational members, more broadly, need to be skilled communicators. They need to argue, convince, and persuade both their internal and external stakeholders (e.g., Cornelissen 2020). They need to design communicative artefacts (e.g., reports, websites, advertisements, charts, office space, architecture, etc.) in ways that resonate with audiences and imbue these artefacts with affordances conducive to organizational objectives. At the same time, they need to be aware that meanings are constantly negotiated and resisted, and affordances become appropriated and transformed. For instance, moving from individual to open and shared offices (e.g., Tann and Ayoko, Chapter 6), in order to facilitate communication and teamwork might be interpreted as an attempt to cut costs, and employees may find creative ways to resist and circumvent the collaborative practices that the new material affordances of their office environment suggest. Official framings of corporate decisions may become challenged, and employees may create their own multimodal narrative of events by appropriating corporate imagery and logos (e.g., Bell 2012).

It is simply impossible to list and discuss all the managerial activities that relate to multimodality and meaning. However, we wish to highlight a few selected, important topic areas as an illustration and case in point. The first reflects issues of *organization design* (e.g., Buchanan 2008; Burton et al. 2006; Daft 2015; Mintzberg 1980). We here include both the design of (invisible) organizational structures and processes as well as their (visible and tangible) visual and material manifestations. Hierarchies, for instance, exist as ideas and cognitive schemata that guide the behaviour of organizational members: questions such as who can make decisions on which issue and whom do I need to inform/involve before I can move forward? At the same time, these hierarchies are also manifestly visible in organizational charts, organizational dress, and organizational architecture. The same is true for processes that guide activities in pursuit of a specific outcome: what does the sequence of activities from customer inquiry to product delivery look like and what are the important interfaces and 'bottle necks' in this process? Again, these processes can be multimodally instantiated through specific material (in bricks-and-mortar shops) and virtual (on websites) 'pathways' from entrance to exit (e.g., Boeriis, Chapter 8). Rules on different steps in the process may be written down in elaborate handbooks, or they may be taped to the desks of retail clerks. Different ways of designing the materiality of organizations have specific implications that include both desired outcomes and potential undesirable side effects (e.g., Ravelli, Chapter 7). Managers need to be aware of these implications before they make decisions on costly construction projects.

A second area of management in which multimodality features heavily is *leadership and the coordination of distributed efforts* for shared objectives, both internally and with external audiences. Literature on strategy-as-practice (e.g., Jarzabkowski and Spee 2009; Suddaby, Seidl, and Lê 2013; Vaara and Whittington 2012), for instance, has shown how participants in strategy meetings make heavy use of available spaces and multimodal artefacts, such as pens, notepads, reports, information sheets, computer screens, and presentation slides (e.g., Jarzabkowski, Burke, and Spee 2015). Additionally, managers use their own bodies as semiotic resources to persuade and convince others (e.g., Gylfe et al. 2016). While the importance of multimodality has been extensively documented in strategy processes, it extends into other areas of organization and management, and managers need to be capable of using a variety of multimodal resources constructively and generatively. Every organizational interaction relies, to a certain degree, on multimodal resources. This includes, on a smaller scale, the weekly 'Jour Fixe' in which organizational members report on their progress as well as coordination between supervisors and trainees in surgical theatres for purposes of performance assessment and learning (Bezemer and Tahim, Chapter 9). On a broader scale, it involves large shareholder assemblies in which managers present their visions for the future as well as organizational efforts to increase sexual health literacy among their audiences (van Leeuwen and Zonjic, Chapter 3). It covers the on-site meeting in (shared) physical spaces as much as virtual meetings on video, in which each participant brings in their own (real or fictional) space in the background. Again, managers need to be aware of how the multimodal resources available to people during these processes affect the process itself as well as its outcomes.

A third area of management that relies on multimodality is *accounting and accountability*. Beyond classical financial accounting as a visual practice (e.g., Davison 2015; Quattrone 2009), we here understand accounting in a broader sense as including all activities by which organizations legitimate their conduct toward internal or external audiences. Organizations and their management are accountable to other actors, such as government agencies, investors, customers, or the public more broadly. Such accountability, has, in recent years, been constantly extended from purely financial performance to broader, non-financial indicators. The balanced scorecard (BSC), for instance, has become a prominent tool to achieve the integration of financial and non-financial objectives within organizations (e.g., Kaplan and Norton 2015). Such scorecards rely heavily on visual representations and allow for creative engagement, ordering, interrogation, and motivation (Busco and Quattrone 2015). In addition to such internal tools, organizations design and publish a variety of reports to address their diverse audiences (e.g., Breitbarth, Harris, and Insch 2010; Davison 2002; Höllerer et al. 2013). They present themselves favourably on their websites (e.g., Laba, Chapter 4); they also publish value statements to convey desirable identities (e.g., Björkvall, Chapter 5), strategy reports to communicate aspired achievements (e.g., Brandtner et al. 2017), and codes of governance and conduct to indicate their willingness to comply with societal expectations (e.g., Leixnering and Bramböck 2013). The (multimodal) design of these artefacts strongly affects their reception and organizational success. Managers are, therefore, challenged to better understand the affordances and potentials of multimodal communication.

Benefits of social semiotic tools and insights for the management of organizations

Considering such omnipresence of multimodality in organizational life, we suggest that *organizational semiotics* has the potential to make life considerably easier for managers in several regards. Particularly, we argue that interactions between social semioticians and managers, as well as other organizational members, can serve the purposes of *educating, elucidating,* and *consulting.*

First, engaging with organizations semiotically can have *educating* effects. While many managers deal with multimodal communication intuitively, relying on knowledge that they have gained during their education in business schools as well as their practical knowledge, or employ professional consultants for more important communicative efforts, they are usually not fully aware of the scope, potential, and challenges of multimodality. Social semioticians can, therefore, help raise awareness for the centrality of multimodality in organizations and the impact of multimodality on organizational members. They could further sensitise practitioners to the potentials and dangers of multimodal communication (see also Höllerer et al. 2019). Scientific collaboration with social semioticians can put multimodality center-stage in managerial considerations and lead to a more conscious and reflective engagement with multimodal texts and artefacts. For instance, architectural designs are often based on considerations of functionality and/or prestige but rarely is such functionality assessed systematically with a focus on the meanings that the built environment conveys. Multiple chapters in this volume (see Boeriis, Chapter 8; Ravelli, Chapter 7; and Tann and Ayoko, Chapter 6) show what a multimodal analysis of architecture and office design can reveal. This first effect of raising awareness may lead to a stronger interest from managers and decision makers in multimodal aspects of organization and organising.

Second, social semiotic perspectives on organizational issues may have *elucidating* effects. Social semioticians are routinely socialised outside business schools and are, therefore, somewhat 'external' to the standard body of knowledge that managers share. They escape the normative isomorphism (e.g., DiMaggio and Powell 1983) that leads to the convergence of organizational structures and practices due to similarities in managerial training. This affords a more critical and reflective attitude toward taken-for-granted organizational problems and solutions. Engagement with social semioticians may, therefore, enable organizational decision makers to 'think outside of the box' and reflexively realise the isomorphic tendencies in their decision-making (e.g., Laba, Chapter 4; Björkvall, Chapter 5). Systematic analysis and critique of current organizational practices by social semioticians may engender new perspectives, ideas, and ways forward – provided that decision makers and researchers enter into a dialogue at eye level (see also our more practical considerations below). Beyond the necessary interaction during research projects, the insights of social semioticians can also enhance the 'multimodal literacy' of decision makers and enable them to apply social semiotic methods themselves. This could complement business school education and enable better management decisions in the long term. Social semiotic insights, as manifested throughout this volume, point to the crucial multimodal aspects for the long-term success of organizations. They might help practitioners design multimodal artefacts more consciously and deftly.

Finally, engagement between social semioticians and decision makers could also take on aspects of *consulting*. Social semiotics could provide organizations with additional tools for everyday management (see also Höllerer et al. 2019) or make organizational members more aware of their use of multimodal resources, thereby opening avenues for further improvement. For instance, multimodal artefacts can be employed to store and retrieve tacit and elusive knowledge (e.g., Tahim and Bezemer, Chapter 9; Toraldo, Islam, and Mangia 2018) that would be difficult to verbalise. Such elusive knowledge might, however, be multimodally transmitted through sketches, prototypes, and infographics. In order to do so, organizational practitioners need to become more familiar with the 'toolbox' of social semioticians. Multimodality can also be utilised to elicit cognitive and affective responses from crucial stakeholders. This is immediately relevant for information campaigns. In this regard, direct collaboration between social semioticians and practitioners (e.g., van Leeuwen and Zonjic, Chapter 3) might be a valuable exercise. Björkvall (Chapter 5) shows how the 'affective civil servant' is constructed through multimodal organizational communication in the attempt to frame public authorities as open, committed, and courageous. If such attempts are to succeed, organizational decision makers are well advised to learn more about how multimodality works and how it can be strategically employed to convince and persuade. Interactions with social semioticians may, therefore, equip managers and decision makers with the required tools to purposefully design organizations and meanings in a way that facilitates the achievement of organizational goals.

Creating and sustaining mutually beneficial research relationships between social semioticians and (business) organizations

Doing multimodal research that is not solely based on secondary or publicly available data but, rather, on deep immersion in 'natural' organizational settings – such as in observatory, participatory, or ethnographical research designs (e.g., Rouleau, De Rond, and Musca 2014; Smets et al. 2014) – requires an appreciation of the various complexities of working with actual organizations (and, therefore, with people within organizations) and the wide range of sensitivities that need to be accommodated and interests that need to be balanced. Such issues go well beyond matters of university ethics in data collection or the practicalities of obtaining the rights for reproducing and publishing material. Among other things, researchers need to be aware of potentially conflicting rationales and objectives, divergent perceptions regarding the value of academic and commercial work, questions of confidentiality in the context of data access and analysis, and/or vastly different time horizons and expectations regarding results, findings, and outcomes. After all, doing research in real-world settings implies a multiplicity of social relationships that need to be carefully initiated, crafted, nurtured, and sustained.

This section draws from the authors' experience in working with a range of organizations across the private, public, and non-profit sectors in order to elucidate and elaborate some of these points, culminating in a few pieces of practical advice for effective engagement with organizations and their representatives when doing multimodal research in organizational and corporate settings. The following sections are structured according to different phases of the research process, although some issues and points of advice are clearly relevant throughout the entire process.

Getting in touch and building relationships

More often than not, initiating contact and gaining access to (business) organizations proves a considerable challenge not only for social semioticians but also for experienced organization and management researchers – and in this way often inhibits applied and engaged scholarship. In many cases, roadblocks are grounded in the different rationales at play between potential partners. This can be as fundamental as mutual resentments (i.e., 'capitalist corporations' vs. 'ivory tower academics') that prevent collaboration in the first place or very different expectations for the outcome of a potential collaboration. Both are indicative of a lack of mutual trust and prohibitive of the kind of research we envisage here and, therefore, need to be overcome. Additional obstacles are more practical in their nature and often revolve around finding the right partner organization and getting a foot in the door.

One useful strategy, rather than cold-calling any organization, is to make use of brokers and intermediaries (such as the university's alumni network) or champions of particular ideas (such as leaders of specific change projects within an organization) who can vouch for the researchers, facilitating access and overcoming gatekeepers. Good examples for this approach are a recent (multimodal) Stanford Graduate School of Business case study on the large-scale reorganization and restructuration of one the largest banks in Central and Eastern Europe (Sutherland et al. 2020) as well as, of course, the studies underlying various chapters in this book. Many universities these days have dedicated research and engagement offices that are keen to help with finding an interested partner organization and establish a first point of contact; teaming up with other academics, for instance from a business school, in order to form a multidisciplinary team that 'speaks the language' of business organizations might also be a promising approach. And sometimes, an organization may have a specific problem or need and seeks social science academic expertise on this, though this is still rare. In fact, creating trust is, therefore, one of the main tasks at the beginning of (and throughout) any such relationship. Even if access is granted – for instance, based on external pressure – it is highly likely that a lack of trust toward researchers will lead to them only ever seeing and hearing the 'official' accounts as produced by the organization's public relations machinery rather than authentic insights into the actual day-to-day workings of the focal organization.

Once initial contact is established, the first round of conversations is of crucial importance. It is important that the researcher is clear on what the multimodal research project is focused on, what commitment will be needed from the side of the partner organization; what the timelines are, and what the envisaged outcome will be (not in terms of analysis, obviously, but in terms of 'products'). In other words, adequately positioning the research is pivotal; it is essential to identify what the mutual benefits could be and explore why the organization should be interested. Successful research in real-world settings is regularly a two-way partnership, so the interests, concerns, and needs of the partner organizations have to find a place in the design of the research project. The more this can be anticipated prior to the first round of conversations, the better. On the other hand, researchers are not, cannot be, and, in our view, also should not act in the capacity of, a more 'sophisticated' (but usually cheaper) business consultancy. It is, therefore, equally important to be transparent, on both sides, about the kind of insights each partner is interested in scientifically and how and where these insights will be disseminated.

The best way to shape the future partnership is to proactively suggest potential research design options and foreshadow specific deliverables also for the partner organization. In addition to sharing academic outcomes (such as publications, in which many practitioners may have an interest), a way that has worked well for us is to suggest formats that benefit the organization. This can include acting as 'critical friends', for instance, during a change process in an organization (selling the value of the critical outsider view) and offering feedback workshops with decision makers. All of this will require extra work, but quite often, the rewards for the researcher along the way are more than worth it. In addition to advanced data access, such conversations early on help to establish a respectful partnership, set the tone between the partners involved, and further build trust. In time, a record of successful partnerships will also facilitate access to other organizations, as networks of potential testimonials grow. Above all, discussing methodological design options and potential deliverables will assist in clarifying mutual expectations that are ideally codified in a short memorandum of understanding, summarising the cornerstones of the research partnership.

Doing research in organizational settings

Trust and agreement on mutually beneficial protocols continues to be crucial during the phase of actually conducting research in organizational and corporate settings. For instance, a researcher often operates in sensitive or high-pressure settings; carefully creating adequate processes and protocols for non-invasive data collection will be important in such contexts as is the handling of intellectual property, commercial interests, and issues of privacy and confidentiality. Developing a shared understanding of what can go into the public domain (via research publications) and what needs to stay within the partner organizations is a delicate matter and a balancing act that highlights the often-problematic trade-offs between commercial interests and academic freedom.

All this helps in further nurturing and leveraging the growing relationship with key actors within the focal organization. For instance, once working 'in the field', the researcher might become aware of additional data sources or internal documents that s/he wishes to access. Getting in-kind support (for instance, the opportunity to access a company's historical records) or even mobilising financial support is something that might become an opportunity once the partnership unfolds. In our own work, we have been modest in asking for such support prior to or in the early phases of the project (unless there are substantial deliverables for the organization agreed upon) but often have received support at a later stage once we presented first insights or have ended up conducting company-funded follow-up research. Of course, every collaboration is different in this respect, but it is certainly something to consider.

Finally, one of the most important challenges is to make sense of organizational settings and to differentiate the unremarkable from the remarkable, surprising, and counterintuitive. This is anything but trivial, and it will take time. To fully understand the inner workings of an organization, it is necessary to deeply immerse oneself in its daily practices, to understand standard processes (such as workflows, lines of communication, hierarchies, flow of resources), and to collect and analyse data that is not directly related to the core of the multimodal project (for instance, via focused interviews). In other words, it is crucial for the researchers to sensitise themselves to the research setting. Too often, we have seen colleagues missing out on research opportunities due to not 'doing their homework' prior to entering organizational settings they were insufficiently familiar with. The good news here is that such engagement pays off twice: by learning the 'language' of a specific organization and developing the capacity and willingness to actively listen to what is going on around them, researchers develop a sensitivity toward what is important in the empirical field, but they also learn how to talk to organizational members in their own language. This increases mutual understanding and trust and increases the ability of researchers to give back something of value (see below).

Even further down the line in ongoing research, we regard it as good practice to regularly create and maintain ample feedback loops. Not only is such feedback (for instance as interim reports) to the benefit of the partner organization and something that can be positioned as a deliverable upfront, but it also helps the researcher in terms of quality assurance (plausibility and robustness checks of preliminary insights and findings).

Giving back and staying in touch

Successful research collaborations are almost always a two-way relationship, and (business) organizations rarely just open their doors for us to observe and study them in detail without having an interest in the outcomes. And why would they? As much as researchers are concerned with collecting data and getting their analysis and findings published, the organizations granting access and sharing their resources (e.g., funding, productive time of their employees, etc.) equally wish to get something out of it – or at least wish to drive home a few core learnings.

One important aspect for research, therefore, is to give back. Considering the very different time horizons for managerial decision-making and for publishing in academic outlets in the social sciences, this is not something that emerges naturally. Rather, we have to think about feasible ways of giving back during the entire collaboration and, of course, in particular, toward its end. There are manifold ways of doing so: interim and final reports, executive summaries of key insights, training workshops with key stakeholders in the organization, or 'fireside chats' with decision makers, to name but a few. While researchers can manage expectations and even suggest formats that they feel most comfortable with and that distract least from the core of the research project, it is always good to have an open ear for what is most beneficial for the partner organization. This, however, requires a certain 'literacy' in their language (see above), and, again, their choice of preferred feedback format might help researchers to understand them even better.

Often, researchers are concerned, or even worried, when it comes to communicating critical feedback – when insights have the potential to challenge current practices or reveal something unfavourable about the organization. This indeed has to be handled carefully in the dissemination of findings to the outside world (note that there are always different ways of saying the very same thing). It is crucial to respect whatever agreement the partnership is based on (issues of confidentiality, etc.). However, organizational decision makers themselves do not usually expect praise from research; they wish to receive the critical outsider view and are interested in what might be referred to as 'critical consulting'. Different audiences might call for different emphases. So, our advice is to definitely not hide these critical aspects but, rather, bring them to the table early on during internal feedback sessions. Of course, such feedback (and any communicated research findings) should always constitute a fair, just, and comprehensive view of the organization and not only focus on selected (negative) glimpses of organizational realities, despite the critical voice that academia has to play. Well aware of our own values and the prejudices that we as researchers might bring to the table, we argue for a careful and more neutral stance in order to respect the values in place in the settings we empirically study.

Eventually, once data collection is finished, or the entire project and research collaboration has ended, we continue to see a lot of value in staying in touch and nurturing emerging networks with practitioners. It is indeed interesting to see how organizations 'digest' and incorporate feedback from academia, although often they do so indirectly and sometimes with a considerable time lag. Nourishing relationships with the people interviewed, talked to, or worked with in organizational settings can, therefore, be a rewarding experience and might even lead to follow-up research projects with the focal organization or other organizations that are in some way connected to the former partner organization.

Summing up, we wish to repeat that any engagement and collaboration of this type needs to be based on an equal footing. Practitioners should not be treated as 'objects' of research but partners; researchers should not become 'hired hands' doing the bidding of their paymasters but (scientific) experts whose critiques and suggestions feed back into the organization. An equal partnership between social semioticians and practitioners gives practitioners a chance to benefit from the critical and imaginative stance that independent academic researchers can still afford and gives social semioticians a chance to benefit from the insights and experience of practitioners and to make a difference to the world 'out there'.

Concluding remarks

Our objective in this chapter was to make a compelling case for *organizational semiotics* as a research program and perspective that is beneficial for both social semioticians and organizations – and also an inspiring complement to organization theory. For this purpose, we have built our arguments in several steps.

First, we have pointed to common interests between social semioticians and researchers of organizations: both communities are fundamentally concerned with the tensions between *functionality* and *symbolism*, between *the material* and *the discursive*, and with issues of *innovation, dynamism*, and *(re)contextualisation*. This provides a solid basis for synergies in the study of multimodal organizational realities.

Building on these common interests, we have, in a second step, outlined the opportunities that an engagement with organizations provides for social semioticians. We have argued in detail that organizations not only provide fertile empirical soil for the application of semiotic insights but that organization theory also provides theoretical concepts that are an organic complement to the theoretical foundations of social semiotics. We have discussed particularly relevant issues on the *intra-organizational* and *inter-organizational* levels as well as at the interfaces of *organizations* and *their broader cultural and institutional environments*. For each of these areas of research, we have provided examples for existing and/or potential research from an organizational semiotics perspective. Additionally, we have suggested that an engagement with organizations does not necessarily imply an 'instrumental' agenda of improving performance and, ultimately, profit. Organizations are, beyond their immediate objectives, central members in broader society, and, these days, many of them, in fact, strive to actively improve societies.

Third, we have presented ideas about why organizations should be interested in insights stemming from social semiotics. Our argument was that managerial work is, in many respects, semiotic work. Specifically, we have highlighted three central areas in which the management of organizations can benefit from a more in-depth and systematic engagement with multimodality: *organizational design, leadership and the coordination of effort*, and *accounting and accountability*. We have further identified three processes or mechanisms through which organizational semioticians can have a direct real-world impact on organizations and their management: *educating* about multimodality, its potential, and its influence on organizations; *elucidating* taken-for-granted ways of employing multimodality from a 'critical outsider' perspective; and *consulting* to and with organizations for more effective and reflexive uses of multimodal resources.

Fourth, and finally, we have also provided a few selected insights on the practicalities of 'doing' *organizational semiotics* – that is, collaborating with real-world organizations. Here, we have highlighted different aspects related to *getting in touch, conducting the research*, and *giving back*.

We realise that many of the arguments presented here (and in Chapter 1) may sound great in theory, whereas the 'devil', as always, is in the details. In the remainder of this volume, therefore, we give voice to a variety of researchers that have engaged with organizations and organizational issues from a social semiotic perspective to illustrate the practical feasibility and value of our suggestions. Just like the contemporary organizational landscape – and its topics and issues – the contributions to this volume are diverse, with different empirical foci, conceptual foundations, and methodological approaches. They illustrate the potential breadth and variety of contributions that organizational semiotics can make. We hope that the research presented in the following chapters completes and complements our foundational concepts and presents organizational semiotics as an inspiring, inclusive, and relevant field of study.

References

Abrahamson, E., and G. Fairchild. (1999). "Management fashion: Lifecycles, triggers, and collective learning processes." *Administrative Science Quarterly* 44(4): 708–740.

Adler, P.S., P. Du Gay, G. Morgan, and M.I. Reed (Eds.). (2014). *The Oxford Handbook of Sociology, Social Theory, and Organization Studies: Contemporary Currents*. Oxford Handbooks.

Ahrne, G., and N. Brunsson. (2008). *Meta-organizations*. Edward Elgar Publishing.
Alvesson, M., and D. Kärreman. (2000). "Taking the linguistic turn in organizational research: Challenges, responses, consequences." *The Journal of Applied Behavioral Science* 36(2): 136–158.
Astley, W.G., and R.F. Zammuto. (1992). "Organization science, managers, and language games." *Organization Science* 3(4): 443–460.
Barley, S.R., and G. Kunda. (1992). "Design and devotion: Surges of rational and normative ideologies of control in managerial discourse." *Administrative Science Quarterly* 37(3): 363–399.
Barry, D., and S. Meisiek. (2010). "Seeing more and seeing differently: Sensemaking, mindfulness, and the workarts." *Organization Studies* 31(11): 1505–1530.
Bartunek, J.M., and S.L. Rynes. (2014). "Academics and practitioners are alike and unlike: The paradoxes of academic–practitioner relationships." *Journal of Management* 40(5): 1181–1201.
Bell, E. (2012). "Ways of seeing organisational death: A critical semiotic analysis of organisational memorialisation." *Visual Studies* 27(1): 4–17.
Bell, E., S. Warren, and J.E. Schroeder (Eds.). (2014). *The Routledge Companion to Visual Organization*. London: Routledge.
Beyes, T., and C. Steyaert. (2012). "Spacing organization: Non-representational theory and performing organizational space." *Organization* 19 (1): 45–61.
Boxenbaum, E., T. Daudigeos, J-C. Pillet, and S. Colombero. (2018a). "Multimodal construction of a rational myth: Industrialization of the French building sector in the period of 1945 to 1970." In M.A. Höllerer, T. Daudigeos, and D. Jancsary (Eds.), *Multimodality, Meaning, and Institutions. (Research in the Sociology of Organizations, Vol. 54B)*. Bingley: Emerald Publishing Limited, 3–36.
Boxenbaum, E., C. Jones, R.E. Meyer, and S. Svejenova. (2018b). "Towards an articulation of the material and visual turn in organization studies." *Organization Studies* 39(5–6): 597–616.
Brandtner, C., M.A. Höllerer, R.E. Meyer, and M. Kornberger. (2017). "Enacting governance through strategy: A comparative study of governance configurations in Sydney and Vienna." *Urban Studies* 54(5): 1075–1091.
Breitbarth, T., P. Harris, and A. Insch. (2010). "Pictures at an exhibition revisited: Reflections on a typology of images used in the construction of corporate social responsibility and sustainability in non-financial corporate reporting." *Journal of Public Affairs* 10(4): 238–257.
Bromley, P., and J.W. Meyer. (2015). *Hyper-organization: Global Organizational Expansion*. Oxford University Press.
Buchanan, R. (2008). "Introduction: Design and organizational change." *Design Issues* 24(9): 2–9.
Burns, T., and G.M. Stalker. (1961). *The Management of Innovation*. Oxford: Oxford University Press.
Burton, R.M., B. Eriksen, D.D. Håkonsson, and C.C. Snow. (2006). *Organization Design: The Evolving State-of-the-art* (Vol. 6). Springer Science & Business Media.
Busco, C., and P. Quattrone. (2015). "Exploring how the balanced scorecard engages and unfolds: Articulating the visual power of accounting inscriptions." *Contemporary Accounting Research* 32(3): 1236–1262.
Comi, A., and J. Whyte. (2018). "Future making and visual artefacts: An ethnographic study of a design project." *Organization Studies* 39(8): 1055–1083.

Cooren, F., E. Vaara, A. Langley, and H. Tsoukas. (Eds.). (2014). *Language and Communication at Work: Discourse, Narrativity, and Organizing. Vol. 4.* Oxford University Press.

Cornelissen, J. (2020). *Corporate Communication: A Guide to Theory and Practice.* SAGE.

Cornelissen, J.P., R. Durand, P.C. Fiss, J.C. Lammers, and E. Vaara. (2015). "Putting communication front and center in institutional theory and analysis." *Academy of Management Review* 40(1): 10–27.

Czarniawska, B., and B. Joerges. (1996). "Travels of ideas." In B. Czarniawska and G. Sevon (Eds.), *Translating Organizational Change.* New York: de Gruyter, 13–48.

Daft, R.L. (2015). *Organization Theory and Design.* Cengage learning.

Davison, J. (2002). "Communication and antithesis in corporate annual reports: A research note." *Accounting, Auditing & Accountability Journal* 15(4): 594–608.

Davison, J. (2015). "Visualising accounting: An interdisciplinary review and synthesis." *Accounting and Business Research* 45(2): 121–165.

Davison, J., C. McLean, and S. Warren. (2012). "Exploring the visual in organizations and management." *Qualitative Research in Organizations and Management* 7(1): 5–15.

Deetz, S. (2003). "Reclaiming the legacy of the linguistic turn." *Organization* 10(3): 421–429.

Diamantopolou, S. and S. Ørevik (Eds.) (2022). *Multimodality in English Language Learning.* London: Routledge.

DiMaggio, P.J., and W.W. Powell. (1983). "The iron cage revisited: Institutional isomorphism and collective rationality in organizational fields." *American Sociological Review* 48(2): 147–160.

Djonov, E., C-I. Teseng, and F.V. Lim. (2021). "Children's experiences with a transmedia narrative: Insights for promoting critical multimodal literacy in the digital age." *Discourse, Context and Media* 43: 1–12.

Doran, Y. (2018). *The Discourse of Physics: Building Knowledge through Language, Mathematics and Image.* London: Routledge.

Drori, G.S., M.A. Höllerer, and P. Walgenbach (Eds.). (2014). *Global Themes and Local Variations in Organization and Management.* London: Routledge, Taylor & Francis Group.

Eisenman, M. (2013). "Understanding aesthetic innovation in the context of technological evolution." *Academy of Management Review* 38(3): 332–351.

Eisenman, M. (2018). "A multimodal investigation of the institutionalization of aesthetic design as a dimension of competition in the PC industry." In M.A. Höllerer, T. Daudigeos, and D. Jancsary (Eds.), *Multimodality, Meaning, and Institutions. (Research in the Sociology of Organizations, Vol. 54A).* Bingley: Emerald Publishing Limited, 183–217.

Erjansola, A.M., J. Lipponen, K. Vehkalahti, H.M. Aula, and A.M. Pirttilä-Backman. (2021). "From the brand logo to brand associations and the corporate identity: visual and identity-based logo associations in a university merger." *Journal of Brand Management* 28(3): 241–253.

Etzioni, A. (1964). *Modern Organizations.* New York: The Free Press.

Fairclough, N. (1993). "Critical discourse analysis and the marketization of public discourse." *Discourse & Society* 4(2): 133–168.

Deng, Y., and Feng, D. (William). (2022). "From researchers to academic entrepreneurs: A diachronic analysis of the visual representation of academics in university annual reports." To appear in *Visual Communication*. DOI: 10.1177/14703572221102180

Gaskins, R. (2012). *Sweating Bullets: Notes about Inventing PowerPoint*. San Francisco: Vinland Books.

Gehman, J., M.G. Grimes, and K. Cao. (2019). "Why we care about certified B corporations: From valuing growth to certifying values practices." *Academy of Management Discoveries* 5(1): 97–101.

Greenwood, R., C. Oliver, T.B. Lawrence, and R.E. Meyer. (2017). "Introduction: Into the fourth decade." In R. Greenwood, C. Oliver, T.B. Lawrence and R.E. Meyer (Eds.), *The SAGE Handbook of Organizational Institutionalism*. London: SAGE, 1–24.

Gylfe, P., H. Franck, C. Lebaron, and S. Mantere. (2016). "Video methods in strategy research: Focusing on embodied cognition." *Strategic Management Journal* 37(1): 133–148.

Halliday, M.A.K. and J.R. Martin. (1993). *Writing Science: Literacy and Discursive Power*. London: The Falmer Press.

Hinings, B., and R.E. Meyer. (2018). *Starting Points: Intellectual and Institutional Foundations of Organization Theory*. Cambridge: Cambridge University Press.

Höllerer, M.A., D. Jancsary, R.E. Meyer, and O. Vettori. (2013). "Imageries of corporate social responsibility: Visual recontextualization and field-level meaning." In M. Lounsbury and E. Boxenbaum (Eds.), *Institutional Logics in Action, Part B*. Bingley: Emerald Group Publishing Limited, 139–174.

Höllerer, M.A., P. Walgenbach, and G.S. Drori. (2017). "The consequences of globalization for institutions and organizations." In R. Greenwood, C. Oliver, R.E. Meyer, and T.B. Lawrence (Eds.), *The SAGE Handbook of Organizational Institutionalism*. London: SAGE, 214–242.

Höllerer, M.A., T. Daudigeos, and D. Jancsary (Eds.) (2018a). *Multimodality, Meaning, and Institutions. (Research in the Sociology of Organizations, 54A and 54B)*. Bingley: Emerald Publishing Limited.

Höllerer, M.A., T. Daudigeos, and D. Jancsary. (2018b). Multimodality, meaning, and institutions: Editorial. In M.A. Höllerer, T. Daudigeos, and D. Jancsary (Eds.), *Multimodality, Meaning, and Institutions. (Research in the Sociology of Organizations, Vol. 54A)*. Bingley: Emerald Publishing Limited, 1–26.

Höllerer, M.A., D. Jancsary, and M. Grafström. (2018c). "'A picture is worth a thousand words': Multimodal sensemaking of the global financial crisis." *Organization Studies* 39(5–6): 617–644.

Höllerer, M.A., T. van Leeuwen, D. Jancsary, R.E. Meyer, T.H. Andersen, and E. Vaara. (2019). *Visual and Multimodal Research in Organization and Management Studies*. London: Routledge, Taylor & Francis Group.

Iedema, R. (2001). "Resemiotization." *Semiotica* 37(1–4): 23–40.

Iedema, R. (2003a). "Multimodality, resemiotization: Extending the analysis of discourse as multi-semiotic practice." *Visual Communication* 2(1): 29–57.

Iedema, R. (2003b). *Discourses of Post-bureaucratic Organization*. Amsterdam: Benjamins.

Jarzabkowski, P., and A.P. Spee. (2009). "Strategy-as-practice: A review and future directions for the field." *International Journal of Management Reviews* 11(1): 69–95.

Jarzabkowski, P., A.P. Spee, and M. Smets. (2013). "Material artifacts: Practices for doing strategy with "stuff"." *European Management Journal* 31(1): 41–54.
Jarzabkowski, P., G. Burke, and A.P. Spee. (2015). "Constructing spaces for strategic work: A multimodal perspective." *British Journal of Management* 26: S26–S47.
Jewitt, C., and G. Kress. (2003). Multimodal Literacy. New York: Peter Lang.
Jones, C., and F.G. Massa. (2013). "From novel practice to consecrated exemplar: Unity Temple as a case of institutional evangelizing." *Organization Studies* 34(8): 1099–1136.
Kaplan, R.S., and D.P. Norton. (2015). *Balanced Scorecard Success: The Kaplan-Norton Collection (4 Books)*. Cambridge, MA: Harvard Business Review Press.
Kieser, A. (1997). "Rhetoric and myth in management fashion." *Organization* 4(1): 49–74.
Knight, S. (2018). "The spectacular power of big lens." *The Guardian*, May 10, 2018.
Kress, G. (2010). *Literacy in the New Media Age*. London: Routledge.
Kress, G., C. Jewitt, J. Ogborn, and C. Tsatsarelis. (2001). *Multimodal Teaching and Learning: The Rhetorics of the Science Classroom*. London: Continuum.
Kvåle, G. (2016). "Software as Ideology: A multimodal critical discourse analysis of Microsoft Word and SmartArt." *Journal of Language and Politics* 15(3): 259–273.
Lawrence, P., and J. Lorsch. (1967). *Organization and Environment: Managing Differentiation and Integration*. Cambridge, MA: Harvard University Graduate School of Business Administration.
Ledin, P., and D. Machin. (2016). "Strategic diagrams and the technologization of culture." *Journal of Language and Politics* 15(3): 322–336.
Lefsrud, L., H. Graves, and N. Phillips. (2020). "'Giant toxic lakes you can see from space': A theory of multimodal messages and emotion in legitimacy work." *Organization Studies* 41(8): 1055–1078.
Leixnering, S., and S. Bramböck. (2013). "Public-corporate-governance-kodizes: Die Köpenickiade der Beteiligungsverwaltung." *Zeitschrift für öffentliche und gemeinwirtschaftliche Unternehmen: ZögU/Journal for Public and Nonprofit Services* 36(2–3): 170–190.
Leonardi, P.M., and S.R. Barley. (2010). "What's under construction here? Social action, materiality, and power in constructivist studies of technology and organizing." *Academy of Management Annals* 4(1): 1–51.
Machin, D. (2004). "Building the world's visual language: The increasing global importance of image banks in corporate media." *Visual Communication* 3(3): 316–336.
Macken-Horarik, M., K. Love, L. Unsworth, and C. Sandiford. (2017). *Functional Grammatics: Re-conceptualizing Knowledge about Language and Image for School English*. London: Routledge.
Meyer, J.W., and P. Bromley. (2013). "The worldwide expansion of 'organization'." *Sociological Theory* 31(4): 366–389.
Meyer, J.W., and B. Rowan. (1977). "Institutionalized organizations: Formal structure as myth and ceremony." *American Journal of Sociology* 83(2): 340–363.
Meyer, R.E. (2014). "'Relocalization' as micro-mobilization of consent and legitimacy." In G. Drori, M.A. Höllerer, and P. Walgenbach (Eds.), *The

Glocalization of Organization and Management: Global Themes and Local Variations. New York and London: Routledge, 79–89.
Meyer, R.E., and M.A. Höllerer. (2010). "Meaning structures in a contested issue field: A topographic map of shareholder value in Austria." *Academy of Management Journal* 53(6): 1241–1262.
Meyer, R.E., and E. Vaara. (2020). "Institutions and actorhood as co-constitutive and co-constructed: The argument and areas for future research." *Journal of Management Studies* 57(4): 898–910.
Meyer, R.E., M.A. Höllerer, D. Jancsary, and T. van Leeuwen. (2013). "The visual dimension in organizing, organization, and organization research: Core ideas, current developments, and promising avenues." *Academy of Management Annals* 7(1): 487–553.
Meyer, R.E., D. Jancsary, and M.A. Höllerer. (2021). "Zones of meaning, Leitideen, institutional logics: And practices: A phenomenological institutional perspective on shared meaning structures." In M. Lounsbury, D.A. Anderson, and P. Spee (Eds.), *On Practice and Institution: Theorizing the Interface: Volume 70*. Emerald Publishing Limited, 161–186.
Miller, D., R. Greenwood, and R. Prakash. (2009). "What happened to organization theory?" *Journal of Management Inquiry* 18(4): 273–279.
Mintzberg, H. (1980). "Structure in 5's: A synthesis of the research on organization design." *Management Science* 26(3): 322–341.
New London Group. (1996). "A pedagogy of multiliteracies: Designing social futures." *Harvard Educational Review* 66(1): 60–92.
O'Halloran, K.L. (2005). *Mathematical Discourse: Language, Symbolism and Visual Images*. London and New York: Continuum.
Painter, C., J.R. Martin, and L. Unsworth. (2013). *Reading Visual Narratives: Image Analysis of Children's Picture Books*. London: Equinox.
Perrow, C. (1991). A society of organizations. *Theory and Society* 20(6): 725–762.
Phillips, N., T.B. Lawrence, and C. Hardy. (2004). "Discourse and institutions." *Academy of Management Review* 29(4): 635–652.
Putnam, L.L., and S. Boys. (2006). "Revisiting metaphors of organizational communication." In S.R. Clegg, C. Hardy, T.B. Lawrence, and W.R. Nord (Eds.), *The Sage Handbook of Organization Studies*. 2nd edition. SAGE publications, 541–576.
Quattrone, P. (2009). "Books to be practiced: Memory, the power of the visual, and the success of accounting." *Accounting, Organizations and Society* 34(1): 85–118.
Quattrone, P., M. Ronzani, D. Jancsary, and M.A. Höllerer. (2021). "Beyond the visible, the material and the performative: Shifting perspectives on the visual in organization studies." *Organization Studies* 42(8): 1197–1218.
Ravelli, L., and R. McMurtrie. (2016). *Multimodality in the Built Environment: Spatial Discourse Analysis*. London: Routledge.
Roderick, I. (2016). "The politics of office design." *Journal of Language and Politics* 15(3): 274–287.
Rose, D., and J. Martin. (2012). *Learning to Write, Reading to Learn: Genre, Knowledge and Pedagogy in the Sydney School*. Sheffield, United Kingdom: Equinox Publishing.
Rouleau, L., M. de Rond, and G. Musca. (2014). "From the ethnographic turn to new forms of organizational ethnography." *Journal of Organizational Ethnography* 3(1): 2–9.

Sandner, K. (1990). *Prozesse der Macht. Zur Entstehung, Stabilisierung und Veränderung der Macht von Akteuren in Unternehmen*. Berlin, Heidelberg, New York: Physica.

Schoeneborn, D. (2011). "Organization as communication: A Luhmannian perspective." *Management Communication Quarterly* 25(4): 663–689.

Smets, M., G. Burke, P. Jarzabkowski, and P. Spee. (2014). "Charting new territory for organizational ethnography: Insights from a team-based video ethnography." *Journal of Organizational Ethnography* 3(1): 10–26.

Strang, D., and J.W. Meyer. (1993). "Institutional conditions for diffusion." *Theory and Society* 22(4): 487–511.

Suchman, M.C. (1995). "Managing legitimacy: Strategic and institutional approaches." *Academy of Management Review* 20(3): 571–610.

Suddaby, R., D. Seidl, and J.K. Lê. (2013). "Strategy-as-practice meets neo-institutional theory." *Strategic Organization* 11(3): 329–344.

Sutherland, M., S. Soule, S. Leixnering, and M.A. Höllerer. (2020). *ERSTE Group: Transformation of a Banking House – Change, Leadership, Space. Case OB 101*. Stanford Graduate School of Business, Stanford: Stanford University.

Tolbert, P.S., and L.G. Zucker. (1996). "The institutionalization of institutional theory." In S.R. Clegg, C. Hardy, and W.R. Nord (Eds.), *Handbook of Organization Studies*. London: SAGE, 175–190.

Toraldo, M.L., G. Islam, and G. Mangia. (2018). "Modes of knowing: Video research and the problem of elusive knowledges." *Organizational Research Methods* 21(2): 438–465.

Tufte, E.R. (2006). *The Cognitive Style of PowerPoint Pitching Out Corrupts Within*. Cheshire, Ct: Graphics Press.

Unsworth, L. (Ed.) (2008). *Multimodal Semiotics: Functional Analyses in Contexts of Education*. London/New York: Continuum.

Vaara, E., and R. Whittington. (2012). "Strategy-as-practice: Taking social practices seriously." *Academy of Management Annals* 6(1): 285–336.

Van Leeuwen, T. (2005). *Introducing Social Semiotics*. London: Routledge.

Van Leeuwen, T. (2008). *Discourse and Practice: New Tools for Critical Discourse Analysis*. New York: Oxford University Press.

Van Leeuwen, T. (2021). *Multimodality and Identity*. London: Routledge.

Van Leeuwen, T., and G. Rasmussen. (2022). "The human touch: Analyzing online and offline shopping. Special issue." *Discourse & Communication* 16(2): 149–159.

De Vaujany, F.X., A. Adrot, E. Boxenbaum, and B. Leca (Eds.). (2019). *Materiality in Institutions: Spaces, Embodiment and Technology in Management and Organization*. London: Palgrave Macmillan.

Vith, S., A. Oberg, M.A. Höllerer, and R.E. Meyer. (2019). "Envisioning the 'sharing city': Governance strategies for the sharing economy." *Journal of Business Ethics* 159(4): 1023–1046.

Wasserman, V., and M. Frenkel. (2011). "Organizational aesthetics: Caught between identity regulation and culture jamming." *Organization Science* 22(2): 503–521.

Wasserman, V., and M. Frenkel. (2015). "Spatial work in between glass ceilings and glass walls: Gender-class intersectionality and organizational aesthetics." *Organization Studies* 36(11): 1485–1505.

Wedlin, L., and K. Sahlin. (2017). "The imitation and translation of management ideas." In R. Greenwood, C. Oliver, T.B. Lawrence and R.E. Meyer (Eds.), *The SAGE Handbook of Organizational Institutionalism*. London: SAGE, 102–127.

Weick, K.E. (1995). *Sensemaking in Organizations* (Vol. 3). London: SAGE.
Zeitz, G., V. Mittal, and B. McAulay. (1999). "Distinguishing adoption and entrenchment of management practices: A framework for analysis." *Organization Studies* 20(5): 741–776.
Zhao, S, E. Djonov, and T. van Leeuwen. (2014). "Semiotic technology and practice: A multi-modal social semiotic approach to PowerPoint." *Text & Talk* 34(3): 349–375.
Zilber, T.B. (2017). "The evolving role of meaning in theorizing institutions." In R. Greenwood, C. Oliver, R.E. Meyer, and T.B. Lawrence (Eds.), *The SAGE Handbook of Organizational Institutionalism*. London: SAGE, 418–446.
Zilber, T.B. (2018). "A call for "strong" multimodal research in institutional theory." In M.A. Höllerer, T. Daudigeos, and D. Jancsary (Eds.), *Multimodality, Meaning, and Institutions. (Research in the Sociology of Organizations, Vol. 54B)*. Bingley: Emerald Publishing Limited, 63–84.
Zuckerman, E.W. (1999). "The categorical imperative: Securities analysts and the illegitimacy discount." *American Journal of Sociology* 104(5): 1398–1438.

3 The resemiotisation of health information in a family planning organization

Theo van Leeuwen and Nikolina Zonjic

Introduction

In this chapter, we analyse the health promotion practices of Family Planning New South Wales (FPNSW), a non-profit organization delivering clinical and health promotion services in the area of sexual and reproductive health across the Australian state of New South Wales. We describe how health promotion materials (web pages, videos, brochures, posters, etc.) are developed by the organization and how, in the process, medical information is translated 'multivocally' (Ferraro, Etzion, and Gehman 2015) to address different population groups – people from culturally and linguistically diverse (CALD) backgrounds, Aboriginal and Torres Strait Islander people, and young people from both of these backgrounds. Such translations change predominantly verbal 'factsheets' into a range of rich, multimodal texts that aim at making information more accessible and acceptable to the communities addressed but also add further layers of meaning, translating social and cultural diversity into semiotic diversity.

From the point of view of organizational communication, FPNSW's health promotion work is an example of communication to stakeholders, more particularly to the 'market'. Cornelissen (2020, 5) defines communication with stakeholders as seeking to 'establish and maintain favourable reputations with stakeholder groups upon which the organization is dependent' and the market as 'a defined group for whom a product is or may be in demand (and for whom organization creates and maintains products and service offerings)' (10). However, as our analysis will show, FPNSW primarily promotes women's health and 'health literacy', rather than itself as an organization. Even though all FPNSW's health promotion resources feature the organization's logo, other sources of reliable health information and services are presented as just as valid. Nevertheless, as we will see, FPNSW's approach to health promotion does have elements in common with marketing, such as the use of focus groups 'aimed at anticipating consumer desires' and the use of advertising strategies such as 'constructing narratives of satisfactory future experiences' (Beckert 2021, 9).

Our analysis will focus on the process of developing health promotion resources as well as on the outcomes of this process, the resources themselves – on practice as well as product. To do so, we use Iedema's concept of 'resemiotisation', which relates the stages of practices to the way they are semiotically realised. In a study of the planning of a new health facility, Iedema (2001, 2003) showed how this practice began with meetings in which architects, planners, bureaucrats and future users tentatively worked toward a sense of agreement (with some interests gradually marginalised or silenced); then moved to written documents that were not only more formal and general but also more authoritative and non-negotiable than the spoken discourses they resemiotised; then to architectural drawings, which were even less negotiable, as by this time, significant resources had been committed; and finally, to the brick and mortar of the completed facility. Iedema used detailed linguistic and semiotic analyses as explicit evidence for his account of the practice by showing, for instance, how tentative formulations ('Um, but yes basically we do want it to be kept separate, so that eh the other patients don't get sort of affected by people who were brought in') transformed into the authoritative and imperative directives of the written documents ('the patient admission needs to allow discrete transfer of patients'), and how 'qualifiers' ('welfare workers working with students') transformed into 'classifiers' that were no longer negotiable ('student welfare workers').

While Iedema's work was published in journals of semiotics and visual communication, a similar study by Comi and Whyte (2018) was published in an organization studies journal. Like Iedema, Comi and Whyte traced an architectural project through the stages of its development, and, focusing in particular on the use of visual artefacts, they showed how each stage was characterised by specific kinds of visuals – a stage of 'imagining' by impromptu sketches; a stage of 'testing' by drawings that were still flexible and able to be annotated so that they could reflect 'combatting proposals and counterproposals' (Comi and Whyte 2018, 1069); a stage of 'stabilising', using more definite printed drawings and a report; and a stage of 'reifying', using elaborate cardboard models and detailed perspectival drawings. However, their method was primarily ethnographic and did not use detailed semiotic analysis of these drawings and models as evidence for positing the stages.

In this chapter, we combine the two methods, starting with an account of the *practice*, based on ethnographic research, then moving to a semiotic analysis of the *products*. The final section of the chapter then discusses how semiotic analyses can contribute to understanding practices and specifies the transformations realised by each stage of the process. It should also be mentioned that the chapter is the outcome of a collaboration between the health promotion manager of FPNSW and a semiotician with a particular interest in visual communication. It is, therefore, also informed by a practical aim – seeking ways of improving both practice and product.

Practice

In this section, we describe how the production of reproductive and sexual health information materials at FPNSW is organised based on the in-house expertise of one of the authors, on interviews with staff conducted by a research assistant of the other author, on reports from FPNSW community consultations, and on FPNSW design approval documentation.

At FPNSW, the production and distribution of health information resources is the responsibility of the health promotion team. In doing so, the team relies on up-to-date medical information about reproductive and sexual health supplied by the clinical team, which is, in turn, informed by the FPNSW research team, which is responsible for staying abreast of recent developments in the field, liaising with research partners (e.g., universities) and engaging in original research. The first stage of the practice, therefore, identifies an issue about which information is needed and provides relevant information about it. The information about cervical screening used in producing the videos, as discussed later in this chapter, for instance, resulted from new, nationally implemented changes to cervical screening and was prepared in collaboration with the Cancer Institute NSW.

The health promotion team then resemiotises this information, ensuring, on the one hand, that the information remains clinically accurate but, on the other hand, making it accessible to and understandable for the communities they aim to reach. As one staff member put it:

> As a health organization we are very focused on ensuring our content is evidence-based, clinically correct and current […] Our challenge is to use that research, that clinical information, and translate it into information resources for the community […] We have to think very carefully about how we translate research into key messages, calls for action, and information that builds individuals' and communities' capacity to take control of their own health through understanding issues.

This resemiotisation is informed by three key objectives: (1) making the information clear and understandable; (2) making it multimodal through the use of layout, typography, colour, images and diagrams, and, in the case of web resources, interactivity; (3) making it culturally appropriate to the relevant communities.

Making the information clear and understandable means rewriting the clinical information according to 'plain English' principles. The guidebook used at FPNSW advocates using short, clear sentences and everyday words without the use of jargon and aiming at Year 7 readability. It is assumed that the communities addressed 'may speak English as a second language, have very low levels of literacy, and are likely to be on a mobile'. It also means translating the information in a range of relevant languages – in Sydney, where the main office of FPNSW is located, more than 250 languages are spoken, and, according to the latest census, 36% of Australia's population speaks a language other than English at home.

Making the information multimodal means that the resources are not only rewritten but also graphically or audio-visually designed. 'People increasingly rely on images to comprehend the world and themselves' (Slutzkaya, Simpson, and Hughes 2012, 3), especially when they have low levels of literacy. Visuals not only include images of people who will be recognised as 'like us' by the communities addressed, but also images that can familiarise people with relevant objects (e.g., contraceptive devices) and information graphics that provide clear and easily understandable explanations. In this respect, the 'Easy English' guide used at FPNSW is somewhat less than helpful, as it offers more 'don'ts' than 'dos', e.g., 'some illustrations or cartoons can be viewed as childish', or 'avoid the use of tables, maps or diagrams. These can be hard to understand'. The health promotion team, therefore, arranges group consultations with members of the relevant communities, asking questions such as 'What types of images do you prefer (pictures, cartoons, illustrations, drawings, photographs)? Why?' or 'Does putting information in coloured circles makes it easier to read?'

To be effective, health information needs to take into account that not only language barriers but also cultural barriers may prevent the information from being taken up by the relevant communities. In a study of an HIV/AIDS health promotion campaign in Ghana, McDonnell (2010) described the physical barriers that may prevent information from reaching people (e.g., billboards placed in areas where they are unlikely to be seen) as well as the social and cultural barriers that may prevent information from being acceptable. Such barriers also exist in the communities FPNSW seeks to reach. Social, religious, and cultural norms related to sexuality differ across CALD communities, which can affect the acceptability of sexual health resources for young people (see e.g., Ussher et al. 2017), and Aboriginal and Torres Strait Islander young people may be reluctant to talk about sexual issues, whether from a sense of shame, mistrust of non-Indigenous health workers, or fear that confidentiality may not be kept (Queensland Heath 2013). Yet it is exactly these communities that FPNSW seeks to reach, and for good reasons. Research has shown that people from CALD backgrounds in Australia experience poorer reproductive and sexual health than those from an Anglo-Australian background, e.g., higher rates of sexually transmittable infections (STIs) (Dean et al. 2017) yet have lower rates of STI testing (Grulich et al. 2014). There is also a flood of literature on reproductive and sexual health issues amongst Aboriginal and Torres Strait Islander people – higher rates of STIs, blood borne viruses, cervical cancer, unintended pregnancies, and lower rates of contraceptive use (e.g., D'Costa et al. 2019).

The health promotion team must, therefore, also seek to make sexual health information culturally acceptable to different communities. This is, again, achieved through group community consultations in which participants are, for instance, shown images and asked 'Do you find any of these images offensive or confronting?' or young people are asked to list a number of topics in order of importance (e.g., 'consent', 'STIs and safe sex', 'common myths', 'relationships', 'how to use a condom', 'what virginity means') and then asked why they ordered them the way they did. These consultations help the health promotion team to anticipate what communities need and want from health information, in the same way marketing research serves to anticipate consumers' needs and wants.

The consultations may initiate new directions. To give just one example, materials for people with disabilities had, until 2015, used cartoon drawings of disabled people, which was intended to protect them from stigma. However, when people with disabilities were consulted, they rejected this approach and told FPNSW staff, 'We're sick of graphics. Why can we only have graphics for all this stuff? We want real faces, photos.' As a result, Belinda Mason, a well-reputed photographer, was engaged to create a series of photographs of LGBTIQ people with disabilities, as part of a new resource, 'Outing Disability', which included audio stories and a documentary. 'I think now we can actually safely put people out here. But it depends on what we are talking about, what age group we're talking with', as the staff member responsible commented. Following these consultations, the health promotion team writes a detailed brief for the designer and prepares a budget. Once the budget is approved, outside designers, photographers, or videographers are commissioned to produce the resources.

To summarise:

- The first stage of the process has the organization's research and clinical teams identify clinical issues and provide up-to-date medical information.
- In the second stage of the process, the health promotion team targets specific communities and rewrites the information for these communities.
- The third stage involves planning a strategy and testing this strategy with the relevant communities.
- In a fourth stage, the health promotion team writes a detailed brief for the designer and prepares a budget.
- The fifth stage is the actual production of the resource, for which the health promotion team brings in outside designers, photographers, or videographers.
- The sixth stage consists of distributing the resources to relevant community centres, general practice clinics, and so on, and uploading it on the internet.

Each of these stages draws on specific semiotic resources in specific ways. The content provision stage uses specialist written language. The rewriting stage uses 'plain English'. The strategy design stage uses spoken language in the community consultations and written reports to summarise the outcomes of the consultations, the latter in a spreadsheet format, with questions and issues listed vertically and the comments of individual participants entered in the columns. The design brief stage resemiotises these, using a spreadsheet type format that includes suggested images. The production stage, finally, uses the rich array of multimodal resources available to graphic designers and audio-visual producers.

The health promotion team's projects have to be approved by the FPNSW Executive, including, at the time of the research, the Medical Director, the Director of Communications, Government and Community Affairs (DCGCA), the relevant Business Director, and the CEO. The approval processes mark transitions between stages. The first is the 'Approval of Text', in which the team's rewrite is checked by the Medical Director for medical accuracy, by the Research Director for copyright issues, as well as by the relevant Business Director, the DCGCA, the CEO, and, where relevant, by external funders or partner organizations. Many detailed changes may be suggested at this stage, some of which reduce the relative informality of the health promotion team's rewrite; for instance, their use of direct address, 'Otherwise you could still become pregnant' was changed to 'Otherwise the woman could still become pregnant', and 'visit your local GP' was changed to 'visit a local GP' in a brochure about emergency contraception. The second stage is a 'Request for Creative Design', which follows the preparation of the design brief and needs to be approved only by the DCGCA. The third is the 'Design Approval' in which the DCGCA and the relevant Director of Business approve the final product prior to uploading or printing. These approval processes, too, use specific semiotic resources – forms in which the responsible members of the executive can enter brief comments and 'sign offs'.

It can be noted that it is only the words, and not the visuals, that must be approved for medical accuracy, although the visuals may be commented on for other reasons. An image showing a patient undergoing cervical screening in a resource for CALD women, for instance, was judged to show too much of the patient's legs, so the towel covering her legs had to be made longer. Yet visual design contributes significantly to the way medical information is communicated in FPNSW's health information resources. As documented in an earlier report on our research at FPNSW (Crane and Van Leeuwen 2019), a web page titled 'Condoms' included images of a male and a female condom but also an image of a diaphragm, which is not a condom. The health promotion team had wanted to stress that 'condoms are the only method that offer protection from both unintended pregnancy and STIs', and for this reason included the diaphragm, which, like the condom, is a 'barrier' method that protects against unintended pregnancy, but it does not, in fact, protect against STIs. We also noted that of the Medical Director's list of 13 criteria for choosing a contraceptive method, only a few were visualised or visually highlighted. A resource for Aboriginal and Torres Strait Islanders, for instance, only visualised 'effectiveness', 'gender', and 'functionality' (i.e., barrier/implant/pill/intrauterine); a resource for young people visualised only 'effectiveness' and 'functionality'; while a resource for CALD people included more criteria, but omitted illustrating 'STI protection', while visually foregrounding 'effectiveness' by means of highly salient boxes showing effectiveness percentages ('99% effective'). It had been assumed that CALD communities see STIs as being a risk only for promiscuous people. Other important medical criteria, such as 'who fits the device', side effects, and practical criteria, such as cost and availability (e.g., in remote regional areas), were not visualised or visually highlighted at all and, in some cases, were even omitted from the verbal text.

Changes can also occur in the resemiotisation from design brief to actual design. The design brief *Yarning about Girls Business*, a resource about puberty for young Aboriginal girls, for instance, specified including an 'illustration of an Aboriginal girl, speaking the text' and an 'illustration of multiple Aboriginal girls of varied skin tone, body shape and abledness (i.e., one in a wheelchair)', but the designer, herself Aboriginal, did not include these, explaining in an interview that 'they would be too specific' and lack 'a more general appeal across Australia' and that she wanted to focus on symbolic motifs based on Aboriginal art rather than on images of people.

This process we have described is not unique to FPNSW. McDonnell (2010, 1819) distinguishes quite similar stages in his description of the 'flow of work' in the HIV/AIDS campaign in Africa: (1) decide on a theme; (2) collect formative research; (3) choose an audience; (4) develop a variety of campaign concepts and images in collaboration with advertising firms; (5) pre-test mock ups with an audience through focus groups; (6) invite community leaders and stakeholders to give advice; and (7) refine and finalise advertisements. Although he focuses on 'cultural objects' that seek to 'affect beliefs and behaviour', he does not provide a semiotic analysis of the products this practice produces.

In the next section, we provide a detailed analysis of the use of visual communication in three resources developed for specific communities. *Know Your Health: cervical Screening Test* is a set of brochures and videos about cervical screening, produced for CALD people, many of whom are recent immigrants and refugees. *Yarning about Girls Business* is a the already mentioned booklet about puberty produced for young Aboriginal girls. *The Low Down* is a booklet about sexual health and sexual relations produced for young CALD people. All three resources are also published online.

Product

For this section, we have selected three visual analysis 'tools' that we believe are particularly pertinent to understanding the use of visual design in communicating reproductive and sexual health information in accessible and culturally appropriate ways. They are (1) viewer positioning, (2) the distinction between narrative and analytical images, and (3) modality.

Viewer positioning can be strategically used to relate viewers to the people depicted in images. It combines three elements (Kress and Van Leeuwen

2021, 115–143): *contact*, *proximity*, and *attitude*. 'Contact' occurs when depicted people look directly at the viewer. What kind of contact is made (friendly or otherwise, for instance) then depends on their facial expression. 'Proximity' refers to whether portrayed people are shown close up ('close shot') or from a distance ('long shot'). Like contact, proximity indexes interpersonal relations, in images as in real life – the more intimate the relation, the closer we can come; the more formal the relation, the greater the distance we will keep. 'Attitude' relates to the angle from which we see depicted people. The horizontal angle can suggest degrees of involvement or detachment. When the angle is frontal, for instance, the viewer and the depicted person are literally face to face, and maximally involved; however, the more we see depicted people from the side, or even from behind, the greater the sense of detachment. The vertical angle suggests power relations – 'looking up at' or 'looking down on' people – or seeing them at eye level and, hence, relating to them as equals. In short, when it comes to creating a sense of rapport between depicted people and viewers, making viewers think 'these are people like me', or 'these are people I can trust', viewer positioning in images uses the same resources we use in everyday interaction. It can, therefore, be an important tool for getting people to pay attention to the health information provided and avoid some of the cultural and social barriers mentioned by McDonnell (2010), e.g., perceptions that information is produced by elites who do not understand the cultural practices of 'non-elites'.

The *Know Your Health: cervical Screening Test* campaign is produced for CALD people of Middle Eastern origin and provides a new approach to cervical screening that replaced the earlier pap test. It includes videos and brochures that feature images of men and women who appear to be of Middle Eastern origin (see the collage of shots from the videos analysed in Figure 3.1). In four of these videos, men respond to the question 'What is something you do for the special women in your life?' They give answers such as 'Take them out to dinner', 'Share the housework with her', and 'Remind her to have the cervical screening test'. The other videos feature

Figure 3.1 Screen shots from the *Know Your Health: Cervical Screening Test* videos (With permission, FPNSW 2019)

women who are asked 'What is something you forget to do?' They give answers such as 'I forget to call my mother-in-law on her birthday', 'I forget to feed my dog', and 'I forget to get a cervical screening test'. While these videos are oriented to creating awareness of the test, in two other short videos, the same men and women provide information about the test (e.g., 'Four out of five women will have human papillomavirus at some time in their lives. This is known as HPV.'). They are, therefore, not only presented as 'people like us' but also as knowledgeable, health-literate providers of medical information. A longer video shows a consultation between a female doctor and patient and an image of the doctor performing the test, with information provided by a voice over.

Our analysis of the cervical screening has revealed a number of patterns.

- All the depicted community members look at the viewer and are shown frontally and in close shots (head and shoulder shots) and very close shots (closer than 'head and shoulders').
- In the videos aimed at creating awareness, proximity is greater than in the videos aimed at providing information.
- Although the difference is fairly small, women are brought closer to the viewer than men.
- The brochures and the long video also show a doctor, but the doctor does not look at the viewer. She is shown from an oblique angle or from behind, and in a medium shot (approximately from the waist up).

The unspoken but visually evident assumption is (1) that health information will be most effective when it comes from the women's own community and (2) that men must be involved in the decision to have the test. The videos, in fact, replaced an earlier video featuring an Arabic-speaking couple in which only the husband spoke, explaining that he comes from a culture where it is 'difficult to speak about these things' but has realised that 'it is better here' and, therefore, he 'told his wife to have the test'. In other words, this video took into account that, in these communities, the husband was used as an authoritative provider of medical information. In the more recent videos, however, both men and women speak, and both are shown to be health literate. Here, the men are shown as supporting their wives and daughters by reminding them of the test. In both cases, then, the information does not come from medical authorities, and the credibility of the information derives not from the credibility of FPNSW but from the credibility of community members. The one image showing a doctor literally and figuratively 'distances' her.

Yarning about Girls Business, produced for young Aboriginal and Torres Strait Islander girls, provides information on what a period is, on how to use different period products, and on period hygiene. Compared to earlier '*Yarning about*' resources, *Yarning about Girls Business* uses a radically different approach to viewer positioning. Earlier resources had used images of Aboriginal people, but they were drawings rather than photographs, because group consultations had brought out that Aboriginal and Torres Strait Islander people are reluctant to act as the public face for a group. An artist had, therefore, been engaged to draw a number of characters, two of them Elders (one female, 'Aunty Lee', and one male, 'Uncle Peter') and three young people ('Charles', 'Keewa', and 'Janayah'). To avoid the kind of stereotyping still common in cartoons and other entertainment media, the drawings had been based on real models. The inclusion of Elders had been important because of their cultural authority, and the texts had been in dialogue form, with the Elders as providers of medical information, answering the young people's questions in dialogue balloons. There were separate resources for boys and girls, as it can be culturally problematic for Aboriginal women to speak about sexual matters to a man, and vice versa.

The more recent resource, *Yarning about Girls Business*, is still exclusively for girls, as the title indicates. Boys are only briefly mentioned ('Did you know? Boys go through puberty too!'). But the few images of people it contains are highly abstract and do not show any facial features. Rather than seeking to achieve recognition by using images of Aboriginal girls, this resource seeks to achieve recognition by using a visual style that will appeal to Aboriginal girls, a style that combines the visual language of Aboriginal art with the visual language of trendy magazines for teenage girls. The cover of the booklet uses visual motifs that are inspired by Aboriginal art (and produced by an Aboriginal designer) and symbolise the themes of the booklet (see Figure 3.2).

The 'magazine' style is expressed by typography and layout, with pages broken up by mobile phone-shaped boxes containing dialogues between girls. Handwriting-inspired fonts bring a touch of informality and authenticity, and synonyms of the word 'period' are displayed in different, colourful fonts, almost as if they are brand names – 'time of the month' on an old-fashioned banner, for instance, and 'rags' in comic strip style caps on an ascending baseline. Shades of pink and blue used throughout the booklet integrate the two stylistic elements. This leaflet, however much it provides information, also, like advertising, promises future satisfaction, namely the achievement of a successfully hybrid identity, a teenage girl identity that is as Aboriginal as it is in touch with contemporary youth culture. In contrast to the earlier materials, information here is provided not by Elders but by a disembodied authoritative voice and, in text boxes, by peers.

The Low Down, a booklet produced for young CALD people, begins by explaining that a range of caring and consensual sexual relations can be normal and healthy, from a relatively young age, and not only in marriage or in heterosexual relationships. Only once this point has been made does the booklet begin to address issues such as contraception and STIs and myths about sexuality common among young people from CALD backgrounds, such as 'only people who have lots of partners get STIs', 'Males will run out

64 *Theo van Leeuwen and Nikolina Zonjic*

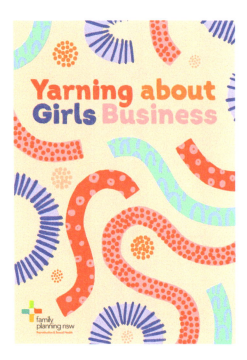

Figure 3.2 Cover of *Yarning about Girls Business* (With permission, FPNSW 2019)

of sperm if they masturbate too much', or 'A female will always bleed the first time she has sex'.

The booklet opens with a large photo of three couples, sitting on a park bench, all smiling happily, sun-dappled trees behind them (Figure 3.3). The image stresses the diversity of sexual relationships. On the left, a girl kisses a boy, sitting on his knees; in the center, a girl sits on the knees of another girl, her arm around her partner; and on the right, a boy sits on the knees of another boy, holding hands with him. They do not look at the viewer and are shown from a certain distance, as though posing on a stage, smiling at each other but not at the viewer, who is, therefore, positioned as an observer who is not (or not yet) part of that group.

The booklet also shows heterosexual couples, and these are shown frontally, at intimate distance (both from the viewer and from each other) and smiling at the viewer. They accompany information on STI prevention, emergency contraception, etc., and so counterbalance information about risks with the promise of a future of happy intimacy. Some show only the lower part of the couples' bodies, which makes their gender somewhat ambiguous, contributing to the inclusivity of the resource.

The booklet contains only one image of a health professional. She is shown from a distance, but frontally and at eye level, smiling invitingly at

Figure 3.3 Pages 1 and 2 of *The Low Down* (With permission, FPNSW 2019)

the viewer. In the final image, a girl holds out a mobile phone, demonstrating her empowerment in actively seeking sexual health information, while her boyfriend looks on in approval, his arm around her.

All three of these resources contain up-to-date, authoritative medical information, but this information is often voiced not by medical authorities but by members of the addressed communities or in non-medical styles of discourse and, where young people are addressed, not by the older generation but by peers. This is most strikingly the case in *Yarning about Girls Business*, which does not represent any health professionals at all and tells readers to talk to 'a friend or family member you can trust', although it also suggests, albeit less saliently, that 'if your period pain is so bad it stops you from going to school or work […] you should go to your doctor, a FPNSW clinic or local Aboriginal Medical Service' and provides a list of contact addresses and telephone numbers. In other words, FPNSW does not only 'advertise' its own services but also those of other reliable providers.

Clearly, in matters of sexual health, medical issues and cultural issues closely intertwine, and FPNSW's resources for young people reflect the way mainstream Australian cultural values around gender and sexuality have evolved over the past half century and continue to evolve, for instance, in relation to gender diversity. These values are not necessarily the same as those traditionally held by many immigrant communities or by some

Aboriginal communities in which homophobia and transphobia have been reported (Korff 2020).

It is equally clear that cultural messages are primarily and most saliently communicated visually through viewer positioning and, in the case of *Yarning about Girls Business*, through a visual style that mixes elements from traditional Aboriginal art with elements from modern magazines for teenage girls, balancing Indigenous culture with mainstream Australian youth culture and, in the case of *The Low Down*, by showing young people whose looks may betray a Middle Eastern background but who are represented as thoroughly integrated in Australian culture and thriving in that identity.

Narrative and analytical visual and the issue of modality

The distinction between narrative and analytical visuals plays an important role in the visual representation of medical and technical information. Analytical visuals show how a whole is made up out of parts and how these parts fit together (Kress and van Leeuwen 2021, 83–102) – usually, but not necessarily, in diagrammatic form, as in the diagrams of the female reproductive organs, which are featured in many FPNSW resources. Narrative visuals (Kress and Van Leeuwen 2021, 44–73), regardless of whether they are drawings or photographs, represent actions or events – processes that unfold over time. In still images, processes are represented by 'vectors' – elements with a sense of directionality, such as arrows or diagonal lines formed by parts of depicted people or things, e.g., an outstretched arm gesturing or holding some kind of tool. Several narrative images can combine in a sequence to show a step-by-step process, whether for purposes of narration or instruction, such as, for instance, in instructional drawings showing how to use a condom or how to insert a tampon. There is always a need to consider whether a particular aspect of sexual and reproductive health is best represented narratively or analytically, for instance, whether 'getting pregnant' is best represented by a dynamic, narrative diagram showing the process of fertilisation or an analytical diagram showing and labelling the female reproductive organs, with the process represented verbally.

Know Your Health: cervical Screening Test uses only narrative images – images in which men and women are seen to speak or listen and, in the case of the doctor, perform the cervical screening test. The brochure does, however, contain a diagram of the female reproductive organs, serving to indicate where the cervix is located. The same diagram can be seen on the desk of the doctor in the long video.

Yarning about Girls Business contains many analytical images, not only the diagram of the female reproductive organs, but also drawings of period products, menstrual cups, and tampons and equally many narrative drawings, showing actions such as showering, washing hands, and inserting a tampon. Images here play a key role in providing technical and practical health information, much more so than in the other two texts we have analysed.

The Low Down, on the other hand, contains only two diagrams. One is a flowchart, hence a narrative visual, explaining in ten steps how to use a condom, with simple icon-style drawings that avoid representing the penis itself. The other is the diagram of the female reproductive organs, which is featured in all the resources we have discussed, but here, only the vulva and the vagina are labelled (the accompanying text also mentions the labia and the clitoris), while the uterus, the fallopian tubes, and so on are neither mentioned in the text nor labelled. In *Yarning about Girls Business*, on the other hand, they are. In other words, *Yarning about Girls Business* represents them as reproductive organs and describes the process of fertilisation ('during sex, if a sperm from a penis meets an egg in the fallopian tube it can travel to the uterus and grow into a baby'), while *The Low Down* represents them as sexual organs, and, on a page about 'Sexual health and the facts', it tells its readers that 'Some people have vaginal sex because they want to have a baby. Other people have sex because it feels good, it is fun and it makes them feel closer to their partner.'

The term 'modality' (Kress and van Leeuwen 2021, 149–173) refers to the degree of realism of an image, not so much in the sense of whether what it depicts actually exists or not, but as in the sense of whether it is represented in realistic detail – with a sense of depth, subtle gradations of colour and light and shade, with or without a background, and so on. The more such means of expression are used, the higher the modality and the more 'photorealistic' the image becomes, regardless of whether it is an actual photograph or not. The realism of such images is, therefore, perceptual, seeking to correspond as closely as possible to our lived experience and to what we would see if we saw the depicted people or scenes in reality. It shows the world in all its diversity and variation. Diagrams, on the other hand, show how things are in general and abstract away from the diversities of specific instances. Its realism is, therefore, cognitive, representing not the surface of things but their defining characteristics, and they can also show body parts or bodily processes that cannot be seen with the naked eye or the photographic lens. Modality is, therefore, an important factor in communicating technical and medical information.

While the images in *Know Your Health: cervical Screening Test* are all photographs that realistically show real people, none of the images in *Yarning about Girls Business* are realistic; they are all abstract, almost icon-like images. This integrates them well with the overall visual style of the booklet and shows a concern with understanding the body and its reproductive functioning rather than a concern with relationships, although there is a brief mention, in fine print, that 'some people might be born one gender, but feel very different inside'. With two exceptions, the images in *The Low Down* are high-modality photographs. Even images of objects, such as condoms, take the form of high-definition photographs rather than icon-style drawings.

As mentioned, modality choices are important. Photographic images can relate information to what we can see and experience in everyday life. Diagrams and drawings aid understanding, but modality choices are also, and at the same time, a matter of taste and style. The modality choices made in FPNSW resources may also result from preferences that have been expressed in community consultations. Young people consulted as part of the production of *The Low Down*, for instance, preferred coloured drawings and photographs and found icons and symbols 'basic and boring', although they also recognised that icons and symbols can 'add to the aesthetics of design and format'. Immigrant women from Afghanistan preferred photographs, seeing them as 'easy to understand', and, as we saw, in the *Know Your Health: cervical Screening Test* resources, photographic images dominated.

Organizational semiotics: practices and products

Resemiotisation is a key concept for organizational semiotics. As we have seen, it results from the staged way in which organizational *practices* are organised, together with the roles and relationships involved, and has its outcome in semiotic *products*, some of which may be intermediary, e.g., design briefs. The practices we have analysed in this chapter involve six stages. They begin with identifying a clinical issue and providing relevant information about it, next move to rewriting the information in 'plain English' and then to designing and testing a communication strategy. This is followed by preparing a design brief, and then by the production and, finally, the distribution of the resource in question. Each stage draws on specific semiotic resources in specific ways. The content provision stage uses specialist written language. The communication strategy stage uses 'plain English' in the rewriting of the medical information. The strategy design stage uses spoken language in the community consultations and spreadsheet-style written reports to summarise the outcome of the consultations. This is then resemiotised in the form of spreadsheet-style design briefs that may include suggested images. The production stage, finally, uses the wide range of multimodal resources available to graphic designers and audiovisual producers. The transitions between the three stages are marked by approval processes that use forms on which the responsible members of the executive can enter brief comments and 'sign offs'.

As the use of semiotic resources changes in the course of this process, so do the meanings that are made with these resources, and this in four fundamental ways (see Van Leeuwen 2008).

1. Information may be *deleted*. We have, for instance, seen that resources for helping people choose a contraceptive method select choice criteria on the basis of what community consultations have shown to be relevant and culturally appropriate. This has, for instance, led to separate

resources for young Aboriginal men and women (see Crane and Van Leeuwen 2019), which select some contraceptive methods as only relevant for boys, others as only relevant for girls. *The Low Down*, on the other hand, addresses young men and women together; although, going by the visuals, some topics (e.g., 'consent') focus mostly on girls, even though the writing uses gender-neutral terms such as 'persons' and 'partners'. We have also seen that diagrams of female reproductive organs may be labelled differently for different groups on the basis of cultural differences between the needs and interests of these groups, as ascertained through community consultation.

2. Information may be *transformed*. Such transformations may be linguistic, as when the informal second person was changed to the more formal third person in the approval process, or visual, as when the source of the information is transformed so that information provided by FPNSW is represented as provided by community members, Aboriginal Elders, or peers, in order to give it the authority and credibility these sources are judged to have in the relevant communities. To give another example, while the design brief of *The Low Down* suggested an 'image of young people in a relationship – it would be good to have an image of a group of young people, but where you can tell two people in the group are a couple', the eventual image showed three couples in diverse relationships (see Figure 3.3).

3. Information may be *added*, often as the result of the basic transformation from verbal to visual information. Visual information inevitably adds detail, particularly when high modality visuals are used. The (formally approved) text of Pages 1 and 2 of *The Low Down*, for instance, says 'People can be attracted to people of the opposite sex, to the same sex, or to both sexes. This is healthy and perfectly normal,' but the concrete details in the photograph not only add a range of more specific ethnic and cultural references and places the 'people' in a sunny outdoor setting but also confronts the viewer much more directly and much less abstractly with the issues at stake (see Figure 3.3).

4. Information may be *rearranged*, as in the case of the reclassification of contraceptive devices, where the diaphragm is (wrongly, as it happens) *visually* co-classified with condoms in the kind of composition, which Kress and van Leeuwen (2021, 76–77) call a 'covert classification', a composition in which people or things are made to look similar (same size, same horizontal and vertical orientation, same background, etc.) to suggest that they belong to the same class of people or things.

Conclusion

We hope we have demonstrated in this chapter not only that resemiotisation plays a vital role in representation and can affect the clinical information

FPNSW seeks to provide but also that analysis can raise issues that may be of practical relevance to organizations. Four issues can be mentioned.

Organizations need to be aware that visuals are not an add-on to make communication 'look good' (Van Leeuwen 2015) but that they play a vital role in making meaning. Individuals and teams involved in all stages of practices of organizational communication need to understand how images and other visuals communicate and have the means to make this understanding explicit, enabling joint enquiries in the way multimodal information is, and should be, provided.

We have shown that visual representation plays a key role in making clinical information appropriate to culturally diverse communities. The concept of 'sexual health' inevitably involves medical as well as moral (and, hence, cultural) issues. Cultural literacy and cultural sensitivity are, therefore, important for all individuals and teams participating in the process and at every stage of that process. Just as effective multimodal meaning-making will benefit from community views as well as from semiotic awareness and analysis, effective and appropriate cultural diversity will benefit both from asking community members questions such as 'Do you find any of the images offensive or confronting?' or 'Is there anything about the resource that worries or upsets you?' and from cultural awareness and analysis.

Training health promotion professionals in semiotic and cultural analysis should empower them to raise awareness and promote dialogue and reflection on multimodal and multicultural communication across the organization at a level equal to that of research and clinical professionals, although this may require a degree of organizational change.

Finally, our analysis has shown the importance of listening to the communities the organization is seeking to reach and of engaging these communities in the process of fostering health literacy. It is important that the multimodal products *themselves* demonstrate that the communities the organization is seeking to communicate with have been listened to and that they are fully included in the multimodal practices of health communication, and, by extension, other forms of communication that are vital to the life of these communities. But self-help with the aid of various kinds of information can only go so far, and it is also important to build the trust in health professionals, which in some communities may be lacking. Our analysis has shown that FPNSW's visual representations of health professionals do not always bring them as 'close' to the communities addressed, literally and figuratively, as is perhaps desirable.

Although we have discussed a specific case, the approach we have followed in this chapter can be applied to other resemiotisation practices as well, including, for instance, processes leading to changes in policies and practices rather than to producing semiotic artefacts such as videos, brochures, and websites. These, too, can be analysed as staged practices that involve people and teams in specific roles and relationships and find their expression in semiotic interactions and artefacts such as meetings, presentations, minutes, policy documents, and so on. These can also benefit from an organizational semiotics approach that inter-relates the ethnographic study of communication practices with the semiotic study of the outcomes of these practices, as we have attempted to do in this chapter.

Acknowledgement

The authors would like to thank Family Planning New South Wales for their participation in the research and its staff members for giving generously of their time. Some of the material in this chapter is also discussed in an article written by van Leeuwen for the journal *Visual Communication* (22,3; in press).

References

Beckert, J. (2021). "The Firm as an engine of imagination: Organizational prospection and the making of economic futures." *Organization Theory* 2: 1–21.
Comi, A., and J. Whyte. (2018). "Future making and visual artefacts: An ethnographic study of a design project." *Organization Studies* 39(8): 1055–1083.
Cornelissen, J. (2020). *Corporate Communication: A Guide to Theory & Practice*. Los Angeles: Sage.
Crane, A., and T. Van Leeuwen. (2019). *The Multimodal Communication of Clinical and Health Promotion Information: A Report to Family Planning New South Wales*. Sydney: Institute for Learning Sciences and Teacher Education, Australian Catholic University.
D'Costa, B., R. Lobo, J. Thomas, and J.S. Ward. (2019). "Evaluation of the Young Deadly free peer education training program: Early results, methodological challenges and learnings for future evaluations." *Frontiers in Public Health* 7(74): 1–11.
Dean, J., M. Mitchell, D. Stewart, and J. Debattista. (2017). "Sexual health knowledge and behaviour of young Sudanese Queenslanders: A cross-sectional study." *Sex Health* 14(3): 254–260.
Ferraro, F., D. Etzion, and J. Gehman. (2015). "Tackling grand challenges pragmatically: Robust action revisited." *Organization Studies* 36(3): 363–390.
Grulich, A.E, R.O. de Visser, P.B. Badcock, A.M.A Smith, J. Richters, C. Risssl, and J.M. Simpson. (2014). "Knowledge about and experience of sexually transmissible infections in a representative sample of adults: The Second Australian Study of Health and Relationships." *Sex Health* 11(5): 481–494.
Iedema, R. (2001). "Resemiotization." *Semiotica* 37(1–4): 23–40.
Iedema, R. (2003). "Multimodality, resemiotization: Extending the analysis of discourse as multi-semiotic practice." *Visual Communication* 2(1): 29–57.
Korff, J. (2020). *Aboriginal People in Australia*. https://www.creativespirits.info/aboriginalculture/people
Kress, G., and T. van Leeuwen. (2021). *Reading Images: The Grammar of Visual Design*. 3rd edition. London: Routledge.
McDonnell, T. (2010). "Cultural objects as objects: Materiality, urban space, and the interpretation of AIDS campaigns in Accra, Ghana." *American Journal of Sociology* 115(6): 1800–1852.

Queensland Health. (2013). *Aboriginal and Torres Strait Islander Adolescent Sexual Health Guidelines.* https://www.health.qld.gov.au/_data/assets/pdf_file/0018/161541/adolescent_sexual_health_guideline.pdf

Slutzkaya, N., A. Simpson, and J. Hughes. (2012). "Lessons from photo elicitation: Encouraging working men to speak." *Qualitative Research in Organization and Management: An International Journal* 7(1): 16–33.

Ussher, J.M., C. Metusela, A. Hawkes, M. Morrow, R. Narchal, J. Estoesta, and M. Monteiro. (2017). *Sexual and Reproductive Health of Migrant and Refugee Women, Research Report and Recommendations for Healthcare Providers and Community Workers.* https://researchdirect.westernsydney.edu.au/islandora/object/uws:40355

Van Leeuwen, T. (2008). *Discourse and Practice: New Tools for Critical Discourse Analysis.* New York: Oxford University Press.

Van Leeuwen, T. (2015). "Looking good: Aesthetics, multimodality and literacy studies." In J. Rowsell and K. Pahl (Eds.) *The Routledge Handbook of Literacy Studies.* London: Routledge, 426–439.

4 Organizational identity design

The evolution of a university web homepage

Nataliia Laba

Introduction

Marketisation is an important social trend impacting many organizations that formerly did not have to 'compete' for market share, not least universities. As a pervasive feature of contemporary public discourses, it has transformed the ways universities present themselves to different audiences. Universities have to compete for, *inter alia*, customers (i.e., students) and resources (i.e., funding) – that is, to offer knowledge as a saleable commodity through creating and maintaining a distinct organizational identity (Saichaie 2011).

While there may be many factors that contribute to organizational identity, two critical considerations can be highlighted. Firstly, as noted by Mumford in their book *The city in history: its origins, its transformations, and its prospects*, whereas organizational identity can be examined as 'anchored historically in time and place, which constitutes distinctiveness' (Mumford 1968, in Jones and Svejenova 2018, 204), it is never entirely fixed, as it undergoes, arguably, inconspicuous changes of formal elements that nevertheless procure subsequent shifts in communicative functions. Secondly, organizational identity emerges from a social practice of brand communication and is presented multimodally by incorporating a wide range of meaning-making resources including, but also going beyond, language (van Leeuwen 2005). With this in mind, this chapter examines how one university has subtly changed the identity of its web homepage – one of the most strategic spaces for brand communication – over time, focusing not just on language but also images, colour, and layout combined in different semiotic modalities. A close examination of these changes will show that the implications are much more profound than they might at first appear, speaking to how the university presents its identity in terms of core functions.

As an entry point to a website, a web homepage is the first contact with the university. A homepage establishes the identity of the institution it represents, communicates the site's purpose, provides a broad composition of the website, and promotes a positive attitude to the university (Djonov and Knox 2014, 174). While these functions are often studied by different fields of research inquiry, prioritising their disciplinary perspectives (e.g., aesthetics in graphic design and information architecture and optimisation in usability studies), this chapter explores the evolution of a selected university website to understand how design as an underlying logic of the page composition shapes the organizational identity of the university and how, in turn, the organizational identity shapes the design of a web homepage. That is, rather than comparing one university web page to another, the focus is on different iterations of the 'same' web page to reveal nuances of design that create subtle shifts in how the university presents itself, how it positions itself relative to its audiences, and how it prioritises some target audiences over others. The chapter uses a multimodal social semiotic approach based on Halliday's (1978) theory of meaning and social context.

Multimodal social semiotic theory understands 'social' as the collection of meaning-making potentials shaping and being shaped by the contexts of culture and situation. 'Semiotic' signifies the resulting configurations of meaning potentials arising from different semiotic principles of organization (Höllerer et al. 2019, 25). By acknowledging the importance of a sign-maker, a social semiotic approach can provide detailed accounts of various semiotic resources and link these accounts to the contexts of culture and situation (Hiippala 2015, 24). Importantly, this approach understands 'meaning' to be complex and of three fundamental types (metafunctions): the representational metafunction (representing experiences and construing our reality), the interpersonal metafunction (negotiating attitudes and constructing the social reality), and the textual metafunction (positioning the elements of discourse and organising the semiotic reality) (Halliday 2013).

The focus of the study is the University of New South Wales, Sydney (UNSW) and its official web homepage <www.unsw.edu.au>. UNSW was founded in 1946 as the first tertiary institution in Australia with an explicit science and technology orientation, merging with the broader Australian university tradition of a 'comprehensive institution' soon after to expand to a full range of course offerings (Davis 2017). UNSW has established itself as a top-tier university, forty-fourth in the 2021 Quacquarelli Symonds (QS) World University Rankings and sixty-seventh in the 2021 Times Higher Education (THE). As a member of the Group of Eight (Go8), a coalition of Australia's leading universities, it is a research-intensive institution educating more than 59,000 students with approximately 7,000 staff (UNSW 2020).

The study compares three versions of the UNSW web homepage from 2000, 2009, and 2021, as described further below, and examines the 'site of the text itself' (Rose 2016) – that is, the web page presented for interaction. The latest version of the page for analysis is dated 22 May 2021. This version reflects the university's new approach to branding rolled out in January 2021 to 'strengthen and clarify [the] brand positioning and value proposition for key audiences to remain competitive and achieve [the university] ambitions' (UNSW, *Brand FAQs* on staff intranet 2020), coinciding with the major restructuring of the university under the COVID-19 response plan.

The analytical focus of the chapter is twofold. First, it considers the key changes of the layout units in terms of their nature and placement. Next, it addresses the representational logic of the identified layout units and analyses their metafunctional implications. The chapter reveals the evolution of organizational identity design within the broader social phenomenon of marketisation and commodification of knowledge. It confirms the shifts in the functionality of the homepage toward vastly promotional discourses targeting prospective students and alumni, making the homepage 'the portal of the future customer' rather than an inventory of resources for current students and staff.

Background: Web pages

Web pages are web-mediated texts – dynamic structural projections defined by the information architecture, web design, and graphic design. Hypertextuality, or the ability to link pages and documents, stands out as one of their most fundamental features, and it opens up navigation possibilities for readers/viewers, who are often referred to as 'visitors'. Additionally, hypertext brings about implications for knowledge construal – information is now a material for visitors to be transformed into knowledge (Kress 2005), inviting collaboration between the author who creates the structures and *an imagined audience* (see Litt 2012) who follows these structures with a great deal of flexibility and in a way that meets their individual needs. Thus, successful navigation and 'good' design are foci of usability studies, information systems studies, and web design studies (e.g., Fang and Holsapple 2011; Pernice 2013).

The database and Hypertext Abstract Machine (HAM) of nodes and links determining the 'look' of a webpage are largely invisible to different audiences. Instead, visitors experience the level of presentation, the so-called 'above the fold' composed of content and navigation. Different disciplines have studied these aspects of content and/or navigation of web pages in relation to functionality and usability (Astani 2013; Yerlikaya and Durdu 2017), (cross-)cultural expression (Estera and Shahjahan 2019; Pauwels 2005), design (Kress 2005; Martinec and van Leeuwen 2009), and so on. Social semiotic studies on web pages have addressed the issues of hypermodal genre (Askehave and Nielsen 2005; Djonov 2007), marketised discourses (O'Halloran, Wignell, and Tan 2015; Zhang and O'Halloran 2013), and student representation (Tomášková 2015; Zhang and Tu 2019; Zhang et al. 2020). Some studies have focused particularly on Australia, one of the top higher education providers for the international market, including Zhang and Tu (2019) on the representation of international students, and Gottschall and Saltmarsh (2017) on promotional videos. Such studies recognise the multimodal nature of websites, incorporating meaning-making resources beyond language, such as composition, typography, and colour (van Leeuwen 2005). However, none have studied the subtle shifts in form and function of different design elements that represent what an institutional website stands for and what such shifts indicate about organizational identity construed on the page.

A key aspect of the design of web pages is that they carry a significant proportion of visual identification for an organization. Visual identification is the 'way in which an organization uses logos, type styles, nomenclature, architecture and interior design, etc. in order to communicate its corporate philosophy and personality' (Balmer 1995, 26). To reflect the concept of visual identification, a myriad of terms, such as corporate visual identity (CVI), visual identity, organizational identity, brand identity, corporate identity, and more, have been adopted from the corporate milieu to the university setting. Whereas some of the terms encompass a broader set of considerations (e.g., corporate culture, design, communication, behaviour, etc., as proposed by Melewar 2003), the common element, *identity*, denotes the core meaning of these synonymous terms – 'the articulation of a brand or group, including all pertinent design formats, such as the logo, letterhead, business card, and website, among others' (Landa 2013, 245) through an assortment of visual and verbal cues by which different audiences can recognise the institution and distinguish it from others (Melewar et al. 2018).

Analytical framework and data

More broadly, organizational identity communication can be understood as a social semiotic practice that involves four inter-related dimensions: the site of production, the site of the virtual artefact, the site of the medium, and the site of audiencing. Such an approach draws on Kress and van Leeuwen's (2001) stratified model of domains of practice in which meanings are made, combined with the insights on design and visuality from web design and graphic design (Landa 2013), empirical approaches to multimodality (Bateman 2008; Bateman, Wildfeuer, and Hiippala 2017), and a range of methods for doing research with visual material as integrated by Rose (2016). Figure 4.1 visualises these inter-relations.

Briefly, Figure 4.1 posits that *the site of production* of a web page includes web design and graphic design considerations in which the semiotic practice is governed by following the semiotic regime of regulatory institutional discourses (see van Leeuwen 2005, 2008). The organizational identity presented for interaction through *the site of the virtual artefact* embeds institutionally specific values across two layers: *page-flow* and navigation/access structures (Bateman 2008). In line with the social semiotic perspective on meaning-making as a social practice, these two layers are understood as 'mediating social interaction between the "makers", the represented materials, and the

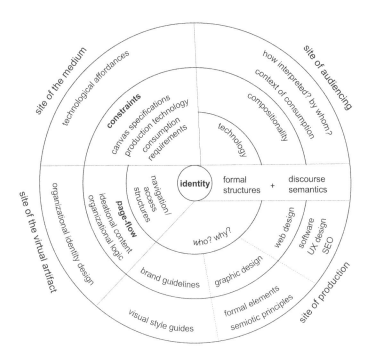

Figure 4.1 Organizational identity communication as a social semiotic practice

(imagined) "readers"' (Bezemer and Mavers 2011, 204). This chapter predominantly addresses the site of the virtual artefact.

The site of the medium includes the material (physical) properties of the medium, affordances of the technology, and its limitations at a given time. In a sense, it is an intermediary between production and audiencing because it has implications for understanding the technological sides of the virtual artefact and the limitations of its consumption.

Lastly, *the site of audiencing* (Fiske, cited in Rose 2016, 38) considers the target audience or by whom the virtual artefact is interpreted. It includes the context of consumption (i.e., the 'where' of interaction with the organizational identity), social identities of the target audience (i.e., their background), the purpose of the interaction, and the canvas used for display (whether the target audience interacts with the virtual artefact through a web browser on a personal computer, phone, etc.).

To annotate and cross-reference the elements of web pages, the genre and multimodality model (GeM) is used (Bateman 2008). The GeM model has proven to be one of the strongest candidates for articulating an account of multimodal design that is sufficiently well-defined and reproducible (Hiippala 2015), particularly from the structural-orientational perspective. The GeM model provides several layers of annotation schema, allowing for sufficiently fine-grained details to be approached as neutrally as possible to make interpretations supportive of empirical investigation. As a foundational layer of analysis, the base layer identifies the 'vocabulary' of the page (Bateman 2008, 108) before interpretative work is carried out. Base level units include text-typographic units (e.g., orthographic sentence, heading), pictorial (e.g., image, video), and diagrammatic (e.g., line, arrow). These are then categorised in the layout layer to reflect both structurally oriented and meaning-making related areas of analysis. Lastly, the discourse semantics layer analyses the meaning potential of the layout units through a trinocular metafunctional view. Together, the layout units and their functional organization construe what Bateman (2008, 176) terms a semiotic mode of the *page-flow*. The *page-flow* combines elements of various materialities (image complexes, text flow, and so on) and adds to the coherence of the overall meaning of the page, which is greater than a sum of meanings of each element, supporting the communicative functions of the page.

This chapter pays attention to the metafunctional foundations of the analysed web pages and is qualitative in nature. It also considers the medium and its materiality to account for a virtual artefact's production and consumption sides. Multimodal research recognises that the material characteristics of visual outputs are important aspects of organizational identity design because the materiality of a visual sign (Kress and van Leeuwen 2021, 224) and canvas (Bateman, Wildfeuer, and Hiipala 2017, 102) impact the shape that the organizational identity takes (i.e., its representational, interpersonal, and textual meanings).

The versions of the UNSW web homepage identified for analysis are based on three indicators of homepage variation: information density (what amount of information is available on the page), layout (how information is structured), and navigation support (what access structures are embedded) (Ryan, Field, and Olfman 2003). The timeline of the available iterations was analysed through the internet Archive's Wayback Machine (http://www.archive.org). Although the university established its web presence in 1997, only the 2000 version became crawlable with the least disruption of the content. Overall, there are eight versions of the web page from 2000 to the time of writing, and three of these that manifest notable changes are selected: 2000, 2009, and 2021 (V1, V2, V3, respectively). Table 4.1 presents the hyperlinks for all versions, with the selected versions in bold.

Analysis and findings

Three 'designs' of the page

The three web pages selected for analysis differ across several dimensions: information density (amount of information present on a page), layout, and navigation styles (see Figures 4.2–4.3). Different versions of the UNSW homepage feature different configurations of base elements

Table 4.1 Historical versions of the UNSW homepage

Number	Date	Link
(V1) 1	02 Dec 2000	https://web.archive.org/web/20001202165400/unsw.edu.au
2	24 Mar 2004	https://web.archive.org/web/20040324154035/http://www.unsw.edu.au/
3	31 Oct 2008	https://web.archive.org/web/20081031005852/http://www.unsw.edu.au/
(V2) 4	24 Oct 2009	https://web.archive.org/web/20091024040212/http://www.unsw.edu.au/
5	17 Jul 2012	https://web.archive.org/web/20120717042139/http://www.unsw.edu.au/
6	14 Jun 2015	https://web.archive.org/web/20150614095543/http://www.unsw.edu.au/
7	06 Oct 2020	https://web.archive.org/web/20201003165121/https://www.unsw.edu.au/
(V3) 8	22 May 2021	https://web.archive.org/web/20210522081258/https://www.unsw.edu.au/

combined into layout units, such as text-flow, image-text complexes, tabled multimedia, and stand-alone deictic expressions (Paraboni and van Deemter 2002) – that is, references to other parts of the same document. V1 is typical of homepages when the web was in its infancy (see Vaughan 2001), including the first interactive elements (through which users have the capacity to 'interact' directly with the site, through clicking on menu options and so on) (Adami 2014).

V2 introduced the carousel design embedded at the top of the viewable area – prominently placed multimedia in the upper half/center of the viewport, alternating automatically through a predetermined pattern with embedded diagrammatic resources that indicate user navigation (right/left arrow-like icons). The carousel enables more than one piece of content to 'occupy the same piece of prime real estate on the homepage' (Pernice 2013, n.p.). V2 makes use of Adobe Flash Player as a browser plug-in that allows playing videos directly from the page. In addition to listing the available information, V2 introduces the university memberships in the footer to enhance legitimacy and enhance cross-promotion and branding of the university.

V3 shows significant changes in information infrastructure, increasing in length from 1.3 to approximately seven screens. It discontinues a carousel design and opts for a single hero image, which delimits the content in the viewport and features a single most 'newsworthy' image instead of several alternating images previously enabled by the carousel design. However, the limited interaction potential of the updated viewport design choice is compensated through the length of the page along the vertical axis (i.e., the audience has to scroll down). On the site of production, such a design solution, in turn, requires more careful consideration of the information to

80 *Nataliia Laba*

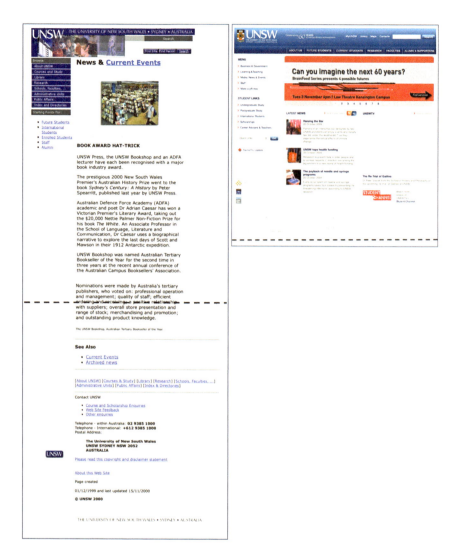

Figure 4.2 Early 'designs' of the UNSW web homepage: (left) V1, (right) V2. *Note.* Above the dotted line is the viewport (the part of the webpage visible on-screen, i.e., without scrolling)

be featured in this guaranteed viewing space. In V3, the spatial correlation between image, verbiage, shape, and colour is more balanced, emphasising visual appeal, text readability, and interactivity.

All CVI elements – corporate name, logo, motto, typography, colour, and graphic shapes – are found on the most recent UNSW web homepage, as prescribed by the accompanying brand guidelines (UNSW, *Brand FAQs* on staff intranet 2020). The nucleus of the university's corporate identity is

Organizational identity design 81

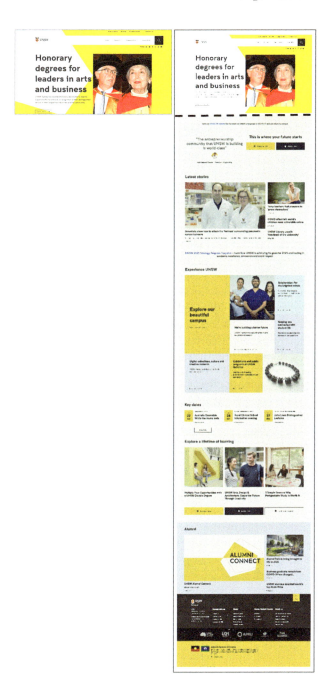

Figure 4.3 V3 of the UNSW web homepage. Note. To the right, the viewport is shown in colour with the webpage 'below the fold' in grey

provided by the corporate name, logo, and motto. These elements ensure identification of the institution, authority of the page, and recognition of the brand. These three CVI elements are present across all analysed versions, comprising the 'heart' of organizational identity and asserting the institution's legitimacy. On the other hand, shifts in typography, colour, and graphic shapes are a 'younger addition' to the university's organizational identity. These elements are the heavy lifters of visual identification of the UNSW brand. Importantly, these structural changes and perceived functions of CVI elements are not dissimilar to the web homepages of other Australian universities. Whereas many studies compare CVI elements across organizations (e.g., Bartholmé and Melewar 2011; van Riel and van den Ban 2001), few comment on consistencies and changes over time within one organization.

Key shifts in form and function

Menu items

Across all analysed versions, some menu items remain consistent with minor updates, such as *logo, name, search,* etc. (Table 4.2). The logo located at the top left of the page enables the interactivity potential of *'return to the top layer of the website'*. The menu items are expressed verbally and usually realised by nouns, verbs, or phrases and point to other parts of the website through several 'interactivity cues' (Adami 2014): *respond to click, respond to hover,* or *respond to type-in and click*. Menu items enable audiences to build their pathways based on their needs and preferences, choosing between, for example, *News and events, Alumni and giving, Study, Research,* and so on.

The menu item *News* appears across all the analysed pages. It is prominently featured in the center of V1 with most verbal text providing details (menu item *News & Current Events*), shifting toward decreased verbal text but maintaining compositional prominence in V2 (menu item *Latest News*) and gradually moving into the below the fold space (i.e., a part of the page one scrolls down to) of V3 (menu item *Latest Stories*), minimising the verbal text to a headline and subheading. It is also preserved as a separate menu item on the top of the page. Although news is not a CVI element, its appearance across all pages demonstrates the assigned importance of notifying different audiences about the university's events and achievements. Table 4.2 highlights continuities and changes of the layout items of the viewport across three designs of the page.

Representationally, the menu items represent relevant communities, with V1 and V2 catering for the needs of a range of key groups, such as future students, current students, staff, alumni, and media. In V3, the representation of communities is delimited to three major groups: (1) Prospective students (both undergraduate and postgraduate) and current students (although these

Table 4.2 Consistencies (in white) and absences (in grey) of the menu items

V1 (2000)	V2 (2009)	V3 (2021)
Logo (wordmark only)	Logo (crest and wordmark)	Logo (crest and wordmark)
	Slogan (Scientia Manu et Mente)	Slogan (Scientia Manu et Mente)
	Login (MyUNSW)	Login (MyUNSW)
The University of New South Wales	The University of New South Wales	UNSW Sydney
Search	Search	[magnifying glass icon]
Research	Research	Research
About UNSW	About Us	About UNSW
News & Current Events	Media, News & Events	News & Events
Future Students	Future Students	Study
Alumni	Alumni & Supporters	Alumni & Giving
Library	Library	
Schools, Faculties, …	Faculties	
Administrative Units	Business & Government	
Enrolled Students	Current Students	
International Students	International Students	
Staff	Staff	
Public Affairs		Engage with Us
	Contacts	[envelope icon] Contact Us
	UNSW TV	Follow [LinkedIn icon] [Twitter icon] [Facebook icon] [Instagram icon] [TikTok icon] [YouTube icon]
Courses and Study	Undergraduate Study	
	Postgraduate Study	

(Continued)

Table 4.2 (Continued)

V1 (2000)	V2 (2009)	V3 (2021)
	Scholarships	
	Career Advisers & Teachers	
	Maps	

are addressed explicitly through one menu item only *MyUNSW*, which also encompasses staff), (2) potential research partners and benefactors, and (3) more general communities (e.g., 'contact us', 'engage with us', i.e., 'anyone'). Staff, an unmistakably crucial part of the university, are not represented via a separate category in the viewport, unlike V1 and V2. The haptically accessible units *About us*, *Contacts*, *Course information*, and *Research* are featured on all versions at the top of the 'real estate' of the homepage, which reflects the major prioritised pathways for potential newcomers. In contrast, the menu item *Library* disappears in V3 – an inconvenience lamented by many staff members. These design choices highlight the underlying function of the page – marketing to prospective and current 'customers' and enrolled students instead of being a functional avenue to find information and 'get the job done' for staff. The options available in menu items show that staff are not 'part of' the visible organizational identity of the institution. Staff members are also infrequently featured in the images present on the page, although their achievements figure prominently as part of news labelled as *Latest stories*.

Logo, motto, and corporate name

The UNSW's logo and corporate name comprise the key layout unit of all analysed versions, establishing the university's identity. Both UNSW's logo and corporate name have undergone some minor representational changes across different versions, but their positioning remains stable across all versions, occupying the top left corner (Figures 4.2 and 4.3), as discussed further below. Upper left-corner logo placement is customary for many corporate institutions. For example, it was a design practice of 94% of the Fortune 500 companies, a ranking of America's largest companies, in 2013 (Jones 2015).

The visual cues of the logo include a shield; an open book with the word 'Scientia' written on it; a red cross and four stars; a lion that appears to be moving (narrative dynamic action); a motto – '*Manu et Mente*' ('knowledge by hand and mind') – written in a ribbon of light blue, and the university's corporate name. The open book signifies the purpose of the institution and is commonly associated with education and erudition (Drori, Oberg, and Delmestri 2017). The use of the coat of arms with heraldic symbols traditionally conveys not only historic pride, but also 'adherence to and validation of strict rules, the authenticity of right, and rigorously authoritative, if not royal, oversight' (Idris and Whitfield 2014, 53). Given that UNSW is a relatively young university with no medieval lineage, the use of heraldry appears to adhere to the founding characteristics of older world-class universities (such as Cambridge, Harvard, and Princeton) that all deploy coats of arms, thus conveying epistemological tradition (see also Drori, Delmestri, and Oberg 2013).

The most recent university's business name is *UNSW Sydney*, introduced in 2017 (following *UNSW Australia*, 2013; *The University of New South Wales*, 1957; and *New South Wales University of Technology*, 1946). The corporate name, thus, invokes a destination narrative (Hansen 2010; Rowley and Hanna 2020) to communicate and cultivate engagement with the destination and reinforce the university's iconic location in the well-known city of Sydney. Such small shifts in naming practices reflect a strategic branding move – localisation of the institutional narrative used to develop a network of positive associations based on the characteristics of the place.

Brand colour

The distinct 'UNSW yellow' or 'hero yellow' started communicating 'a collective sense of optimism for a positive future' (UNSW 2021) in the 2012 iteration of the web homepage. V2 and V3 see minor upgrades in the colour palette on the spectrum of darker and lighter blue that were used primarily for readability purposes (Figure 4.2). As a brand colour, the UNSW yellow is reminiscent of the world-famous beaches of Sydney's eastern suburbs and is selected to convey the purpose of a positive difference. Yellow is also representative of the 'Yellow Shirts' volunteer program run annually at UNSW, known to be a prestigious undertaking recognised on the Australia Higher Education Graduation Statement. The program helps to develop communication skills and teamwork abilities for approximately 170 students each year. In this sense, it is the associative value of colour (Kandinsky 1977, cited in Kress and van Leeuwen 2002, 354–355) in contrast to the direct value derivative from the material (physical) properties of colour that adds to the representational meaning potential of this visual resource as an organizational identity element (and see Pastoureau 2019, on its historical associations).

Ultimately, colour adds to the recognisability of a brand, even on a perceptual level, as it is usually recognised prior to processing any other features of a given artefact (Wheeler 2017), enhancing the positive associations with the brand personality (Aaker, Fournier, and Brasel 2004). As a metafunctionally diversified resource, colour then not only 'means' (representationally) but is also used in certain 'colour acts' (Kress and van Leeuwen 2002), as language expresses speech acts, initiating people to act in a certain way – affiliate with the institution it represents. Therefore, similar to typography, colour has evolved from mostly serving a legibility function to expressing specific meanings and values associated with the brand on the UNSW web homepage.

Social media

The social media (SM) panel, with its high cross-platform interactivity potential deserves special attention. From 2012, SM icons were placed in the footer at the bottom of the page. In V3, the panel is also placed beneath the two-layered menu at the top right of the page – a far more salient location. The form of SM representation sees several textual changes. The first predecessor of social media is a banner-like embedded YouTube image in the 2004 version. In V2, the SM layout unit features the names of SM platforms and SM icons (i.e., verbal text followed by a diagrammatic icon) against continuous black colour (weak framing). In V3, with the proliferation of SM across practically all public domains, the layout unit integrates only SM icons against an unmodulated black and white background, with no accompanying names of the platforms.

As for many universities and other organizations worldwide, SM platform integration enables users to share multimodal messages to an unprecedented number of people, and a key purpose is to compete for prospective students in domestic and international markets (Bélanger, Bali, and Longden 2014). The 'brand from the consumers' practice is an efficient strategy, as the target audience (re-)enters the ecosystem of the organizational identity communication not only reproducing and resharing the messages constructed for them but also by adding new identity values. SM platforms also provide consumers a public and accessible platform to exchange experiences and opinions about the university (somewhat) independently of the brand proprietor (Batey 2012). Generally, these developments indicate a perceptible shift from more *passive consumption* of the presented information to *active participation*, in which the audience has some apparent equality with the university.

Images

Although a detailed metafunctional image analysis is outside the scope of this chapter, it is noteworthy that the function of images as a design choice has changed across different versions of the page. In V1, a limited number of images are 'complementary to a verbal text' (Martinec and Salway 2005, 343), as they tend to add visual meaning to the verbal text they are featured with (e.g., an image of the library interior above the news article 'Book award hat-trick'). In V2, images appear prominently in carousels, as already noted. Other images appear in image-text complexes with images anchoring the verbal content of three pieces of news under *Latest News*.

In V3, the 'hero' image design solution appears to be what the university wants the visitors to see on the first screen; its sole pictorial focus occupying most of the viewport, with an option to read the featured story through the provided menu item *Learn More*. This design solution focuses on aesthetics rather than functionality, offering a clean and modern look to the viewport but not much interactivity potential. Although highly salient (by size, positioning, and representational and interpersonal content of the image, etc.), the hero image is 'haptically inaccessible' (Adami 2014) and is offered for observation and scrutiny rather than interaction. While images are often the focus of content analysis and merit considerable further investigation, as 'front end' elements, they do not fully determine the website's identity. The 'back-end' elements (i.e., the base units combined into layout units) also contribute fundamentally to the overall meaning of the website as well as other elements of CVI.

Metafunctional implications

The selection and placement of different layout units has various metafunctional implications. For the page as a whole and across the three analysed versions, and as already noted, the logo occupies the top left position on the page and is the university coat of arms. In terms of interactivity potential, and depending on the location of the interactant, the logo enables two options: (1) Return to the homepage from any page of the website or (2) return to the viewport of a homepage from 'below the fold'. Thus, this one element has cross-metafunctional potential. Textually, it functions as a 'given', an 'understood point of departure' (Kress and van Leeuwen 2021), as well as an anchor to the homepage, enabling return to a known point of the website. At the same time, it marks the macro-theme, similar to a text opener in verbal text ('this is UNSW'). Representationally, it is an antecedent of organizational identity, endowing the page with the ideological import of the coat of arms as a point of departure, something known or familiar that the audience will instantly recognise and potentially identify with. Interpersonally, it is an enabler of the interaction with the site, each time reinforcing an association with the university. What changes across the three versions, and particularly in the most recent version, is the selection and placement of the other layout units.

From V1 and V2 to V3, there is a fundamental change in representational structures. Earlier versions of the homepage prioritise taxonomies as social constructs, 'representing participants in terms of their more generalised and more or less stable and timeless essence, in terms of class, or structure or meaning' (Kress and van Leeuwen 2021, 76). Classificational processes relate subordinates (elements of the same kind in some sense) to at least one superordinate as an overarching category that can either be shown explicitly

88 Nataliia Laba

OT1 Browse	About UNSW
	Courses and Study
	Library
	Research
	Schools, Faculties,...
	Administrative Units
	Public Affairs
	Index and Directories

OT2 Starting Points For:	Future Students
	International Students
	Enrolled Students
	Staff
	Alumni

OT3 Search	Find Site
	Find Person
	Search

Figure 4.4 Overt taxonomies in the viewport of V1

in overt taxonomies (OT) or implicitly through spatial arrangements and perceptual similarity of subordinates in covert taxonomies (CT).

V1 has a small set of menu items on the left and top right, complemented by an image and text to the center-right (Figure 4.2). The menu items are organised into three OTs: *browse*, *Starting Points For*, and *Search* (Figure 4.4).

In V2, further menu items appear, both on the left side of the page and across the top, also complemented by the carousel image that occupies prominent space in the viewport to the right of the menu items (Figure 4.2, right). These menu items and the latest news are organised in overt taxonomies, whereas two CTs organise the carousel design of the viewport and show university memberships (Go8, Universitas 21) and accomplishments (*Employer of Choice for Women*) (bottom left of the viewport in Figure 4.2, right). These taxonomies are represented in Figure 4.5.

In V3, a small number of menu items are located across the top of the screen (Figure 4.3), in two covert taxonomies and one overt (Figure 4.6). The superordinate of the OT is realised visually by a magnifying glass icon, which, if clicked, also enables general searching by typing in a specific query. The covert taxonomies communicate a broader schema of the website and link to the university's official accounts on six SM platforms. In V3, the 'above the fold' real estate is predominantly occupied by the large hero image (Figure 4.3). 'Below the fold', a further seven screens are available for scrolling and present various options, placed individually, 'floating' on the page (Figure 4.6). These appear as disassembled analytical structures (Kress and van Leeuwen 2021, 83), presenting a visual 'this is', a form of 'free association' (90). Layout units 'float' on the page with no indicative cues about the categories that follow in the subsequent screens. Ordering/sequencing of the overarching categories

OT1 Menu	Business & Government
	Learning & Teaching
	Media, News & Events
	Staff
	Make a Gift Now

OT2 Student Links	Undergraduate Study
	Postgraduate Study
	International Students
	Scholarships
	Career Advisers & Teachers

OT3 Latest News	Item 1
	Item 2
	Item 3

CT1: MyUNSW, Library, Maps, Contacts

CT2: Member Group of Eight, Member Universitas 21, Employer of Choice for Women

Figure 4.5 Overt and covert taxonomies in the viewport of V2

is largely intuitive, and the units are organised visually on the principles of proximity and size in addition to different diagrammatic resources that either demarcate the base elements (e.g., through spacing and discontinuities of colour) or unify them (e.g., through consistent visual elements).

Some ordering of these elements is necessarily indicated by the vertical (top-bottom) content structuring because the most essential information is usually placed at the top of a page as the most salient and highest in the hierarchy of importance (Knox 2007, 33). However, even this prioritisation appears to follow no predetermined logic, beginning with student testimonials and information for future students, moving on to *Latest stories* and *Experience UNSW* information in the form of a grid. Certainly, student testimonials personalise the learning experience and 'create an atmosphere of authenticity and trust' (Askehave 2007, 737). Application details, degree finder, and study inquiry options appear twice, signalling the priorities of the page: to recruit prospective students. There are also some OTs below the fold in V3 – two also relating to students (*This is where your future starts*, and *Key dates*) and one general (*Latest stories*).

Notably, V1 and V2 organise content through predominantly overt taxonomies (e.g., *Browse* and *Starting Points For* in V1; *Menu* and *Student Links* in V2). Thus, the earlier versions provide practical information for future applicants, current students, and staff through 'functional design' (van Leeuwen 2021) that builds on the available generic templates.

However, such taxonomic structures are minimally present in V3, with only three covert taxonomies present in the viewport and with the units

90 *Nataliia Laba*

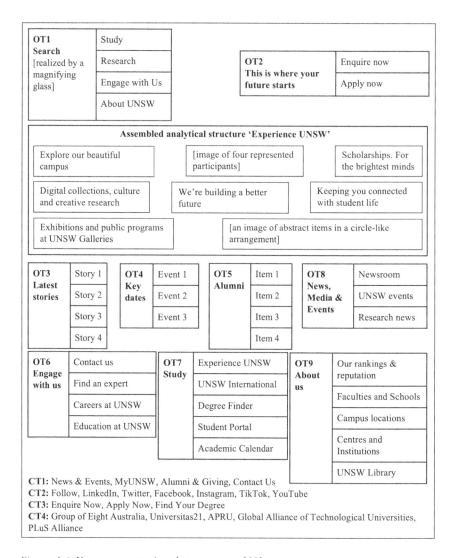

Figure 4.6 Key representational structures of V3

below the fold represented for exploration or 'browsing'. This is one of the key representational differences with the earlier versions. Representationally, the university – at least as seen on its homepage – appears to prioritise prospective students, as it provides information mostly for them. A limited set of classificational processes in V3 reflects the structure of the university in a covert way without making it explicitly visible to different audiences. In a sense, these choices contribute to the organizational identity as that of a community of practice and not a business with a rigid hierarchical infrastructure. Thus, the design of this page reflects an 'identity design' (van Leeuwen 2021) that aims to build affinity with the audience.

Discussion

In many ways, the design changes of the university web homepage over the past 20 years are reflective of recent digital trends and undoubtedly build on available templates seemingly accessible to other universities competing for similar markets. There is an evident increase in interactive elements, a rise of the importance of SM, and more open navigation pathways. A general shift from verbal to visual semiotic modalities is also evident, reflecting the 'increase in the visual and non-verbal orientation of culture at large' (Bateman 2008, 2). Images and non-verbal representation become central.

However, this study demonstrates that brand meaning lies not just in the presence or absence of different visible design elements but also in other details, such as the nature of taxonomies, co-presence of placement to foreground interactive significance, and the nature of the fundamental layout units. In addition, the historical perspective taken in this study enables a detailed understanding of the small changes over time, in which these seemingly inconspicuous shifts have collectively deep significance for what the university stands for and what the website says about it. This provides a basis for comparison with (any) organizational web homepages, academic or corporate.

What is, then, the shape of UNSW's organizational identity? Overall, it is a pretty and somewhat functional 'postcard' to prospective students. Undoubtedly, UNSW has developed a comprehensive strategy to create a distinct appearance for its web homepage, ensured by the content and its ordering, the main CVI elements, and enhanced agency for its audience. The meaning of the communicated identity arises not only from general characteristics of design elements but also from the intricate bundling of meanings across the three metafunctions.

Representationally, the university shifts the emphasis from the provision of explicit institutional knowledge to the presence and (constant) engagement of the student, who plays a more determining part in the construction of brand meaning. Future students are presented as the most valued audience on the page. Interpersonally, the university's role shifts from an author to a facilitator, progressively establishing a more egalitarian relationship with the target audience through a reduced social distance and (more) equal power. Students are 'in charge' of constructing their experiences through effectuated semiotic sequences. A degree of control is, however, exercised as to what experiences can be built (selection from a number of predetermined textual paths) and who is given options to construct these experiences (mostly future students and benefactors rather than staff or current students). Prioritisation is given to the appearance of 'choice' for the future consumer, seeking to 'transfer' control of choice to the customer, in alignment with neoliberal values (Roderick 2021).

Textually, a more comprehensive array of navigational trajectories is available, and various starting points lead to potentially different paths through the remainder of the website. This contrasts with the older versions with highly ordered and structured information, whereby different audiences were required to fit their needs to the organizational categories. Navigation in the more recent version is more fluid and exploratory in nature because there is a lack of hierarchical dependencies between different layout units, and the audience needs to scroll the page to 'discover' its offerings. By interacting with the layout units of the page in this way, the audience engages in an active co-construal of the organizational identity on the site of audiencing.

While there is not necessarily any hierarchical logic in terms of the macrostructure of the page, the overall organizational identity is integrated through design serving as a predominant logic of spatial organization. In other words, whereas these options construe a distinctive image of what UNSW stands for, it is the design that enables this image to emerge. The content and sequencing of layout units signify that potential students are the main interactants with the page, with multimodal messages ordered by the envisaged interests of potential students through their '(*ordering-as*) design' (Kress 2010, 38, italics in original). The sequencing of the messages, thus, reflects the desired manner of engagement with the page, with the target audience having greater agency than before and a high degree of flexibility to construct different pathways based on their (envisaged) needs. In line with Kress's (2005) findings, reading (/traversing) a web page is not enforced; there is neither a pre-set entry point nor a clearly defined reading path for navigation. In this sense, organizational identity design is construed as participatory design – the content of the page is the visual material to be transformed into (customer) experience, in which the audience engages in a co-construal of meaning. The interaction with the proposed corporate identity is, in a sense, more *social* because it offers a set of possibilities for the visitors to construct their experience using a plethora of ways to click, read, and share. However, the scaling of user experience is less predictable because, regardless of the presentation of messages, the valuation may be rejected by some readers (Kress and van Leeuwen 2021, 186). Anecdotal evidence from both staff and students suggests that many simply ignore the multiple pathways offered (through the long list of unrelated items on the eight screens of the homepage) and type their enquiry directly into the search bar.

Overall, UNSW keeps up with digital trends through evident continuous enhancement of the content management systems that draw on the broadening and centralisation of technological affordances of the medium. As demonstrated by the subtle shifts across all three versions, UNSW combines different expressive resources in ways that reflect the university's goals set for its web homepage. Integration of specific layout units into multimodal combinations and their placement on the page is, therefore, a social semiotic practice of the organizational identity design – from the rhetor-institution to the interpreters – the product of which presents an organizational identity seen as 'the outcome of constant transformative engagement' (Kress

2010, 174) by the visitors of the homepage. The analysis shows that the way the university presents itself on its homepage has changed from an authoritative knowledge provider to a seeker of customers in domestic and international student markets.

Conclusions

Among the many purposes of a university homepage (and a website more broadly), marketing the university's organizational identity to domestic and international students is undoubtedly predominant. Despite scholarly chagrin, universities have to respond to the challenges of consumerism and commercialisation of higher education. Whether to compete is no longer a question, and 'how to compete successfully' is on the agenda instead. This trend has several implications.

A first implication addresses how brand labs and marketing teams approach the conceptual side of the university's organizational identity. It is the question of meaning that underlies the formal structures of the site and their ordering and logic, who/whose interests get(s) coverage on the page and whether the communicative goals of the site are clearly defined. The question of the inclusive representation of all university members, not only the prospective students, is central. Being distinct matters but the type of 'distinct' matters more.

A second implication stems from the first and is about communicating realistic expectations of a university degree and providing help with managing these expectations. What values is a modern university expected to communicate? Critical and multimodal discourse analysis has overwhelmingly confirmed the ever-increasing promotional nature of academic discourses permeated by market ideology (e.g., Fairclough 1993; Klassen 2000; Tomášková 2015). A well-communicated brand is a prerequisite to attract more fee-paying students, just as metrics are for obtaining sponsorships and funding. Still, in addition to an idyllic depiction of a *sans-souci* student experience, such a brand could also reflect other factors, such as what it truly means to be a student, including the challenges that a university degree holds, practical information about how degrees are structured, and where students can seek help with academic and non-academic matters, given the growing mental health and well-being issues reported by university students worldwide amid a pandemic (Kohls et al. 2021). Instead, this information is buried in the peripheral corners of the website infrastructure, if at all accessible.

A third implication concerns softening the tensions between aesthetics and functionality of the page. This consideration applies to all four sites of the proposed model of organizational identity communication – the sites of production, virtual artefact, medium, and audiencing. The 'paradox of technology' (Norman 2013, 32) dictates the inevitably growing design complexity as new features emerge and get integrated into the product. The same technology that attempts to simplify a website/page by providing more functions also complicates its form, leading to unusable designs or users opting for a search bar instead of building any trajectories envisaged by an organization. This implication has to do with the usability of websites and can be further evaluated in future studies.

Finally, the informalisation of organizational identity communication needs to be considered, particularly through the role of SM platforms. These are a powerful forum for expanding brand meaning and an important part of a brand's communication strategy (Owyang et al. 2009) to create brand communities and strengthen membership affiliation with the organization. Still, there is limited research on how universities use social networking sites for marketing and student recruitment (Alison and Peruta 2018). This study reveals that the university foregrounds SM on the homepage (the only layout unit featured twice, alongside the *application information* layout unit), but additional research is needed to examine the interaction between users and the university on social media.

Ultimately, organizational identity communication is concerned with the issue of meaning. Studying it through a qualitative lens reveals the seemingly inconspicuous shifts in design elements and their placement. A record of such latent changes helps reveal more profound meanings about what an(y) organization stands for. Whereas diligent documentation of the formal units is an essential step of such a research effort, it is the interpretative effort of the discourse semantics layer that reveals meaning. The expanded GeM model complemented with the metafunctional foundations is one such tool. Organization studies can enrich this research by delving into sociological insights of the historical and cultural contexts of the studied phenomenon of organizational identity communication, placing a new emphasis on social practice, sign-making, and meaning.

Acknowledgements

The author gratefully acknowledges the receipt of an Australian Government Research Training Program Scholarship.

References

Aaker, J., S. Fournier, and S.A. Brasel. (2004). "When good brands do bad." *Journal of Consumer Research* 31(1): 1–16. https://doi.org/10.1086/383419.

Adami, E. (2014). "What's in a click? A social semiotic framework for the multimodal analysis of website interactivity." *Visual Communication* 14(2): 133–153. https://doi.org/10.1177/1470357214565583.

Alison, B.S., and A. Peruta. (2018). "Social media and the university decision. Do prospective students really care?" *Journal of Marketing for Higher Education* 29(1): 67–83. https://doi.org/10.1080/08841241.2018.1557778.

Askehave, I. (2007). "The impact of marketization on higher education genres: The international student prospectus as a case in point." *Discourse Studies* 9(6): 723–742. https://doi.org/10.1177/1461445607082576.

Askehave, I., and A.E. Nielsen. (2005). "Digital genres: A challenge to traditional genre theory." *Information Technology & People* 18(2): 120–141. https://doi.org/10.1108/09593840510601504.
Astani, M. (2013). "A decade of changes in university website design." *Issues in Information Systems* 14(1): 189–196. http://iacis.org/iis/2013/198_iis_2013_189-196.pdf.
Balmer, J.M. (1995). "Corporate branding and connoisseurship." *Journal of General Management* 21(1): 24–46. https://doi.org/10.1177/030630709502100102.
Bartholmé, R.H., and T.C. Melewar. (2011). "Remodelling the corporate visual identity construct: A reference to the sensory and auditory dimension." *Corporate Communications: An International Journal* 16(1): 53–64. https://doi.org/10.1108/13563281111100971.
Bateman, J.A. (2008). *Multimodality and Genre: A Foundation for the Systematic Analysis of Multimodal Documents*. Palgrave Macmillan. https://doi.org/10.1057/9780230582323.
Bateman, J.A., J. Wildfeuer, and T. Hiippala (2017). *Multimodality: Foundations, Research and Analysis: A Problem-oriented Introduction*. De Gruyter. https://doi.org/10.1515/9783110479898.
Batey, M. (2012). *Brand Meaning*. Routledge. https://doi.org/10.4324/9781315733456.
Bélanger, C.H., S. Bali, and B. Longden. (2014). "How Canadian universities use social media to brand themselves." *Tertiary Education and Management* 20(1): 14–29. https://doi.org/10.1080/13583883.2013.852237.
Bezemer, J., and D. Mavers. (2011). "Multimodal transcription as academic practice: A social semiotic perspective." *International Journal of Social Research Methodology* 14(3): 191–206. https://doi.org/10.1080/13645579.2011.563616.
Davis, G. (2017). *The Australian Idea of a University*. Melbourne University Press.
Djonov, E. (2007). "Website hierarchy and the interaction between content organization, webpage and navigation design: A systemic functional hypermedia discourse analysis perspective." *Information Design Journal* 15(2), 144–162. https://doi.org/10.1075/idj.15.2.07djo.
Djonov, E., and J.S. Knox. (2014). "How to analyze webpages." In S. Norris and C.D. Maier (Eds.), *Interactions, Images and Texts: A Reader in Multimodality*. De Gruyter Mouton, 171–194. https://doi.org/10.1515/9781614511175.
Drori, G.S., G. Delmestri, and A. Oberg. (2013). "Branding the university: Relational strategy of identity construction in a competitive field." In L. Engwall and P. Scott (Eds.), *Trust in Higher Education Institutions*. Portland Press, 134–147.
Drori, G.S., A. Oberg, and G. Delmestri. (2017). "Forest and trees, institutional dynamics and artifacts: On visual organizational indicators of global and historical cultural patterns." In G. Krücken, R.E. Meyer, and P. Walgenbach (Eds.), *New Themes in Institutional Analysis: Topics and Issues from European Research*. Edward Elgar Publishing, 224–252.
Estera, A., and R.A. Shahjahan. (2019). "Globalizing whiteness? Visually re/presenting students in global university rankings websites." *Discourse: Studies in the Cultural Politics of Education* 40(6): 930–945. https://doi.org/10.1080/01596306.2018.1453781.
Fairclough, N. (1993). "Critical discourse analysis and the marketization of public discourse: The universities." *Discourse & Society* 4(2): 133–168. https://doi.org/10.1177/0957926593004002002.

Fang, X., and C. Holsapple. (2011). "Impacts of navigation structure, task complexity, and users' domain knowledge on Web site usability: An empirical study." *Information Systems Frontiers* 13(4): 453–469. https://doi.org/10.1007/s10796-010-9227-3.

Gottschall, K., and S. Saltmarsh. (2017). "'You're not just learning it, you're living it!' Constructing the 'good life' in Australian university online promotional videos." *Discourse: Studies in the Cultural Politics of Education* 38(5): 768–781. https://doi.org/10.1080/01596306.2016.1158155.

Halliday, M.A.K. (1978). *Language as Social Semiotic: The Social Interpretation of Language and Meaning*. Arnold.

Halliday, M.A.K. (2013). "Meaning as choice." In L. Fontaine (Ed.), *Systemic Functional Linguistics: Exploring Choice*. Cambridge University Press, 15–36.

Hansen, R.H. (2010). "The narrative nature of place branding." *Place Branding and Public Diplomacy* 6(4): 268–279. https://doi.org/10.1057/pb.2010.27.

Hiippala, T. (2015). *The Structure of Multimodal Documents: An Empirical Approach*. Routledge. https://doi.org/10.4324/9781315740454.

Höllerer, M.A., T. van Leeuwen,, D. Jancsary, R.E. Meyer, T.H. Andersen, and E. Vaara. (2019). *Visual and Multimodal Research in Organization and Management Studies*. Routledge. https://doi.org/10.4324/9781315455013.

Idris, M.Z., and T.W.A. Whitfield. (2014). "Swayed by the logo and name: Does university branding work?" *Journal of Marketing for Higher Education* 24(1): 41–58. https://doi.org/10.1080/08841241.2014.919979.

Jones, S.L. (2015). "A re-examination of Fortune 500 homepage design practices." *IEEE Transactions on Professional Communication* 58(1), 20–44. https://ieeexplore.ieee.org/document/7097096.

Jones, C., and S. Svejenova. (2018). "The architecture of city identities: A multimodal study of Barcelona and Boston." In M.A. Höllerer, T. Daudigeos, and D. Jancsary (Eds.), *Multimodality, Meaning, and Institutions (Research in the Sociology of Organizations, 54B)*. Emerald Publishing Limited, 203–234. https://doi.org/10.1108/S0733-558X2017000054B007.

Klassen, M.L. (2000). "Lots of fun, not much work, and no hassles: Marketing images of higher education." *Journal of Marketing for Higher Education* 10(2): 11–26. https://doi.org/10.1300/J050v10n02_02.

Knox, J. (2007). "Visual-verbal communication on online newspaper home pages." *Visual Communication* 6(1): 19–53. https://doi.org/10.1177/1470357207071464.

Kohls, E., S. Baldofski, R. Moeller, S. Klemm, and C. Rummel-Kluge. (2021). "Mental health, social and emotional well-being, and perceived burdens of university students during COVID-19 pandemic lockdown in Germany." *Frontiers in Psychiatry* 12. https://doi.org/10.3389/fpsyt.2021.643957.

Kress, G.R. (2005). "Gains and losses: New forms of texts, knowledge, and learning." *Computers and Composition* 22(1): 5–22. https://doi.org/10.1016/j.compcom.2004.12.004.

Kress, G.R. (2010). *Multimodality: A Social Semiotic Approach to Contemporary Communication*. Routledge. https://doi.org/10.4324/9780203970034.

Kress, G.R., and T. van Leeuwen. (2001). *Multimodal Discourse: The Modes and Media of Contemporary Communication*. Arnold.

Kress, G.R., and T. van Leeuwen. (2002). "Colour as a semiotic mode: Notes for a grammar of colour." *Visual Communication* 1(3), 343–368. https://doi.org/10.1177/147035720200100306.

Kress, G.R., and T. van Leeuwen. (2021). *Reading Images: The Grammar of Visual Design*. 3rd edition. Routledge. https://doi.org/10.4324/9781003099857.

Landa, R. (2013). *Graphic Design Solutions*. 5th edition. Cengage Learning.

Litt, E. (2012). "Knock, knock. Who's there? The imagined audience." *Journal of Broadcasting & Electronic Media* 56: 330–345. https://doi.org/10.1080/08838151.2012.705195.

Martinec, R., and A. Salway. (2005). "A system for image-text relations in new (and old) media." *Visual Communication* 4(3): 337–371. https://doi.org/10.1177/1470357205055928.

Martinec, R., and T. van Leeuwen. (2009). *The Language of New Media Design: Theory and Practice*. Routledge. https://doi.org/10.4324/9780203068984.

Melewar, T.C. (2003). "Determinants of the corporate identity construct: A review of the literature." *Journal of Marketing Communications* 9(4): 195–220. https://doi.org/10.1080/1352726032000119161.

Melewar, T.C., P. Foroudi, K. Dinnie, and B. Nguyen. (2018). "The role of corporate identity management in the higher education sector: An exploratory case study." *Journal of Marketing Communications* 24(4): 337–359. https://doi.org/10.1080/13527266.2017.1414073.

Mumford, L. (1968). *The city in history: Its origins, its transformations, and its prospects*. Harcourt Brace Paperback.

Norman, D. (2013). *The Design of Everyday Things: Revised and Expanded Edition*. Basic Books.

O'Halloran, K.L., P. Wignell, and S. Tan. (2015). "Online university branding: A multimodal social semiotic approach." In G. Rossolatos (Ed.), *Handbook of Brand Semiotics*. Kassel University Press GmbH, 280–327.

Owyang, J.K., J. Bernoff, T. Cummings, and E. Bowen. (2009). "Social media playtime is over." *Forrester*, 16 March, 2020. https://www.forrester.com/report/social-media-playtime-is-over/RES47665.

Paraboni, I., and K. van Deemter. (2002). "Towards the generation of document-deictic references." In K. van Deemter and R. Kibble (Eds.), *Information Sharing: Reference and Presupposition in Language Generation and Interpretation*. CSLI Publications, 329–354.

Pastoureau, M. (2019). *Yellow, a History of Colour*. Princeton University Press.

Pauwels, L. (2005). "Websites as visual and multimodal cultural expressions: Opportunities and issues of online hybrid media research." *Media, Culture & Society* 27(4): 604–613. https://doi.org/10.1177/0163443705053979.

Pernice, K. (2013). "Carousel usability: Designing an effective UI for websites with content overload." *NN/g Nielsen Norman Group*, 14 September 2013. https://www.nngroup.com/articles/designing-effective-carousels/.

Roderick, I. (2021). "Recontextualising employability in the active learning classroom." *Discourse: Studies in the Cultural Politics of Education* 42(2): 234–250. https://doi.org/10.1080/01596306.2019.1613020.

Rose, G. (2016). *Visual Methodologies: An Introduction to Researching with Visual Materials*. 4th edition. SAGE Publications.

Rowley, J., and S. Hanna. (2020). "Branding destinations: Symbolic and narrative representations and co-branding." *The Journal of Brand Management* 27(3): 328–338. https://doi.org/10.1057/s41262-019-00180-8.

Ryan, T., R.H.G. Field, and L. Olfman. (2003). "The evolution of US state government home pages from 1997 to 2002." *International Journal of Human-Computer Studies* 59(4): 403–430. https://doi.org/10.1016/S1071-5819(03)00113-7.

Saichaie, K. (2011). "Representation on college and university websites: An approach using critical discourse analysis." Doctoral dissertation, University of IOWA. IOWA Research Online. https://ir.uiowa.edu/etd/1071/

Tomášková, R. (2015). "A walk through the multimodal landscape of university websites." *Brno Studies in English* 41(1): 77–100. https://doi.org/10.5817/BSE2015-1-5.

University of NSW. (2020). *UNSW Annual Report 2020*. University of NSW. https://www.unsw.edu.au/about-us/the-university/annual-reports.

University of NSW. (2021). *UNSW Visual Style Guide*. University of NSW. January, 2021. https://joom.ag/0cBe

Van Leeuwen, T. (2005). *Introducing Social Semiotics*. Routledge.

Van Leeuwen, T. (2008). *Discourse and Practice: New Tools for Critical Discourse Analysis*. Oxford University Press.

Van Leeuwen, T. (2021). *Multimodality and Identity*. Routledge. https://doi.org/10.4324/9781003186625.

Van Riel, C.B., and A. van den Ban. (2001). "The added value of corporate logos: An empirical study." *European Journal of Marketing* 35(3/4): 428–440. https://doi.org//10.1108/03090560110382093.

Vaughan, J. (2001). "Three iterations of an academic library web site." *Information Technology and Libraries* 20(2): 81–92. https://www.proquest.com/scholarly-journals/three-iterations-academic-library-web-site/docview/215832160/se-2.

Wheeler, A. (2017). *Designing Brand Identity: An Essential Guide for the Whole Branding Team*. 3rd edition. John Wiley & Sons.

Yerlikaya, Z.O., and P.O. Durdu. (2017). "Usability of university websites: A systematic review." In M. Antona and C. Stephanidis (Eds.), *Universal Access in Human–Computer Interaction: Design and Development Approaches and Methods*. Springer Verlag, 277–287. https://doi.org/10.1007/978-3-319-58706-6_22

Zhang, Y., and K.L. O'Halloran. (2013). "'Toward a global knowledge enterprise': University websites as portals to the ongoing marketization of higher education." *Critical Discourse Studies* 10(4): 468–485. https://doi.org/10.1080/17405904.2013.813777.

Zhang, Z., S. Tan, P. Wignell, and K. O'Halloran. (2020). "Addressing international students on Australian and Chinese university webpages: A comparative study." *Discourse, Context & Media*. 36: 100403. https://doi.org/10.1016/j.dcm.2020.100403.

Zhang, Z., and W. Tu. (2019). "Representation of international students on Australian university websites: A critical multimodal discourse analysis." *Ibérica* 37: 221–244. https://hdl.handle.net/1959.11/27996.

5 The emotional civil servant
On the multimodal construction of affect in 'platform of values' texts of Swedish public authorities

Anders Björkvall

Introduction

In the early 2000s, public authorities in Sweden started producing identity-oriented texts labelled 'platform of values' (Swedish *värdegrund*, in English 'vision and values'), and this development is now accelerating with the majority of Swedish public authorities displaying their 'platform of values', commonly including 'value words' (*värdeord*), on their websites or as internal documents. Describing the organization, and its employees in particular, the 'value words' always have positive connotations. According to a recent study, the three most common 'value words' are 'open/openness' (*öppen/öppenhet*), 'respect/respectful' (*respekt/respektfull*) and 'commitment/committed' (*engagemang/engagerad*), and the top ten list also includes 'courage/courageous' (*mod/modig*) (Nyström Höög 2020, 222). Arguably, in terms of semantics, these words relate to a realm of affective meaning potentials and are construed as part of *affective practices* (Wetherell 2012) that are supposedly present at or promoted by public authorities. The 'value words' can also be described as both vague and open to various interpretations.

Importantly, many of these 'platform of values' texts are highly multimodal and involve quite an elaborate use of colours, images, and illustrations in combination with language. Not underestimating the affective potential of language, previous research in organizational and management studies have highlighted how the multimodal and visual aspects of artefacts in organizations can offer key insights into organizational change as well as into the dominating ideologies and the steering and control of organizations (Höllerer, Daudigeos, and Jancsary 2018; Höllerer et al. 2019). The affective potential of images in the media has been extensively researched in fields such as semiotics, media, and communication studies (Motschenbacher 2020; Zieba 2020). However, recent research within organizational studies also emphasises the importance of images when communicating and construing affective meanings and atmospheres in organizations (Lefsrud, Graves, and Phillips 2019). Briefly, from a semiotic perspective, one of the *affordances* (Kress 2010) of images is that they have a well-developed potential to represent, mediate, and offer affective meanings.

From a historical perspective, the textual landscape of public administration in Sweden has predominantly been characterised by monomodal and linear texts and genres and, in later decades, influenced by the plain language movement's call for linguistic clarity, directness, and simplicity. In relation to the construction of a civil servant ethos based on objectivity and rationality rather than organizational loyalty and affective commitment, there have been rules, regulations, and explicit instructions to follow that have primarily relied on the semiotic mode of writing. It is hardly a coincidence that the introduction of more multimodal texts goes hand in hand with offers of affect that construe civil servants as emotional subjects filled with, for instance, 'courage' and 'commitment' rather than predominantly rational subjects who are part of a rule-based public administration.

With these developments as a backdrop, this chapter offers a critical understanding of the functions of the 'affect-driven civil servant' in multimodal 'vision and values' texts of public authorities in Sweden, along with a discussion about the professional and affective practices of which they are a part. Two research questions are addressed: first, how are *multimodal affective affordances* construed in the 'platform of values' genre? Second, what are the broader implications of the type of affective identities that are being ascribed to civil servants? In other words, the chapter will address affect as an organizational value in terms of multimodality and from the perspective of civil servants and professional practices (as part of organizational, identity-oriented changes in public authorities).

Affect, organizations, and multimodal discourse

An interest in the role of affect and emotion is by no means new to organizational and management studies. Fotaki, Kenny, and Vachhani (2017) describe how a focus on the affective aspects of organizations can open up new issues to explore, for instance, by placing emphasis on bodily experiences rather than purely cognitive or linguistic experiences. This focus requires methodological development, but it also brings different theoretical perspectives on organizations and organizational life to the field. A special issue of *Organization* entitled *Thinking Critically About Affect in Organization Studies* highlights a broad spectrum of affect research in the field. For instance, Dashtipour and Vidaillet (2017) depart from psychoanalysis when discussing the complex relationship between affect and working life. Michels and Steyaert (2017) draw on the concept of affective atmospheres when analysing bodies in organizational space as part of an urban art intervention in the streets of Berlin, and Ashcraft (2017) uses affect theory to formulate a critique of what she calls 'Neoliberal U', i.e., neoliberal university practices with their well-known 'Rules of Excellence'. Again, affect is used as a way of formulating a critique different to what has been accomplished by more established theoretical frameworks for critical analysis. Pullen, Rhodes, and Thanem (2017) address Deleuze and Guattari's concept of *becoming* when theorising the affective trajectory of 'becoming-woman' in gendered organizations, whereas Beyes and De Cock (2017) focus on the affective potential of colours in organizations. What unites this research, apart from offering a wide array of productive as well as intriguing perspectives on affect in organizations, is that, partially for the reasons explained above, none of it engages thoroughly with semiotic, linguistic, or discursive invitations to engage in affective practices.

However, studies have been conducted in which linguistic or multimodal artefacts themselves are given more attention when exploring the role of affect in organizations. One example is Moisander, Hirsto, and Fahy (2016), who examine how emotions interact with processes of meaning-making and power when a powerful institutional actor – the Finnish government – tried to legitimise Finland joining the Economic and Monetary Union (EMU). In this endeavour, Moisander, Hirsto, and Fahy (2016, 965) underline the importance of understanding the strategic use of discourse:

> This discursive emotion work entails mobilizing – organizing and using – both emotions and meanings as resources strategically: assembling the discursive field in a way that (1) eliminates, invalidates, and incapacitates emotions that drive resistance and (2) makes available, evokes, and promotes emotions that enable actors to gain support for their institutional objectives. In these discursive strategies, explicit appeals to emotions constitute only one form of emotion work.

Thus, the *management of emotion* is important in their analysis, which is also in line with the construction and offers of affect in the 'platform of values' texts analysed in the present chapter.

Whereas Moisander, Hirsto, and Fahy (2016) do not delve into the multimodal construction of texts, the multimodality of organizational texts is at the core of the analysis presented by Lefsrud, Graves, and Phillips (2019). Their methodology incorporates the design of multimodal messages and the recipients' interpretations and reactions and stresses the theoretical assumption that images (in combination with language) are powerful emotional triggers: 'Our model can be helpful to scholars engaged in values work because it enables them to more convincingly explicate how words and images trigger the processes of identification and associated emotional processes that underpin values work' (Lefsrud, Graves, and Phillips 2019, 1072). This relates directly to the position taken here in the analysis of the construction of affective potentials in 'platform of values' texts.

Theoretical considerations

Much of the research on affect discussed above has been performed in organizational and management studies, but there is also an expanding strand of research in social semiotics and critical multimodal discourse studies in which discursive constructions of affect through texts and other multimodal artefacts are the object of analysis (Björkvall, Van Meerbergen, and Westberg 2020; Milani and Richardson 2020; Westberg 2021). In varying degrees, this research aligns with Wetherell's (2012) view of affect as not only lived, embodied, and 'pre-discursive' but also as a type of discursive meaning-making. Wetherell (2012, 19) defines affective practice as 'a configuration where body possibilities and routines become recruited or entangled together with meaning-making and with other social and material figurations'. In other words, the construction of affect is analytically graspable in the shape of social practice and as meaning-making. This theoretical assumption is fundamental to the analysis conducted in the present chapter, which focuses on the 'affect-driven civil servant' as a type of multimodally constructed identity offered or prescribed in texts. Key to this understanding is the sociality of affect, which is, here, understood as 'a relation to others, a response to a situation and to the world' (Wetherell 2012, 24). Motschenbacher (2020), in an analysis of multimodal affective regimes in a specific area in Florida, continues Wetherell's line of argument:

> What distinguishes 'affect' from other terms such as 'emotion' or 'feeling' is not just its broader coverage. The latter terms are generally used to describe the emotional experiences of an individual (feeling) subject, while 'affect' is more strongly tied to collective experiences. […] Affect is thus not about the private, internal feelings of individuals, but a mechanism that publicly unites individuals through shared experience. […] Affect is, therefore, a relational concept – a phenomenon that plays a role in the formation of group identities and belonging.
> (Motschenbacher 2020, 3)

A couple of theoretical points can be made here. First, Motschenbacher and Wetherell clearly state that they treat affect as something social and shared, while reserving feelings and emotion for individuals. For instance, in the case of 'happiness' as a multimodally realised meaning potential in 'platform of values' texts, it is not the 'private' and 'internal' feelings of civil servants that are most interesting from the perspective of social semiotics and multimodal discourse analysis but, rather, the social construction of affective potentials as part of affective and professional practices (Bhatia, 2017) in the public authorities in which the texts and artefacts constitute only one of many affective components.

Second, Ahmed (2014) discusses the *performative* aspect of affect as part of her analysis of the politics of emotion. Drawing on Butler (1993), Ahmed (2014, 92) describes how the representation of affects (in texts) 'rather than simply naming something that already exists, works to generate that which it apparently names'. For the 'platform of values', this implies that not only are their affective dimensions to be viewed as a (normative) representation of affective situations in a public authority, but they also have the potential to generate affects that can transform the professional practices. Therein lies part of the ideological power of affective practices in public authorities. Thus, a critical analysis of affects must ask the question of what implications for future affective identities the 'platform of values' may have.

Third, affect as social practice is connected to meaning-making, which is the concern of semiotics and multimodality. The concepts and tools from these fields are also potentially productive for the analysis of affect, which will be discussed below. And finally, definitions of affect in the literature discussed above tend to be somewhat vague rather than exhaustive. There is a point to this: affect is construed as an embodied but still social experience as well as a way of exploring meaning-making, organizational life, and power. For the purpose of the present analysis, affect is defined as a relational, intersubjective, and performative meaning potential that is part of the existing or promoted affective professional practices in an organization. Again, it should be noted that in no way does this definition claim to include the feelings or emotions of specific individuals in an organization but is directed toward social and professional practices, including the texts and artefacts in use in any given public authority. It can also be noted that the working definition of affect applied here does not place the *representations* of affects at the core of the analysis to the same extent as, for instance, Martin and White's *appraisal* framework (2005, 45–52). Instead, the analysis aims at identifying offers of affects in texts that may fuel and encourage certain professional practices and identities rather than others (see affective affordances below).

As previously mentioned, in the context of the 'platform of values' analysed here, affective practices are also intrinsically connected to working life in public authorities. Bhatia's (2017) critical genre analysis (CGA) framework can be used to theorise different organizational levels toward which an analysis of affect can be directed: *text, genre, professional practice,* and *professional culture*. Affect can be relevant on all these levels, which are inter-connected. At the highest level, that of professional culture, the identities construed on other organizational levels are played out and employed as part of strategic, everyday action. This culture is constituted by a number of professional practices, i.e., actions that are considered successful within specific professional communities. 'Platform of values' is a type of professional practice, which, among other things, construes certain affects as being appropriate or required from civil servants. Genres and texts are part of these professional practices and include the artefacts that make up an organization along with their (generic) multimodal construction, meaning potentials, uses, and interpretations.

The present analysis is primarily oriented toward texts, including the genre aspect of the 'platform of values' and the professional practices of which they are a part. However, the relation between these concepts needs further consideration. More precisely, there is a need for a multimodal concept that connects the textual and generic construction of the 'platform of values' with affective potential. To this end, the present analysis applies the concept of *affordance* in a slightly modified semiotic sense. Affordance is derived from Gibson's (1977) ecological psychology in which it is concerned with perception, more precisely, the possibilities and constraints that can be perceived by an animal (including humans) in the environment. Regarding social semiotics, multimodality, and human meaning-making, Kress (2010) uses affordance in a more specific way to discuss the *gains* and *losses* when representing a type of meaning potential using one semiotic mode rather than another. This is a key issue in multimodality with implications for our understanding of, for example, the use of diagrams or graphs rather than linear writing in mass media texts or in educational contexts. Graphs afford comparisons, for instance, whereas linear text affords making arguments or explaining causal relations.

In an analysis of affective, discursive potentials at international airports, Björkvall, Van Meerbergen, and Westberg (2020) introduce the concept of *affective* affordance, which refers to the ways in which certain affects are invited rather than others in and through the use of different semiotic resources and modes in artefacts. In the present analysis, the concept is used as a means of thinking about how images and other visual representations in combination with key formulations in the written parts of the 'platform of values' texts invite certain affects from civil servants. It is important to emphasise that the construction of such affordances is never only down to representations of, for instance, the practices, environments, or affective behaviour of the depicted persons; it is always a matter of the position from which a text or artefact is viewed, read, and interpreted. In epistemological terms, Westberg (2021, 227) refers to this as an *interpretative position*, which, in his analysis, is that of 'a reluctant recipient of the NMR's [*Nordiska Motståndsrörelsen*, the Nordic Resistance Movement, a Swedish Nazi organization] propaganda'. In the case of the affective affordances of the 'platform of values' texts analysed here, the interpretative position is that of current or prospective civil servants at the public authority in question.

As discussed above, previous research in the field of organizational studies has focused on the use of images because of their well-developed potential to construe and offer affective and emotional meanings. Of course, semiotics and media studies also have a long tradition of exploring the affective potential of images (Barthes 1977; Hodge and Kress 1988; Kress and van Leeuwen 2020; Messaris 1997). However, what is new about the analysis presented here is that it not only identifies the key affective affordances in 'platform of values' texts but also connects them with the affective professional practices of public authorities. In other words, the affordances and the use of images and other visual formats, as well as the implications of the affective identities offered or ascribed to civil servants today, are addressed and explored. However, it should be noted that in no way does the analysis aim to say anything about the texts' cognitive and emotional effects on individual civil servants but only relates to the collective affective potential that the texts construe.

Method and data

Methodologically, the analysis connects both to what Höllerer et al. (2019, 49–70) call the *archaeological* and *practice* approach to visual and multimodal artefacts in organizations. Both these approaches analyse artefacts as manifestations of the cultures and subcultures in an organization. However, whereas the former primarily addresses the semiotic analysis of the artefact itself, the latter also focuses on the situated use of artefacts as part of social action in professional practice (see Björkvall 2018; Björkvall and Nyström Höög 2019; Nyström Höög and Björkvall 2018). The present analysis is guided by a search for multimodal affective affordances in 'platform of values' texts and is, therefore, primarily related to the archaeological approach. However, in order to gain an understanding of the 'platform of values' texts as part of professional practice, the analysis is also informed by a two-hour, video-recorded focus group discussion involving seven senior civil servants/ managers from public authorities in Sweden – all of whom have substantial experience in value work and producing 'platform of values' texts at their respective public authorities. In the analysis presented here, the focus group data is drawn upon selectively, whereas the study is presented in more detail in Nyström Höög and Björkvall (2018).[1]

The basic data comprise 230 'platform of values' and related texts (e.g., texts labelled 'vision' and 'strategy') from a total of 154 public authorities in Sweden, all collected from websites or via email correspondence in 2016. Because the aim of the analysis is to identify and discuss multimodal affective affordances, 42 texts were selected in which images and other resources were regarded as carrying some affective potential in relation to the written parts and the overall semiotic construction of the texts (see below). It is from this primary corpus of 42 texts that the analytical examples presented here have been extracted. These examples represent different ways in which multimodal affective affordances are realised at the textual level as different textual formats that integrate image, layout, and language.

The text analysis comprises three parts. First, previous research (Björkvall 2018; Björkvall and Nyström Höög 2019; Nyström Höög 2020; Nyström Höög and Björkvall 2018) have identified a number of genre features of 'platform of values' texts, one of which is particularly relevant for the analysis of affective affordances. One of the most salient *speech acts* in this genre is non-modalised *statements* with the function of *demand* (or *command*) through a process of *interpersonal grammatical metaphor*. As described by van Leeuwen (2005, 117–119), the type of speech acts used is a key feature of the dialogic functions of any given text (as part of any given genre). Halliday and Matthiessen (2014, 136) describe this dialogicity in quite direct terms. Statements – 'we are committed' – imply an offering of information and have 'acceptance' as a preferred response. Commands – 'be committed' – on the other hand, are a demand for goods and services (in this case, a type of affective service). Thus, commands and demands are usually more face-threatening and relate more directly to, for instance, power relations: it is easier for managers than employees to command and demand as part of workplace interaction.

The explicitness of commands makes them less usable in the exercise of 'soft power' (Mulderrig 2011), in which hierarchical power relations are not as explicit. This is where the interpersonal grammatical metaphor of *mood* enters the picture (Halliday and Matthiessen 2014, 698–707). From the perspective of a civil servant working for a public authority whose 'platform of values' text clearly states that 'we are committed', this is not only a declaration of how employees in the organization *are* – it is a command: you *must* align with the affective professional practice of being 'committed' in order to be a well-functioning part of the public authority (Björkvall 2018). The lexical and grammatical realisation of the command is exactly the same as that of a statement, hence the term *grammatical metaphor*. Thus, the first part of the analysis identifies key sentences with affective potential. These sentences are not primarily treated as declarative (making a statement about something) but as prescriptive (aimed at directing physical or mental action). In other words, the affective affordance of these 'commands as statements' are assumed to be quite intrusive in the realm of identity, in the sense that they are likely to be interpreted as commands from the perspective of civil servants.

This intrusiveness of the language-based affective affordances spills over into the visual representations when the analysis is brought into a multimodal context. The multimodal analysis draws on research on the emotional and affective potential of stock photos (Machin 2004; Zieba 2020), social semiotic accounts of emotive and affective meanings of images (Feng and O'Halloran 2012), and the basic analysis of image acts as either the *offer* or *demand* type suggested by Kress and van Leeuwen (2020). To a certain extent, it is the classical verbal anchoring of (interpersonal) visual meaning potentials proposed by Barthes (1977) that informs most of the multimodal analysis of affective potentials. This way, the verbal parts of the 'platform of values' texts interpersonally anchor the affective meaning potentials of the images: visually represented affects are not just offered, they command the viewer in the construal of their identity.

Finally, the results of the text-oriented affective analysis were related to the role of the 'platform of values' genre in the professional practices of public authorities as bureaucratic organizations. Here, the secondary data – the focus group discussions – are drawn upon and so are insights from previous organizational research on steering and control in (neo-)bureaucratic organizations.

Results

The primary corpus of 42 'platform of values' texts comprises three main multimodal formats – all with affective affordances from the perspective of a current or prospective civil servant. The predominant format is the *affect as positive*

Figure 5.1 'Platform of values' from the Swedish National Road and Transport Research Institute (VTI)

collaboration format, exemplified in Figure 5.1. Typically, stock photo-like images of 'happy' civil servants, often taking part in different kinds of collaboration, are matched with verbal statements such as 'we are committed'. The second format is the *modelled* format (Figure 5.2). Here, visual diagrams or other types of models are used to connect the different partially affective properties of the ideal civil servant. The final format is the *ambience* format. Images of environments (rather than people) at a public authority or nature or cityscapes interact with the verbal representations of how the employees 'are'.

Affect as positive collaboration

While there is plenty of research on representations of emotions and affects in images (e.g., Feng and O'Halloran 2012; Zieba 2020), the present analysis is framed by the particular affective affordances from the perspective of civil servants. However, representations must also be taken into account. It is clear from the focus group discussion with senior civil servants/managers that, for them, 'platform of values' texts and practices are, above all, internally and not externally oriented artefacts and processes (Nyström Höög and Björkvall 2018). The 'values' texts often highlight collaboration as a key component of the professional practices of the public authorities, but these collaborative practices are infused with (representations of) affects such as 'happiness' and, as Nyström Höög (2020, 222) shows, 'open/openness', 'respect/respectful', 'commitment/committed', and 'courage/courageous'. Of course, all these affects have positive connotations. In terms of multimodal affordances in the genre of 'vision and values', it appears to be easier to offer, for instance, 'happiness' through images than through lexicogrammar: statements such as 'we are happy' were not found in the data. However, there is an abundance of images of 'happy' civil servants. Feng and O'Halloran point to the well-developed visual resources for representing 'happiness' (see Martinec 2001):

> Happiness is perhaps the easiest to represent among the basic emotions [...]. In our data, happiness is mostly represented as [mouth: corners up] [...] and [eyes: narrowed/closed] [...]. The mouth may be open or closed, but the smile or laughter is easy to recognize [...]. [Cheeks: raised] may also be employed and is represented by wrinkles in the cheek area.
> (Feng and O'Halloran 2012, 2076)

The 'platform of values' text of the Swedish National Road and Transport Research Institute (VTI) (Figure 5.1), illustrates how multimodal affective affordances are construed in this genre. VTI is a research institute in the form of a public authority (just like, for instance, most universities in Sweden). In a highly salient position on the cover of the text is an image of inter-connected hands – a type of *narrative process* in the terminology suggested by Kress and van Leeuwen (2020), with meaning potentials such as 'unity'. This is a well-known motif with a long history, and it has been used in political and propaganda posters. For instance, one version is found in Frederic Henri Kay Henrion's 1944 poster *Allied Hands Breaking Swastika*. The image is also interdiscursively connected to a vast amount of stock image with similar motifs, mostly pointing in the direction of 'team building' and 'unity'. In the present organizational context, its meaning potential of, for instance, 'unity' is recontextualised, but an affective offer of collective 'pride' is probably also realised, which is also reflected in the writing that follows (see below).

Underneath the inter-connected hands are two other images: one of a man in a lab-like environment and one of a pair of working shoes. The man is not overly 'happy', perhaps, but the corners of his mouth are at least pointing upward (Feng and O'Halloran 2012, 2076).

The women on the right in Figure 5.1 fulfil all of Feng and O'Halloran's criteria for representing 'happiness': corners of their mouths up, eyes narrowed, raised cheeks. They are also looking straight at the viewer; this is what Kress and van Leeuwen (2020, 115–121) call a demand image, demanding that the viewer makes contact with the represented participant and potentially align themselves with them. The directness of this image is matched by the verbally realised affective potential of this text. In a key passage with the heading 'employeeship' (*medarbetarskap*), the description of the desired affective properties of civil servants is partially realised as metaphors of mood and partially as statements explicitly modalised for obligation (through the use of the modal auxiliaries *wants* and *shall*; see Halliday and Matthiessen 2014, 177–178).

> **VTI wants to have proud** and committed employees who work according to a common platform of values in a collaborative organization. The workplace shall be characterized by openness, mutual personal respect, and shared responsibility as well as a good balance between work and leisure.
>
> **Commitment, collaboration, competence,** and a sense of humour are signs of good employeeship at VTI.(Author's translation from original Swedish into English here and elsewhere; original boldface.)

Three of the words from Nyström Höög's (2020) overall top ten list of 'value words' appear in the text: 'Committed/commitment', 'openness', and 'respect'. In addition, the text also states that the public authority 'wants' to have 'proud' employees. Whereas 'proud' and 'happiness' have a rather obvious affective meaning potential, 'committed', 'openness', and 'respect' are more ambiguous. They could be interpreted as being more general values. This is a challenge for any analysis of affect: how is affective potential to be differentiated from other values or evaluations? In this case, however, from the perspective of a civil servant, the 'value words' would point to a sensitive, mentally oriented approach to the professional practices and other persons at the public authority. They would offer a type of affective stance.

From a multimodal perspective, the verbal parts of VTI's 'platform of values' interact with the visual parts when multimodal affective affordances are construed. As mentioned above, the meaning potential of the inter-connected hands is anchored by the recurring verbal descriptions of collaboration at the public authority. This collaboration is not only a rational, competent collaboration but also a professional practice infused with affective potentials. Collaboration at VTI requires employees to ascribe to affects such as 'pride', 'commitment,' and 'openness' in their professional affective practice. The 'happy' women are not only role models (Van Leeuwen 2005, 56–57), but they also embody the 'happiness' that is required by the public authority.

From the perspective of a civil servant working at the public authority, it appears to be difficult to totally reject this prescribed affective professional identity in favour of, say, a more rational, rule-oriented, and procedurally based identity. Unlike rules and formal procedures, affects have the potential to get under the skin of civil servants, due to their performative properties (Ahmed 2014) – that is, the potential to control the future affective behaviour of civil servants. One of the participants in the focus discussion describes this affective intrusiveness: 'To us, it [the "platform of values"] is not primarily a communicative artefact, it is something you feel, a backbone to your work.' Not only are the professional practices in the public authorities prescribed as affective in the 'platform of values' texts but the experience of the 'platform of values' itself is also potentially affective. The multimodal analysis proposed here can be usefully complemented by further ethnographic research to verify whether this is the case and, if so, to what extent.

Affect as modelled identity

The most generic textual feature of 'platform of values' texts is the bullet point list that showcases a number of typical value statements such as 'we are open'. From a multimodal perspective, the bullet point list gives salience to the values statements in relation to the surrounding text elements (Kress and van Leeuwen 2020). In addition, the list format allows for the exclusion of cohesive devices and conjunctions that are necessary when, for instance, arguing, explaining, or problematising in other types of texts. In other words, it is not necessary to explain how and why being 'open', 'brave', and 'customer oriented' are connected. Rather, these are listed as independent building blocks that make up the value-based identities of the public authority. In text-linguistic terms, the bullet point list affords the exclusion of logical connectors between clauses (Djonov and van Leeuwen 2013, 14).

The bullet point list can also be multimodally enhanced, extended, and presented as a type of diagram of modelled identities, as in Figure 5.2. The 'value words' of the Riksbank (Sweden's central bank) are listed on the left of the diagram, whereas the three columns topped with circular, anthropomorphic illustrations are marked with 'I' (*jag*) in red, 'my manager' (*min chef*) in blue, and 'my colleagues' (*mina kollegor*) in orange.

Höllerer et al. (2019, 115) state that 'analytical diagrams show the parts of a whole and how they fit together to form that whole, linking participants on the basis of metonymy, part–whole relations'. In Figure 5.2, the horizontal axis – the 'value words' – intersects with the vertical axis – the I and the two other represented professional identities – and the square of the intersection contains bullet point lists that state the direct implications of the 'value words' for each respective identity.

The 'value words' in the leftmost column translate (from the top) into English as 'result', 'initiative', 'competence', 'collaboration', and 'job satisfaction'. In terms of affect, the final vertical line is of interest: 'Job satisfaction' (*arbetsglädje*). Many of the listed value statements place themselves in between more external social actions and inter-subjective, affective practices. For example, the former category contains 'I […] treat others like I would like to be treated' and 'my colleagues […] are there for me and

The emotional civil servant 111

Figure 5.2 'Platform of values' from the Riksbank (Sweden's central bank)

others'. The latter category contains grammatical metaphors that prescribe affective stances: 'I [...] am approachable'; 'my manager [...] shows respect and concern = provides security'; 'laughs and drinks coffee with us'; and 'my colleagues [...] show respect and concern'. All these connect to affective moods and practices at the public authority and, again, all of them have positive connotations.

The overall semiotic construction of the text in Figure 5.2 elaborately sets up these affective practices as parts of a prescribed and multimodally represented civil servant identity. The affective affordances are construed through the format of the diagram: a specific civil servant identity is offered multimodally, in which the affects constitute parts of a visually (although schematically) represented human body. These prescribed affective identities have consequences. For instance, a manager who does not laugh during a coffee break with other employees does not measure up to the affective standards and neither does the civil servant who is 'introverted' rather than 'approachable'. In terms of the entire identity package represented in Figure 5.2, the multimodal design concedes that the affective properties of the prescribed employees' identities are presented as being just as important as having 'competence' (*kompetens*) or delivering 'results' (*resultat*), presented in other boxes of the Riksbank's identity kit.

Affect and ambience

The final type of affective affordance in the 'platform of values' texts is the least multimodal in the sense that images alone carry most of the affective meaning potential. In the examples shown in Figures 5.3 and 5.4, both have written components that contain bullet point lists defining common 'value words'. The text in Figure 5.3, aimed at internal target groups of the Swedish Board of Agriculture (a public authority), thematises strategy processes and values such as sustainability, gender equality, and non-discrimination. The bullet point list in Figure 5.4, from the Swedish Geotechnical Institute, defines common 'value words' such as 'quality' (*kvalitet*) and 'impartiality' (*opartiskhet*). Put briefly, the bullet point design of both Figures 5.3 and 5.4 connects to a vast number of other documents and texts from public authorities.

However, the text from the Geotechnical Institute (Figure 5.4) is distinctly different from that of the Board of Agriculture in at least one significant aspect: a connotative and, arguably, affective layer is added through the image of a seagull flying across open water that forms the full background to the writing. In this and similar 'platform of values' texts, images

natur- och kulturmiljöer, initiativ för smarta byar och samhällen (smarta landsbygder), bioekonomi och klimatomställningar eller liknande temaområden som är viktiga för landsbygdernas utveckling. Där det är relevant kan Leader stödja lokala insatser för att utveckla kustsamhällen, den lokala fiskenäringen, vattenbruk, fisketurism eller vattenmiljön. Leader kan även stödja projekt som stärker jämställdhet, integration, arbetsmarknaden eller land-stad-relationen.

Övergripande principer

Strategin ska också i alla sina delar sträva efter de övergripande principer som gäller inom EU. Det handlar om grundläggande rättigheter och tillgänglighet men också om hållbar utveckling.

- **Hållbar utveckling** – hållbar utveckling enligt unionens arbete för att bevara, skydda och förbättra miljöns kvalitet och med hänsyn till principen att förorenaren betalar.
- **Likabehandling och icke-diskriminering** – bekämpa diskriminering på grund av kön, ras eller etniskt ursprung, religion eller övertygelse, funktionshinder, ålder eller sexuell läggning och inte stödja åtgärder som bidrar till någon form av segregering.
- **Jämställdhet mellan kvinnor och män** – undanröja ojämlikhet och främja jämställdhet mellan kvinnor och män samt integrera ett genusperspektiv.

Läs mer om övergripande principer i Fördraget om Europeiska Unionens funktionssätt.

Strategiprocessen

Strategiprocessen leds av ett trepartnerskap bestående av representanter från privat, ideell och offentlig sektor som tillsätter en skrivargrupp. Initiativet att starta en strategiprocess kan komma från olika håll – det kan vara en leaderförening, lokala företagare, kommunen, lokala LRF, föreningar eller andra intressenter som vill engagera sig i den lokala utvecklingen. Ju bredare förankring desto bättre! Den legitima grunden för Leader är nätverkande och ett starkt underifrånperspektiv.

Ju bättre skrivargruppen lyckas skapa en bred intressentbas desto bättre förankrad blir strategin. Det skapar goda förutsättningarna för utveckling.

Figure 5.3 Handbook for the strategy process for leaders 2023–2027 from the Swedish Board of Agriculture (extract)

The emotional civil servant 113

Figure 5.4 'Platform of values' from the Swedish Geotechnical Institute (SGI)

of landscapes or nature invite affects on a more abstract level rather than, for instance, the boxes with affective potentials from the Riksbank in Figure 5.2. Such visual resources are also often used in advertising or in other promotional texts, in which they play on affects such as 'the love of nature' or 'a sense of freedom'.

Of course, it could be claimed that the open water and the seagull in Figure 5.4 mainly have aesthetic functions or just represent another value of the authority rather than having any particular affective potential. From the perspective of social semiotics, few elements in multimodal texts in organizations are merely decorative or exclusively representative ('this is what nature looks like'). Returning to the interpretative position (Westberg 2021) of current or prospective civil servants at the Swedish Geotechnical Institute, the visuals in the texts in Figure 5.4 rather offer a 'sense of nature' as part of professional identity, an affective relationship to (Swedish) nature to be shared by all the civil servants at the authority. This affective 'sense of nature' forms a background to all the other shared values of the public authority as presented in Figure 5.4. Interdiscursively, this connects to other descriptions of Swedes' highly affective relation to nature (see Beery 2013), as drawn upon in Figure 5.4. This way, it can be argued that the affective relationship to nature is incorporated into the overall professional identities offered at the Swedish Geotechnical Institute.

Arguably, the type of connotative affective potential illustrated in Figure 5.4 is less explicit than those potentials illustrated in Figure 5.1 (VTI) and Figure 5.2 (the Riksbank). It adds a type of ambience (however, not in the more technical sense of the term from systemic functional theory; see Painter, Martin, and Unsworth 2014) to the text – an affective meaning potential that can easily be left untapped by a reader/viewer, particularly in cases in which the images have no obvious connections to the verbal parts of the text. Nevertheless, the potential for such a connection is there.

Affective civil servants in the neo-bureaucratic organization

The semiotic and multimodal analysis has shown that there are multiple ways that affective affordances are construed in 'platform of values' texts. However, the results of the analysis need to be related to other levels in the organization of public authorities, i.e., to their professional practices and cultures (Bhatia 2017). Reed (2011) discusses a well-known dichotomy between *rational* and *post-bureaucratic* organizations and concludes that most modern organizations are actually a bit of both. Thus, it is often more appropriate to talk about *neo-bureaucratic* organizations in conjunction with specific *control regimes*. These regimes rely, for example, on *discursive identities* and *committed subjects* (Reed 2011, 243) that, in relation to Bhatia's (2017) model, all relate to the level of professional culture in which the preferred identities are more generally played out. In terms of discursive identities and committed subjects, civil servants can no longer be described only as being, above all, rule-abiding and rational subjects concerned with the core duties of their public authority. Instead, they are supposed to loyally *live*, *think*, and *act* in accordance with the core values of their public authority. Arguably, such extensive and highly personal commitments come close to the affective identities that are multimodally afforded in 'platform of values' texts. In other words, the affective affordances of 'platform of values' texts both reflect and enforce the professional cultures of the public authorities.

In light of such interpretations, affective texts and practices become part of strategies for organizational steering and control in neo-bureaucratic organizations that can no longer be governed through explicit rules, regulations, and authoritative texts. Reed (2011) discusses the potential gap between top-level management and highly qualified front-line workers in many organizations today. In order for management to govern employees in a less rule-based organizational context, there is a need for committed civil servants who have integrated specific values – and affective practices – as part of their identities. Arguably, the professional practices of public authorities can no longer only be guided by the rational execution of core duties; they must also be affective in order to promote ongoing identity work among civil servants. Again, 'platform of values' texts are both a consequence and a generator of such affective professional practices.

To some extent, the focus group data support the idea that the affective affordances of a 'platform of values' are connected to organizational control. First, there is the idea that 'platform of values' texts are part of a process of distancing a public authority from its traditional administrative and formal organizational identity. For instance, when one of the participants stated that they had an ambition to 'make it [the "platform of values"] less [of a product of an] administrative authority and more of a [genuine] platform of values', it aligns well with Reed's (2011) description of a neo-bureaucratic authority in the process of moving away from a more traditional bureaucratic-administrative *modus operandi* into something else, in which value work is key.

Second, and directly related, changed forms of control are also addressed, and one participant explained that one of the functions of the 'platform of values' is that the public authority now requires 'us to govern ourselves as employees', and the 'platform of values' provides tools to achieve this. Finally, when these kinds of statements are matched with statements that explicitly focus on affects and emotions, this strengthens the idea that affective practices as part of value practices play a role in the steering and control of public authorities in Sweden today. One of the focus group participants explicitly stated that 'our employees should live and feel the platform of values [of the public authority]', To sum up, the empirical data from the focus group discussion support the interpretations based on research on steering and control in organizations.

There are other ways of making sense of the affective civil servant identities in 'platform of values' texts. One of them concerns a public service *ethos*. For example, a general decline in citizens' trust in civil servants and public institutions in the Western world has led to calls for a more ethical bureaucracy (Maesschalck 2004). The focus group discussion indicated that a concern about civil servants' ethics and attitudes has played a role in the development of value practices and texts in public authorities in Sweden. For example, an ethical common ground was highlighted by a participant as being a driver for developing a 'platform of values' at their authority: '[These are] ethics that we agree on.' The 'platform of values' was also described as 'an attitude, a responsible attitude'. Ethics always involve the consideration of other people's reactions and well-being, and it is not that far-fetched to state that the affective affordances of 'platform of values' texts are connected to a more general movement in the direction of construing more ethically aware civil servants. In a similar vein, Du Gay (2011, 24) makes the case that an 'ethics of enthusiasm' has developed in public administration, which is quite different from the rational self-denial that was previously the guiding principle for Swedish civil servants.

To sum up, it can be argued that a new public service ethos requires a type of civil servants' *pathos*, in which affective practices of, for instance, 'commitment', 'happiness', and 'courage' are key components. These affective practices are part of an ethical identity package in which 'platform of value' texts both reflect and construe the professional practices of civil servants.

Discussion

The analysis has shown how affect-driven civil servant identities are offered in the form of multimodal, affective affordances. Based on findings from the focus group discussion, along with insights from organizational research on bureaucratic steering and control, it was argued that affective affordances of 'platform of values' texts relate to and enforce forms of steering and control of neo-bureaucratic public authorities and partially also relate to ethical issues in public administration.

Two aspects stand out. First, there is a need for multimodal perspectives and methods to understand the specific affective functions and affordances of values texts in public administration. Second, the affective identities – the results of the affective affordances – offered or prescribed to civil servants in and through 'platform of values' texts and practices have concrete implications for civil servants and, in the long run, also for the general public when it is interacting with public authorities.

Starting with multimodal perspectives, affect and the potential implications for our understanding of organizations, Lefsrud, Graves, and Phillips (2019) and others have highlighted the fact that visual representations can function as emotional triggers differently to their verbal counterparts.

For instance, this affective affordance of images has been exploited by the advertising industry for years (Barthes 1977; Cook 2001; Messaris 1997), although the analysis of the 'platform of values' texts adds something that is quite new to organizational and management studies (Höllerer, Daudigeos, and Jancsary 2018; Höllerer, Jancsary, and Grafström 2018; Höllerer et al. 2019): an integrated multimodal perspective on texts as multimodal ensembles (Kress 2010), in which language, image, and various textual formats, for example, combine to construe affective potentials. The analysis has highlighted the integrated semiotic constructs in these texts, for which grammatical metaphors of mood constitute the foundation. For instance, 'I am approachable' (*jag bjuder på mig själv*), meaning 'I must be approachable in the "platform of values" practice', is integrated into a visual model that represents a civil servant of the Swedish Riksbank (Figure 5.2). 'Approachability' is construed as an affective stance – a way of feeling and affectively being. It is an integrated, prescribed component in the overall identity of the civil servant. In this respect, the semiotic resources combine into powerful affective affordances with direct implications for the identities of civil servants as part of their organization.

Based on the analysis presented, and not in any way suggesting other possibilities in other contexts, a preliminary inventory of the semiotic resources used (in combination) for construing affective affordances in Swedish 'platform of values' texts can be proposed. First, it can be concluded that language plays an important role in these affective, multimodal ensembles. 'Value words' are used in grammatical configurations, often as grammatical metaphors, that offer, or prescribe, affective identities and practices. In particular, this was illustrated by the analysis of the text from VTI (Figure 5.1) and the Riksbank (Figure 5.2). A second type of semiotic resource is naturalistic visual representations of persons participating in affective practices or expressing affects. These can be used quite independently, in the shape of affective demand images as in Figure 5.1 but are usually combined with verbally realised affective potential that more explicitly points to the importance of certain affective behaviour on the part of civil servants.

A third relevant semiotic resource that can have a more independent role in multimodal ensembles are naturalistic representations of nature that add a connotative layer, a type of ambience, to a 'platform of values' text that draws on civil servants' 'love of nature' and the like. Finally, visual shapes and lines are an important resource for setting up affective affordances, for example, in Figure 5.1 (left), where four arms were inter-connected, and in Figure 5.2, where a part–whole structure was used to construe certain types of affective identities.

All these semiotic resources have a history, and they also connect to semiotic practices in other domains. As pointed out in the analysis, the inter-connected arms in Figure 5.1 connect to similar representations in art, for instance. However, it is striking how many of the resources have similar uses in advertising and other types of commercial texts. This is perhaps not surprising, as advertising has always strived to evoke affect and emotion as a first step toward consumption, but it is worth pointing out that these semiotic resources have now fully moved into the textual landscape of public authorities.

As illustrated by the analysis, the theoretical concepts and tools of social semiotics and multimodal critical discourse studies are able to reveal the critical role of 'platform of values' texts in creating affective identities for civil servants. However, the analysis presented does not capture the embodied aspects of affective practices, which have been the reason why many researchers in the humanities and social sciences have turned to the study of affect and emotion. Even though the 'platform of values' texts and the embodied, affective practices that they are supposed to evoke are, here, considered to be part of the same professional practice, other methods are needed to analyse the latter. In other words, while the present analysis has mainly been archaeological (Höllerer et al. 2019) and text-oriented, it would undoubtedly be of interest to delve further into how the 'commitment', 'happiness', and 'openness' of the afforded civil servant identities are played out in the professional practices of public authorities. In an era in which meetings and other professional practices may increasingly be performed online, such questions are all the more important because of our currently limited understanding of such affective potential in the online context. Such an investigation would require more ethnographically and practice-oriented methods and collaborations between, for instance, text- and artefact-oriented multimodalists and those from, for instance, multimodal conversation analysis.

As previously mentioned, the results of the analysis raise questions concerning the role of the civil servant as part of a public administration traditionally guided by virtues such as rationality and transparency. There are several potential challenges connected to this development. When professional texts and practices become partially affective, questions of personal integrity vs. organizational steering and control are raised. As is clear from (discourse-oriented) affect research, affects are difficult to both define and encircle, but at the same time, they are key to human action and identity. In the context of public authorities, affect as a means of organizational control potentially delves deeper into the integrity of civil servants than any rule or regulation. Arguably, for any civil servant, there is a difference between delivering potentially difficult official decisions to a citizen because the rules of the public authority require it and delivering the same decision based on, for instance, 'courage' as a core value of the public authority (whether or not the civil servant actually feels courageous). Of course, because there is still a legal basis for decision-making in public administration, this is not a strict question of either delivering rule-based decisions or entirely affect-based decisions, although it would appear that the latter is gaining ground. There is also a democratic aspect to this. The general public usually expect a prompt and rational response when interacting with civil servants, as representatives of a public authority and, through rules and regulations, the general public usually knows what to expect. However, it is much more difficult to predict any type of affect-based response – supposedly guided by a 'platform of values' that may differ between the respective public authorities – given by civil servants.

Zietsma and Toubiana (2018, 430) state that 'emotions represent a critical way that we can understand the cross-level influences of institutions, individual persons and social groups', and Zietsma et al. (2019, 1) claim that 'because emotions are central to organizational processes and social behaviour, they should be seen as central to organization theory'. This chapter has demonstrated that, in Swedish 'platform of values' texts, multiple semiotic resources are used to construe positive collaboration, to model identity, and to identify a guiding ambience and, thus, has illustrated how social semiotic and multimodal approaches can provide important perspectives and tools for analysing and understanding the role of affects in organizations. It is hoped that by doing so, the chapter has also contributed to the development of a more independent research field of organizational semiotics.

Note

1 The data are from the larger project *The archaeology of a new genre: vision and values texts of public authorities in Sweden*, supported by the Riksbankens Jubileumsfond (The Swedish Foundation for Humanities and Social Sciences) [grant number P15-0119].

References

Ahmed, S. (2014). *The Cultural Politics of Emotion*. Edinburgh: Edinburgh University Press.

Ashcraft, K.L. (2017). "Submission' to the rule of excellence: Ordinary affect and precarious resistance in the labor of organization and management studies." *Organization* 24(1): 36–58.

Barthes, R. (1977). "Rhetoric of the image." In *Image – Music – Text*. New York: Hill and Wang, 32–51.

Beery, T.H. (2013). "Nordic in nature: Friluftsliv and environmental connectedness." *Environmental Education Research* 19(1): 94–117. https://doi.org/10.1080/13504622.2012.688799

Beyes, T., and C. De Cock. (2017). "Adorno's grey, Taussig's blue: Colour, organization and critical affect." *Organization* 24(1), 59–78.

Bhatia, V.K. (2017). *Critical Genre Analysis: Investigating Interdiscursive Performance in Professional Practice*. Abingdon, Oxon: Routledge.

Björkvall, A. (2018). "Critical genre analysis of management texts in the public sector: Towards a theoretical and methodological framework." In D. Wojahn, C. Seiler Brylla, and G. Westberg (Eds.), *Kritiska text- och diskursstudier*. Huddinge: Södertörns högskola, 57–79.

Björkvall, A., and C. Nyström Höög. (2019). "Legitimation of value practices, value texts, and core values at public authorities." *Discourse & Communication* 13(4): 398–414.

Björkvall, A., S. Van Meerbergen, and G. Westberg. (2020). "Feeling safe while being surveilled: The spatial semiotics of affect at international airports." *Social Semiotics*: 1–23. https://doi.org/10.1080/10350330.2020.1790801

Butler, J. (1993). *Bodies that Matter: On the Discursive Limits of "Sex"*. New York: Routledge.

Cook, G. (2001). *The Discourse of Advertising*. London: Routledge.

Dashtipour, P., and B. Vidaillet. (2017). "Work as affective experience: The contribution of Christophe Dejours' "psychodynamics of work"." *Organization* 24(1): 18–35.

Djonov, E., and T. van Leeuwen. (2013). "Between the grid and composition: Layout in PowerPoint's design and use." *Semiotica* 197: 1–34. https://doi.org/10.1515/sem-2013-0078

Du Gay, P. (2011). "Problems of involvement in Post-Bureaucratic Public Management." In S. Clegg, M. Harris and H. Höpfl (Eds.), *Managing Modernity: Beyond Bureaucracy?* Oxford: Oxford University Press, 11–29.

Feng, D., and K.L. O'Halloran. (2012). "Representing emotive meaning in visual images: A social semiotic approach." *Journal of Pragmatics* 44(14): 2067–2084.

Fotaki, M., K. Kenny, and S.J. Vachhani. (2017). "Thinking critically about affect in organization studies: Why it matters." *Organization* 24(1): 3–17.

Gibson, J. (1977). "The theory of affordances." In R. Shaw and J. Brandsford (Eds.), *Perceiving, Acting, and Knowing: Toward an Ecological Psychology*. Hillsdale, NJ: Erlbaum, 62–82.

Halliday, M.A.K., and C.M.I.M. Matthiessen. (2014). *Halliday's Introduction to Functional Grammar*. 3rd edition. Abingdon, Oxon: Routledge.

Hodge, B., and G. Kress. (1988). *Social Semiotics*. Ithaca, NY: Cornell University Press.

Höllerer, M.A., T. Daudigeos, and D. Jancsary. (2018a). *Multimodality, Meaning, and Institutions*. Bingley, UK: Emerald Publishing Limited.

Höllerer, M.A., D. Jancsary, and M. Grafström. (2018b). "'A Picture is Worth a Thousand Words': Multimodal Sensemaking of the Global Financial Crisis." *Organization Studies* 39(5–6): 617–644.

Höllerer, M.A., T. van Leeuwen, D. Jancsary, R.E. Meyer, T. Hestbæk Andersen, and E. Vaara. (2019). *Visual and Multimodal Research in Organization and Management Studies*. Abingdon, Oxon & New York: Routledge.

Kress, G. (2010). *Multimodality: A Social Semiotic Approach to Contemporary Communication*. London: Routledge.

Kress, G., and T. van Leeuwen. (2020). *Reading Images: The Grammar of Visual Design*. 3rd edition. London: Routledge.

Lefsrud, L., H. Graves, and N. Phillips. (2019). "Giant toxic lakes you can see from space": A theory of multimodal messages and emotion in legitimacy work." *Organization Studies* 41(8): 1055–1078.

Machin, D. (2004). "Building the world's visual language: The increasing global importance of image banks in corporate media." *Visual Communication* 3(3): 316–336.

Maesschalck, J. (2004). "The impact of new public management reforms on public servants' ethics: Towards a theory." *Public Administration* 82(2): 465–489.

Martin, J.R., and P.R.R. White. (2005). *The Language of Evaluation: Appraisal in English*. Basingstoke: Palgrave Macmillan.
Martinec, R. (2001). "Interpersonal resources in action." *Semiotica* 135(1/4): 117–145.
Messaris, P. (1997). *Visual Persuasion: The Role of Images in Advertising*. Thousand Oaks: Sage.
Michels, C., and C. Steyaert. (2017). "By accident and by design: Composing affective atmospheres in an urban art intervention." *Organization* 24(1): 79–104.
Milani, T.M., and J.E. Richardson. (2020). "Discourse and affect." *Social Semiotics*: 1–6. https://doi.org/10.1080/10350330.2020.1810553.
Moisander, J.K., H. Hirsto, and K.M. Fahy. (2016). "Emotions in institutional work: A discursive perspective." *Organization Studies* 37(7): 963–990.
Motschenbacher, H. (2020). "Affective regimes on Wilton Drive: A multimodal analysis." *Social Semiotics*: 1–20. https://doi.org/10.1080/10350330.2020.1788823..
Mulderrig, J. (2011). "The grammar of governance." *Critical Discourse Studies* 8(1): 45–68.
Nyström Höög, C. (2020). "Core values in public administration: Tools for openness and democracy?" *CADAAD Journal* 11(2): 213–234.
Nyström Höög, C., and A. Björkvall. (2018). "Keeping the discussion among civil servants alive: 'Platform of values' as an emerging genre within the public sector in Sweden." *Scandinavian Journal of Public Administration* 22(3): 17–38.
Painter, C., J.R. Martin, and L. Unsworth. (2014). *Reading Visual Narratives: Image Analysis of Children's Picture Books*. London: Equinox.
Pullen, A., C. Rhodes, and T. Thanem. (2017). "Affective politics in gendered organizations: Affirmative notes on becoming-woman." *Organization* 24(1): 105–123.
Reed, M.I. (2011). "The post-bureaucratic organization and the control revolution." In S. Clegg, M. Harris, and H. Höpfl (Eds.), *Managing Modernity. Beyond Bureaucracy?* Oxford: Oxford University Press, 230–256.
Van Leeuwen, T. (2005). *Introducing Social Semiotics*. London: Routledge.
Westberg, G. (2021). "Affective rebirth: Discursive gateways to contemporary National Socialism." *Discourse & Society* 32(2): 214–230. https://doi.org/10.1177/0957926520970380
Wetherell, M. (2012). *Affect and Emotion: A New Social Science Understanding*. London: Sage.
Zieba, A. (2020). "Visual representation of happiness: A sociosemiotic perspective on stock photography." *Social Semiotics*: 1–21. https://doi.org/10.1080/10350330.2020.1788824
Zietsma, C., and M. Toubiana. (2018). "The valuable, the constitutive, and the energetic: Exploring the impact and importance of studying emotions and institutions." *Organization Studies* 39(4): 427–443.
Zietsma, C., M. Toubiana, M. Voronov, and A. Roberts. (2019). *Emotions in Organization Theory (Elements in Organization Theory)*. Cambridge: Cambridge University Press. https://doi.org/10.1017/9781108628051

6 Communicating in space

Relating the physical and the social in open-plan offices

Ken Tann and Oluremi B. Ayoko

Introduction

Material space has generally been neglected in organizational studies despite the fact that it is an important part of organizational experience (van Marrewijk and Yanow 2010). This is largely due to a persistent tendency by scholars to conceptualise the material separately from the social aspects of organization. However, there is growing evidence that suggests space and interaction are inseparably bound in social practice (e.g., Lefebvre 1991; Orlikowski 2007; van Marrewijk 2009). This is especially important given that particular office space designs, such as the open-plan office, claim to transform the use of space in the name of improving communication (Ayoko and Ashkanasy 2020). Furthermore, in light of post-COVID-19 social distancing and health concerns, the open-plan office, as we know it, will be different in the future, and understanding the organizational implications of current open-plan offices will help inform post-COVID-19 designs in addressing anxieties about shared spaces in the future.

Open-plan designs are commonly believed to remove barriers to communication; however, this notion is based on a conception of space as a mere vessel for containing interactions and of material features as little more than obstructions to communication (Kim and de Dear 2013). However, studies in social semiotics (e.g., Kress and van Leeuwen 2006; Lim 2020; Ravelli and McMurtrie 2016; van Leeuwen 2005) have shown that the actual configuration of a built environment, including its material aspects such as walls and partitions, is socially meaningful to its occupants and associated with different discourses. This paper draws on social semiotics to investigate how management discourses are communicated through the design of one particular office type, the open-plan office, and how the employees respond and communicate by manipulating that space in actual use.

Using the case study of the Asia-Pacific regional office of an American multinational corporation, we first examine the relationship between space and organizational communication. We then introduce an analytical framework based on social semiotics and demonstrate how it accounts for three distinct but interdependent aspects of communication. Finally, we apply the

DOI: 10.4324/9781003049920-6

framework to the open-plan office to analyse the complexities of organizational communication in practice and suggest some of their implications in the post-COVID-19 work environment.

Rise of the open-plan office

Open-plan offices were introduced in the 1950s to promote collaboration (Kim and de Dear 2013) and reduce the cost for office space (Davis, Leach, and Clegg 2011). They became popular with management because of their lower cost (Chigot 2003), reduced time in setting up and renovation (Brennan, Chugh, and Kline 2002), and easier line-of-sight supervision (Baldry 1997). Such offices marked a shift from relatively insulated cell offices to work environments characterised by a lack of full-height walls between individual workspaces and lack of access to individual windows (see Bodin, Danielsson, and Bodin 2009). While popular with management, they were often controversial with employees, and complaints about noise and stress persisted in mainstream media as recently as 2019 (Sailer and Thomas 2021). The open-plan office presents a challenge to workplace activities, primarily because without traditional partitions, multiple practices overlap in the same physical space, and employees are constantly engaging with one another throughout the workday. It should be noted here that the nomenclature 'open-plan' can refer to a wide variety of actual office types, not least practices of 'hot desking' or the more recent style adopted by companies, such as Google, in which diverse functions are included and employees are relatively free to choose which functions they avail themselves to (Wakabayashi 2021). This is discussed further below.

Communicating in open-plan offices

The design of open-plan offices is known to affect organizational communication, with implications for work design, interpersonal processes, distractions, human resource practices, and leadership (Ayoko and Ashkanasy 2020). Managers, on the one hand, advocate adopting open-plan offices to encourage teamwork and to reduce office hierarchies (Baldry 1997) and argue that removing partitions improves communication and interaction (Brennan, Chugh, and Kline 2002) as well as cohesiveness between employees (Chigot 2003). Critics, on the other hand, argue that open-plan offices lead to increased noise, poor privacy (Regoeczi 2003), and conflict (Ayoko and Härtel 2003). However, studies on the effectiveness of open-plan offices unhelpfully yield inconclusive results, largely because they tend to treat open-plan designs as homogenous, ignoring variations in their actual configuration, how the layout is used in practice, and whether the layout fits the type of organization (Sailer and Thomas 2020).

Furthermore, studies focusing on management decisions only provide half the picture, as employees in open-plan offices actively engage with the space by personalizing it to express their feelings and identity (Ashkanasy, Ayoko, and Jehn 2014) as well as ownership of that space (Brown, Lawrence, and Robinson 2005, 578) by using physical markers such as personal objects or by modifying and rearranging aspects of their environment to construct, communicate, and maintain their territorial boundaries (Brown 2009). In this sense, the physical environment is not an immutable influence on behaviour but lends itself as a resource for meaning-making in organizational interactions, as it is 'negotiated' and 'reconfigured' dynamically by the movements and actions of its inhabitants (Lim 2020, 46). Hence, to understand why open-plan designs work in some cases and not others, as well as the tensions and trade-offs in open-plan offices, scholars require a more nuanced approach that considers the office as a combination of simultaneously social and spatial realities (Sailer and Thomas 2020). We will, therefore, demonstrate using an example of how a specific workspace is used by both management and employees alike to negotiate the social reality of work.

An ethnographic approach to the open-plan office

To understand how the material aspects of workspaces can be used to create and constrain meanings in actual practice, we take a 'strong' multimodal approach (Zilber 2018) by combining ethnography and social semiotics to analyse both the 'in situ interaction, and the practical, political and historical complexities that constitute it' (76). We documented the physical layout of the office, such as the presence of partitions, furniture, and artefacts during a site visit and conducted a series of in-depth ethnographic interviews with an employee who played a key role in the setting up of the office. The layout is used as a prompt for the unstructured interviews to obtain an insider account of its significance and how it is used by the occupants in practice.

Our key informant has worked for two years in an accounting team of an American multinational corporation and experienced the whole process of setting up a shared service center (SSC) in its Asia-Pacific regional office located in a multistory commercial building. We selected the informant based on her role in the company, as she was employed specifically to assist in setting up the SSC. She was extensively consulted in management decisions around the design of the workspace throughout the process and provided the management with feedback on employees' workplace experience.

The SSC is designed to coordinate and standardise accounting procedures between its US head office and in-country offices across six countries by locating their representatives in a common open-plan office. However, the representatives work virtually with other members of their individual in-country teams who continue to liaise with customers overseas. This situation presents an interesting challenge in fostering the identity of the SSC as a team. As the SSC was newly set up within a pre-existing office space, it presented management with an opportunity to implement a new design within that space, incorporating new features and furniture.

The SSC occupies a relatively small area in the shared space and is comprised of a general ledger (GL) team with eight members, an accounts payable (AP) team with six members, and an accounts receivable (AR) team with 13 members. To accommodate the incoming SSC, part of the regional open-plan office space that originally housed the local finance team has been refurbished, so the creation of the SSC, therefore, involves a shift in both physical and social arrangement in the organization. The locations of SSC personnel are marked by filled circles on the office layout in Figure 6.1.

Figure 6.1 shows part of the office that our informant accesses regularly, featuring a shared office on one side of the corridor for the center director and two team managers, an open-plan area on the other side for the team members, and a traditional cell office at the far corner for the finance vice-president. The SSC director discusses the office layout with our informant, who, in turn, provides the director with informal feedback from her co-workers. In her role mediating between management and other employees, our informant provides an insider perspective on how management discourses were formulated and disseminated and how employees experience and use the office space after they have moved in.

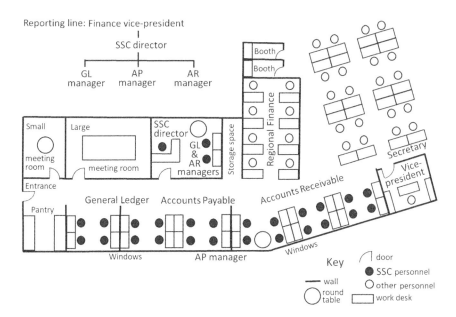

Figure 6.1 SSC office layout and reporting line

Social semiotics of the work environment

To explore the meanings created through the use of the material space, we draw on social semiotics (Halliday 1978; van Leeuwen 2005) as a tool for analysing features of the space as a meaning-making resource. Instead of looking at space in isolation from speech, our framework (Tann and Ayoko 2020) takes a 'strong' multimodal approach by situating them holistically in social practices and examines how these practices are 'accomplished' (Jancsary et al. 2018) through the combination of different resources, such as visual images (Kress and van Leeuwen 2006) alongside speech (Slade and Eggins 1997), documents (van Leeuwen, Tann, and Benn 2016), and body language (Hood 2017).

Modelled after Systemic Functional Linguistics (see Halliday and Matthiessen 2004), the framework provides a means for investigating how communication constitutes social action by relating meanings to their social context, as shown in Figure 6.2.

In this model, communication consists of three distinct but interrelated kinds of meanings and is systematically related to three aspects of the social context that combine in social practice. *Genre* (Martin and Rose 2008) refers to a specific practice that is taking place at any given moment toward a social goal[1], and can be characterized as a combination of field, mode, and tenor. *Field* refers to the users and uses of the space, which relate systematically to the forms of communication that constitute their functional roles and work tasks, or *representational meanings*.[2] *Mode* refers to the role that

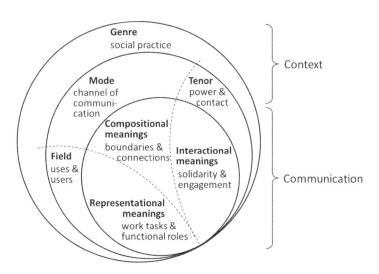

Figure 6.2 Relationship between spatial design and social practice (adapted from Martin and Rose 2007)

the nature of space plays in shaping communication by creating boundaries and connections between things and people, or *compositional meanings*. *Tenor* refers to the relational power and contact between organizational actors as realised through their solidarity and engagement in interaction or *interactional meanings*. The relationship between communication and its context and the multifunctional nature of communication are elaborated in the sections below.

Social context

The framework in social semiotics characterises context according to the three situational aspects of field, mode, and tenor that combine to realise various purposeful social practices (Halliday 1978; Martin 1992; Tann 2017).

Field refers to the instrumental functions that are designated to a space and the people and objects that comprise its legitimate uses and users. As Figure 6.1 shows, the regional office is divided into dedicated spaces designated for different functions, such as corridors, meeting rooms, workspaces, cell offices, storage areas, telephone booths[3], and pantries. Different features and objects can be found within each of these areas to facilitate those functions, such as seating and desks as well as equipment such as computers, telephones, files, and stationery. The function of each space is prescribed by management to the extent that alternative uses, such as having lunch at the desk, are actively discouraged. The areas are also divided with respect to different tasks or work units associated with different functions of the organization. During the planning process, the SSC seats members in each team together, and when new members are recruited, management places them close to the existing members, such that areas used for the organizational functions of GL, AP, and AR can be readily identifiable, as seen in Figure 6.1.

Mode refers to the way meaning is shaped by the nature of its communicative medium, such as how the properties of physical space and speech allow for different kinds of communication. Employees within the SSC interact mainly through speech, electronic forms, instant messaging, and emails as well as manipulations of and movement through the physical environment. On a typical workday, an employee may walk down the corridor to talk face-to-face with a colleague seated at another desk to discuss a spreadsheet displayed on the screen. Generally, different kinds of medium are associated with different purposes: urgent work discussions are usually conducted face-to-face, while private conversations are carried out on instant messaging, and invoices and spreadsheets are uploaded to shared drives, depending on considerations such as access, speed, and responsiveness. Even though many work tasks are completed online, the physical environment remains important to the SSC, in that it is designed to locate representatives of different in-country teams within the same open-plan office.

Tenor refers to the relationship between users interacting in the office, in terms of their relative status, frequency of contact, and solidarity. Employees in this office are allocated to spaces with respect to their position in the organizational structure – the vice-president has a dedicated cell office, while the SSC director shares an office with two managers, and lower ranked employees are located in an open-plan area across the corridor. The physical distance between them is also indicative of their formal social distance and their frequency of contact. For example, an employee in the AP team would generally be seated closer to their team member than someone in the AR team, and closer to the SSC director than the vice-president. While physical proximity to team members can serve an instrumental function, as described above, the relational aspect of seating is made clear whenever the arrangement is violated by individuals. Employees who move to a desk located away from their team (for example during a disagreement with a co-worker) are quickly asked by the director to return to their assigned location to maintain team cohesiveness. Conversely, employees who change teams during job rotations are reassigned to the corresponding desk.

Field, mode, and tenor combine in particular configurations to realise specific social practices known as *genre*, following Tann and Ayoko (2020). For example, the large meeting room on the left of Figure 6.1 may be used for practices such as a team meeting (genre) between the manager and team (tenor) to discuss AP matters (field) face-to-face (mode). Alternatively, the same room may be used by colleagues located in different teams (tenor) to chat about their vacation plans (field) over lunch (genre). In this sense, physical spaces provide a communicative resource that affords the possibility of realizing different social practices (or genres) without necessarily predetermining them.

Multifunctional communication

To develop a rich understanding of the role of these spaces in communication, we first present our on-site observation of how occupants interact in them, in terms of three simultaneous but interdependent forms of meaning-making resources across different communication systems, known as metafunctions (Halliday and Matthiessen 2004; Kress and van Leeuwen 2006; Ravelli and McMurtrie 2016). By distinguishing between the three metafunctions – *representational*, *interactional* and *compositional*[4] meanings – the framework provides a multifunctional lens to relate communication systematically to the three different aspects of the context (see Figure 6.2). In this section, we illustrate this alignment using examples of how the managerial discourse in the SSC is communicated through the open-plan employee workspace, as shown in Figure 6.3.

Representational meanings communicate both 'denotations' and 'connotations' (Ravelli and McMurtrie 2016, 28) in establishing the legitimate tasks and work roles of employees in the office, corresponding to its field.

Communicating in space 129

Figure 6.3 The SSC open-plan employee workspace

Each of the workspaces is pre-fitted with a chair, a monitor, and a laptop docking station, denoting regular uses of the space, such as being seated to access work tasks on the screen. Such features also communicate connotative meanings to occupants that the space is a legitimate workspace. However, its layout acts simultaneously to constrain the possibilities of meaningful activities. For example, the space available between the desks largely confines users to remain within a limited area, while the fixed height of the desk requires the user to remain seated while using it. It is, therefore, uncomfortable for employees to gather or remain standing in the space. The filing cabinet at the side of each workspace can be pulled out and the top is fitted with a bright red cushion, allowing one other person to sit in each space, even though the second person faces away from the desk, and is, hence, not expected to engage with the screen for any extended period. The function of each space is prescribed by management to the extent that the occupant is not allowed to remove or replace any of the furniture. If the employees wish to hold a group discussion, they may relocate to an alternative space dedicated for that function, such as the meeting or breakout rooms. The layout, hence, establishes norms in uses of the space without explicitly prescribing them.

The physical layout also serves to regulate the activity and communication of employees online. The presence of large screen monitors with relatively little cover in an open-plan space promotes surveillance by rendering activities on their computers open to scrutiny by others around as well as anyone walking along the shared corridor. In this way, the representational meanings in employee interactions are regulated by interactional meanings, which demonstrates that, while addressed separately, the metafunctions are inherently interdependent.

Interactional meanings establish how employees relate to one another interpersonally in the office in terms of variables such as 'power', 'social distance', and 'contact' (Ravelli and McMurtrie 2016, 55), construing the tenor of interaction. For example, the location of individuals indicates their relative status in the organization. Two of the managers share an office with the SSC director across the corridor from the rest of the employees. The office is fitted with a large internal window, allowing them to conduct line-of-sight supervision on those in their charge. Internally, the layout construes social distance through the proximity of the managers to the director and distance from the employees, while externally, the visual accessibility to the employees maintains their power over them. However, space constraints in the shared office mean that one of the three managers is located with the team, and during the planning process, the SSC director specified that the AP manager should be located next to a window. Being located next to the window also reduces the direction from which an employee may be monitored. In other words, access to an enclosed space or a window serves both as a symbol of status as well as providing or hindering the ability to exercise that authority.

Within the open-plan workspace, occupants relate to one another as co-workers, as they engage in parallel work with the screens in front of them, although not necessarily with one another. In this sense, they simply 'coexist' in terms of 'social geometry' (Ravelli and McMurtrie 2016, 9) of the default layout. However, the open-plan design also allows for 'impermanence' in the framing of the space (van Leeuwen 2005, 22), whereby occupants may turn their seats around to initiate conversation with the colleague behind them, stand up to engage with someone across the desk, or pull the cabinet out from under the desk to reveal the red cushion as an invitation to a visitor to spend more time interacting. While the presence of rectangular tables, monitor screens, and partitions facilitate computer-mediated interactions more readily, occupants are able to make these adjustments to engage with those physically close by. Nonetheless, such interactions are expected to be temporary arrangements, as standing up or pulling out the cabinet are marked and highly visible actions. The availability of different kinds of interactions, including discussion and surveillance, is shaped by the presence of windows and desk partitions as forms of compositional meanings.

Physical spaces, as a mode of communication, can be used to delineate boundaries and relate parts of the office space as part of its *compositional* meanings. Traditional boundaries in offices take the form of permanent, full-height walls, such as those that mark the vice-president's and SSC director's offices and the meeting rooms, as distinct from the common corridor and open-plan areas. The walls function to strongly frame, or 'segregate', different areas (van Leeuwen 2005, 15) and to delineate functional areas with respect to representational meanings and social status with respect to interactional meanings. A variant to the wall is the internal window that allows visual contact with those across the corridor, enabling the managers to continue engaging the employees in a supervisory capacity. The distinction between the wall and the window is, hence, one of degrees of permeability in 'framing' (Boeriis and Nørgaard 2013) – the window blocks physical movement and the transmission of sound but allows visual communication.

The main characteristic of an open-plan office, such as the one discussed here, lies in the flexibility and removal of weak framing devices that 'separate' different areas (van Leeuwen 2005, 22). With the absence of full-height walls and doors that enable a space to be closed off, the employees' areas allow for both visual and auditory engagement with one another. Framing in such areas is adjusted by temporary partitions of varying height and flexibility, thereby allowing different degrees of communication across them. For instance, the employees' individual workspace in the open-plan area is marked off by low partitions to create a sense of personal space, even though such barriers provide little to no privacy (see Figure 6.3). Movable furniture, such as the cabinet, can also be used to form temporary boundaries to create a sense of enclosure, by creating a largely symbolic barrier from the corridor.

Analyzing multimodal discourses in the office

In the preceding section, we introduced a multifunctional analytical framework that is useful for identifying multiple forms of meaning that are communicated simultaneously in the physical work environment. In this section we demonstrate, using excerpts from our interviews, how employees respond to them when using the space in practice and how the framework can be applied to understand employees' engagement with management discourses.

Collective and individual identities

The management of the SSC ostensibly promotes team cohesion across work units as part of its rationale for adopting an open-plan layout. One way it does this is by standardizing the appearance of office furniture, thus, creating a sense of collective identity through the use of 'rhyme' (van Leeuwen 2005, 17). For example, the bright red low partitions separating employee work desks match the colour of the cushions on the cabinets at the side (see Figure 6.3). The colour scheme distinguishes the SSC from the rest of the office that has a grey scheme, visually identifying its members, and employees are not allowed to remove or replace any of the furniture. In this way, visual cohesion, as part of compositional meanings, identifies those within the SSC as belonging together and creates a boundary between the SSC and the rest of the office space. Such a device enables the management of the SSC to create the interactional meaning of solidarity among its employees.

Nonetheless, employees found it necessary to personalise their workspaces. As our informant describes:

> On our desks we are allowed to decorate as we like, but we are not allowed to have live plants or pets. We usually have mugs and water bottles, ornaments, stationery, additional small storage, small fans, and even stuffed animals. Some of us also display souvenirs from other colleagues' travels.

While desks are designed for the utility of their work, and designate workspaces representationally, they can be differentiated from others through the display of the employee's interests and values as described in the preceding quote. Such strategies have been well documented elsewhere (Brown, Crossley, and Robinson 2014; Monaghan and Ayoko 2019) and point to the foregrounding of interactional meanings through such devices; visitors and passersby are provided with an opportunity to 'bond' (Ravelli and Stenglin 2008) with employees as individuals beyond work. Other functional items, such as an employee's noticeboard, used to display representational meanings of their work tasks, are similarly appropriated:

> The partitions between our desks are low, but it allows for some items to be stuck to them to personalize our workspaces. We would pin up important information that is required for our day-to-day work, like bank codes or accounting cost centres, so that we can refer to them quickly and easily. Besides that, some colleagues might put up pictures of family or pets. This invites conversations when visitors come to the desks and see the pictures.

In both examples of personalisation, we can observe that the interactional meanings that employees create with what they found in their workspace are not simply isolated phenomena but are part of an ongoing chain of communication and negotiation of their solidarity and individuality. The souvenirs are gifts from colleagues sharing travel experiences and displayed as vicarious affirmations of those experiences, while the photos displayed to communicate personal lives prompt further conversations and engagement among colleagues as a form of 'resemiotisation' (Iedema 2003; O'Halloran, Tan, and Wignell 2016).

Open-plan and boundaries

The management of SSC adopted an open-plan and low partitions to facilitate interactions among the SSC employees by replacing strong framing practices ('segregation') with weaker ones ('separation', see van Leeuwen

2005, 15). However, the presence of boundaries is not categorical, as different modalities allow different degrees of 'permeability' (van Leeuwen 2005, 16). Visual boundaries, such as an obstruction to the line of sight do not necessarily also present a boundary to auditory communication, and employees develop different strategies to construct their own boundaries wherever they are not provided by the office design.

By facing work desks toward each other and installing low partitions, the management creates constant visual 'contact' (Ravelli and McMurtrie 2016, 57) between employees, partly as a way to encourage self-policing, as the director frequently asks employees individually about the activities of other employees. Employees also find the need to constantly engage with others distracting, and have developed a way to create visual boundaries mutually:

> As our workstations are in an open-plan office and the partitions are low, we would use our double monitors to block ourselves from each other by putting them next to each other. If we didn't do that, we might end up staring at each other through the workday. Some of us would shift the monitors slightly so that others will not see our screens entirely.

Another aspect of the management discourse is the promotion of verbal interaction. By minimizing physical barriers between employees, verbal interactions can take the form of broadcasts, such that anyone speaking can be heard by everyone else in the vicinity. Unlike visual contact that one can more easily opt out of by turning away or hiding behind an object, passive engagement in conversations can be involuntary. Consequently, employees also developed auditory boundaries to cope with the problem:

> Our bosses encouraged conversation, so sometimes it can get noisy and distracting. I would listen to music on my earphones during these times to avoid conversation so that urgent work can be finished on time. Listening to music during the workday isn't prohibited. In fact, one of my colleagues has a radio on a low but audible volume. Unfortunately, earphones are explicitly discouraged as it prevents bosses or staff from calling us, as I have been warned on a few occasions.

However, as the quote shows, opting out of auditory engagement altogether poses a problem to the management discourse that requires employees to be readily available for verbal communication at all times. In this case, the management exercises its power to regulate and constrain employees' choices in engagement, as an example of how one form of semiosis (i.e., verbal) is used to at times regulate another (i.e., auditory) in the negotiation of tenor.

Surveillance and resistance

Another way that management exercises its power to engage employees visually is by maintaining visual availability of their work desk monitors through the open-plan design. The open-plan area is located opposite the office of the director and managers across the corridor, so employees' monitors are constantly under surveillance as a form of 'control' (Ravelli and McMurtrie 2016, 60) over legitimate uses of the workspace and the interactional meanings that employees are allowed to negotiate online. As our informant explains:

> The director's office is just opposite, and the finance VP would walk by frequently, so some of us like to angle one of our screens so that they will not see part of our screen. This allows for some private conversation through instant messaging or web surfing on the blocked screen. We can minimize the screen quickly if they come by.

By designing the space in the office, management designates legitimate uses and expresses its power by constraining the representational and interactional meanings that can be exchanged by employees. Conversely, by manipulating objects in that space, employees are able to actively 'reconfigure' (Lim 2020) the space to resist and circumvent the management discourse.

Physical spaces also provide an alternative means of communicating voices of resistance when speech is not viable. For instance, employees may vent their frustration with the management by typing uncharacteristically loudly or knocking audibly against the desk when they are placing items on it:

> The shared service center setup was new, and the director was sometimes very demanding and adamant about work processes. Some colleagues can be quite upset if things didn't go well. Typing loudly on the keyboard to vent frustration was very common. We obviously could not talk about it openly, but we could clearly feel their frustration.

The employees may be unable to openly complain about their superiors within earshot, especially in an environment where there is little barrier to sound, but such actions prompt empathy from colleagues who can either hear the knocks, or feel them through the connected furniture, and express their concerns through instant messaging. When meanings are suppressed, the physical environment, in practice, provides users with alternative means to express them through resemiotisation. Such an adaptation of the material environment can only be adequately captured by a multimodal analysis that attends to the full spectrum of communicative resources available and the multiple meanings that they can produce, as the employee in this instance manipulated a physical object whether consciously or subconsciously to create meaning that is clearly acknowledged by others, which would not be considered by studies that rely solely on verbal data.

Communicating in space 135

While the examples so far illustrate how the considerations of field, tenor, and mode shape representational, interactional, and compositional meanings in communication, the three contextual variables have to be located within the routine conventions of social practices (i.e., genre), which provides a temporal dimension to the framework (see Figure 6.2). For example, management discourses about work are not enforced past office hours, because the nature of the social practice changes. When pressed to suggest why there is a change in expectations, our informant offers the following explanation:

> Officially, the company only has a hold over us during business hours from 9 to 6. If we choose to linger beyond 6 pm to finish the work, it's basically our freedom to do so, and some rules, like listening to music or walking around barefooted, don't really apply even though it might still be frowned upon if the bosses are still around.

As the formal work agreement with the organization is between 9 am and 6 pm, employees see themselves in a voluntary role when they remain in the office outside of those hours. Consequently, the nature of the tenor has shifted, ever so slightly, so that managers are no longer expected to exercise as much power to enforce the usual practices. In other words, the field, tenor, and mode of the workplace are not static determinants of behaviour; rather, they shift over time in response to contextual changes because of the conventional nature of social practice. In fact, employees may openly celebrate this shift as a show of solidarity:

> In our section, one of our colleagues usually has her radio on, and past office hours we were less restricted by rules. Work often ended way past 6 pm, so to keep our spirits up, we would encourage her to turn up the volume.

Communicating in the post-COVID-19 office-scape

The reasonably static open-plan office, as described here, has already been supplanted in popularity in some organizations by other types of open-plan spaces, such as those which incorporate 'hot desking' (Elsbach 2003; Morrison and Macky 2017) or those that allow for a greater variety of representational functions (including playing various games, such as ping pong, or even sleeping, e.g. in a designated sleeping pod (Munshi 2017)).

Further, a clear early impact of the pandemic has been a dramatic shift to working from home (Hamouche 2021; Pinnington and Ayoko 2021) and a concomitant decrease in demand for the usual floor space required for open-plan offices, given that fewer staff need to come into the office or do so in a staggered way for only a portion of the working week. Workers are choosing to work remotely from home rather the physical office because working from home saves commuting time and offers more flexibility while avoiding distractions and noise from co-workers, especially in an open-plan office.

However, working from home is not without challenges. The lack of face-to-face interactions in remote work can affect teamwork (Wallace 2020) as well as physical and mental health (Westfall 2020; Xiao et al. 2021)[5], and the office is, therefore, unlikely to disappear altogether. Instead, the open-plan office will more likely be augmented by physical distancing requirements alongside flexible work arrangements that will exacerbate the ongoing changes in work design and interpersonal processes (Ayoko and Ashkanasy 2020). While managers are under pressure to respond quickly to the evolving situation, investment in infrastructure can be costly and difficult to alter once implemented. It is, therefore, necessary to build on our understanding of what has worked so far and why. Based on our analysis thus far, we will briefly suggest how spatial design within the office is likely to be affected by the post-COVID-19 work environment, assuming that working practices of the future will likely combine working from home with working in the office.

In terms of representational and compositional meanings, the strict delineation of teams (that is, between the GL, AP, and AR teams), as already described here, will be difficult to maintain if overall floor space is reduced and working arrangements are flexible. It is likely that the cohesion of the SCC team, as a whole, can be retained (dependent on other changes within the accounting team as a whole, which occupies other areas of the floor in question) through the cohesive devices of consistent design and co-location. But it will be more challenging to retain the specific functions of the teams within the SCC, assuming that there will be less overall floor space allocated, but more space required between individual employees, and that members of different teams might be at work on different days. That is, spatial design will need to be more fluid and other strategies devised to distinguish the identity and achieve the cohesiveness of teams.

Also in representational terms, the assumption that particular functions, such as meetings, must be performed with all participants in situ no longer holds, and the post-COVID-19 workplace will likely have meetings with some participants in the office and others online at home. This means that verbal exchanges, already distracting in the open-plan office, could be even more challenging if the current spatial configuration remains the same, with open lines of sight and the absence of full-height walls. Adjustments will be needed to allow for fully enclosed meeting rooms, both small and large, so that the noise of meetings does not distract others. Thus, the post-COVID-19 workplace is likely to see the reintroduction of some greater physical boundaries between functional spaces.

Such changes also mean that the surveillance performed by managers in the current environment, with clear line of sight over workers' activities, will need to be rethought not only for those working from home but also for those working in the context of a different spatial configuration in the office, with potentially less clear divisions between teams and more segregation of functional spaces.

In interactional terms, as the office becomes less populated and employees increasingly communicate with their co-workers online (see for example Safe Work Australia 2020), traditional markers that management uses to delineate social status and distance will also lose their salience. For example, while windows were formerly used to indicate status in the office, they will have to be regulated differently to promote ventilation for all, due to health concerns.

From the employees' perspective, the sharing of work desks associated with shift rotation would mean that opportunities for personalisation are curtailed. However, the display of personal items is important for establishing territory, rapport, and personal identity (Brown, Lawrence, and Robinson 2005; Byron and Laurence 2015; Wells 2000), and some consideration would need to be given to how this could be achieved in a shared environment, as is also the case for pre-pandemic 'hot desking' (Elsbach 2003; Morrison and Macky 2017).

Conclusion

Until recently, spatial features of the physical work environment have often been neglected in the analysis of organizational behaviour (see Ashkanasy, Ayoko, and Jehn 2015; Monaghan and Ayoko 2019) because there has been a lack of a systematic framework to account for them. Crucially, physical features have often been given piecemeal treatment and conceptualised separately from the social aspects of organizational interactions. However, this study demonstrates that both the physical and social are inseparably implicated in organizational communication. On the one hand, space affects the nature and quality of communication, facilitating or obstructing the kind of communication that can be done. On the other hand, space provides resources for meaning-making and the possibility of resemiotisation to communicate what could not be communicated verbally.

We, therefore, argue that a social semiotic framework provides a way to conceptualise communication more holistically by focusing on how meanings are expressed not only through language but also through space in context. To do so, the framework offers a multifunctional lens to systematically tease apart the representational, interactional, and compositional meanings that are simultaneously at play in a given situation so that each one can be adequately accounted for. However, our analysis also reveals that these three forms of meaning are not mutually exclusive but are, instead, interdependent. Compositional meanings that communicate boundaries and relate parts of the organization to each other simultaneously serve to form identities and encourage solidarity; furniture that serves functionally to facilitate representational meanings is co-opted to communicate interactional meanings and maintain interpersonal relationships. Crucially, the interplay between them can only be fully understood in situated practice[6].

Using the framework, we are able to explore competing voices in the workplace. Design is explicitly used by management to construct desired workplace relations and behaviours, but employees engage dialogically with management discourse by manipulating physical objects to create voices of empathy and solidarity among themselves[7]. It also accounts for how communication changes, even within the same physical space, because of shifts in conventionalised social practices. Finally, the framework reveals gaps in current research, such as how different channels of communication – including physical spaces – affect both work tasks and interpersonal processes and how an ethnographic perspective can reveal nuances of meaning that would otherwise be missed. While our case study focuses on the accounting department of a multinational corporation, future studies can also apply this framework as a common analytical tool to compare how the use of space in workplace communication may differ across industries and organizational cultures, and a more comprehensive ethnographic perspective can enhance the insights that such an approach brings.

For decades, organizations have hopped on the bandwagon of open-plan offices to break down communicative barriers based on a mechanistic understanding of communication that does not take its multifunctional nature into account. Instead of an understanding of space merely as a physical vessel in which communication can be obstructed by its features, our study shows that it is necessary to consider the social practices around the meanings that are made and how space plays an important role in expressing those meanings. This nuanced understanding is all the more important as managers are now redesigning the workspace for a post-COVID-19 world.

Notes

1. See Yates and Orlikowski (1992) for an account of organizational genres as the result of structuration.
2. See Cooren et al. (2011) on the communicative constitution of organization (CCO).
3. These small spaces are surrounded by relatively soundproof glass walls to avoid generating excessive noise in the office; see notes on framing and permeability below.
4. Ravelli and McMurtrie (2017) use 'organizational' for spatial discourse analysis rather than 'compositional'. The latter is preferred here to avoid confusion with 'organizational studies'.
5. There is not enough space here to consider the nature of working from home in full, but see Pinnington and Ayoko (2021), Hamouche (2021), and Yang et al. (2021) for some early studies.
6. See McMurtrie (2017) for another exemplification of this.
7. See Kress (2010) on notions of 'design'.

References

Ashkanasy, N.M., O.B. Ayoko, and K.A. Jehn. (2014). "Understanding the physical environment of work and employee behavior: An affective events perspective." *Journal of Organizational Behavior* 35: 1169–1184.

Ayoko, O.B., and N.M. Ashkanasy. (2020). "The physical environment of office work: Future open plan offices." *Australian Journal of Management* 45(3): 488–506.

Ayoko, O.B., and C.E.J. Härtel. (2003). "The role of space as both a conflict trigger and a conflict control mechanism in culturally heterogeneous workgroups." *Applied Psychology: An International Review* 52(3): 383–412.

Baldry, C. (1997). "The social construction of office space." *International Labour Review* 136 (3): 365–79.

Bodin Danielsson, C., and L. Bodin. (2009). "Differences in satisfaction with office environment among employees in different office types." *Journal of Architectural and Planning Research* 26: 241–257.

Boeriis, M., and N. Nørgaard. (2013). "Architectural discourse: The material realization of framing and discourse in a university building." *International Journal of Language and Communication* 38: 71–100.

Brennan, A., J. Chugh, and T. Kline. (2002). "Traditional versus open office design: A longitudinal field study." *Environment and Behavior* 34(3): 279–299.

Brown, G. (2009). "Claiming a corner at work: Measuring employee territoriality in their workspaces." *Journal of Environmental Psychology* 29(1): 44–52.

Brown, G., T. Lawrence, and S.L. Robinson. (2005). "Territoriality in organizations." *Academy of Management Review* 30: 577–594.

Brown, G., C. Crossley, and S.L. Robinson. (2014). "Psychological ownership, territorial behavior, and being perceived as a team contributor: The critical role of trust in the work environment." *Personnel Psychology* 67(2): 463–485.

Byron, K., and G.A. Laurence. (2015). "Diplomas, photos and tchotchkes as symbolic self-representations: Understanding employees' individual use of symbols." *Academy of Management Journal* 58(1): 298–323.

Chigot, P. (2003). "Controlled transparency in workplace design: Balancing visual and acoustic interaction in office environments." *Journal of Facilities Management* 2(2): 121–130.

Cooren, F., T. Kuhn, J.P. Cornelissen, and T. Clark. (2011). "Communication, organizing, and organization: An overview and introduction to the special issue." *Organization Studies* 32: 1149–1170.

Davis, M.C., D.J. Leach, and Clegg, C.W. (2011). "The physical environment of the office: Contemporary and emerging issues." In G.P. Hodgkinson and Y.J.K Ford (Eds.), *International Review of Industrial and Organizational Psychology* 26. Chichester, UK: Wiley, 193–235.

Eggins, S., and D. Slade. (1997). *Analysing Casual Conversation*. London: Cassell.

Elsbach, K.D. (2003). "Relating physical environment to self-categorizations: Identity threat and affirmation in a non-territorial office space." *Administrative Science Quarterly* 48(4): 622–654.

Halliday, M.A.K. (1978). *Language as Social Semiotic: The Social Interpretation of Language and Meaning*. Victoria & Maryland: Edward Arnold.

Halliday, M.A.K., and C.M.I.M. Matthiessen. (2004). *An Introduction to Functional Grammar*. 3rd edition. London: Arnold.

Hamouche, S. (2021). "Human resource management and the COVID-19 crisis: Implications, challenges, opportunities, and future organizational directions." *Journal of Management & Organization* 1: 16.

Hood, S. (2017). "Live lectures: The significance of presence in building disciplinary knowledge." *Onomázein* 2(1): 179–208.

Iedema, R. (2003). "Multimodality, resemiotisation: Extending the analysis of discourse as multi-semiotic practice." *Visual Communication*: 29–57.

Jancsary, D., R.E. Meyer, M.A. Höllerer, and E. Boxenbaum. (2018). "Institutions as multimodal accomplishments." In M.A. Höllerer, T. Daudigeos, and D. Jancsary (Eds.), *Multimodality, Meaning, and Institutions (Research in the Sociology of Organizations* 54B: 87–117.

Kress, N. (2005). "Engaging your employees through the power of communication." *Workspan* 48(5): 26–36.

Kress, G., and T. van Leeuwen. (2006). *Reading Images: The Grammar of Visual Design*. 2nd edition. London & New York, Routledge.

Kim, J., and R. de Dear. (2013). "Workspace satisfaction: The privacy-communication trade-off in open-plan offices." *Journal of Environmental Psychology* 36: 18–26.

Lefebvre, H. (1991). *The Production of Space*. Oxford: Blackwell.

Lim, F.V. (2020). *Designing Learning with Embodied Teaching: Perspectives from Multimodality*. New York: Routledge.

Markus, M.L. (1994). "Electronic mail as the medium of managerial choice." *Organization Science* 5(4): 502–527.

Martin, J.R. (1992). *English Text: System and Structure*. Philadelphia: John Benjamins Publishing.

Martin, J.R., and D. Rose. (2007). *Working with Discourse: Meaning Beyond the Clause*. 2nd edition. London: Continuum.

Martin, J.R., and D. Rose (2008). *Genre Relations: Mapping Culture*. London: Equinox.

McMurtrie, R.J. (2017). *The Semiotics of Movement in Space: A User's Perspective*. New York: Routledge.

Monaghan, N., and O.B. Ayoko. (2019). "Open-plan office, employees' enactment, interpretations and reactions to territoriality." *International Journal of Manpower*: 228–245.

Morrison, R.L., and K.A. Macky. (2017). "The demands and resources arising from shared office spaces." *Applied Ergonomics* 60: 103–115.

Munshi, N. (2017). Sleeping on the job can improve your work. *Financial Times*, September 13, 2017. https://www.ft.com/content/09067126-3720-11e7-99bd-13beb0903fa3.

O'Halloran, K.L., S. Tan, and P. Wignell. (2016). "Intersemiotic translation as resemiotisation: A multimodal perspective." *Signata* 7(7): 199–229.

Orlikowski, W.J. (2007). "Sociomaterial practices: Exploring technology at work." *Organization Studies* 28(9): 1435–48.

Pinnington, A.H., and O.B. Ayoko. (2021). "Managing physical and virtual work environments during the COVID-19 pandemic: Improving employee well-being and achieving mutual gains." *Journal of Management & Organization* 27(6): 993–1002.

Ravelli, L.J., and R.J. McMurtrie. (2016). *Multimodality in the Built Environment: Spatial Discourse Analysis*. London, England: Taylor & Francis Ltd.

Ravelli, L.J., and M. Stenglin. (2008). "Feeling space: Interpersonal communication and spatial semiotics." In G. Antos and E. Ventola (Eds.), *Handbook of Interpersonal Communication*. Berlin, New York: De Gruyter Mouton, 355–393.
Regoeczi, W. C. (2003). "When context matters: A multilevel analysis of household and neighbourhood crowding on aggression and withdrawal." *Journal of environmental Psychology* 23(4): 457–470.
Safe Work Australia (2020). *COVID-19 Information for Workplaces*. https://www.safeworkaustralia.gov.au/covid-19-information-workplaces/industry-information/office/physical-distancing#heading—6—tab-toc-what_physical_distancing_measures_do_i_need_to_implement_in_my_workplace? Updated September 15, 2020.
Sailer, K., and Thomas, M. (2020). "Socio-spatial perspectives on open-plan versus cellular offices." *Journal of Managerial Psychology* 36(4): 382–399.
Sailer, K., and M. Thomas. (2021). "Socio-spatial perspectives on open-plan versus cellular offices." *Journal of Managerial Psychology* 36(4): 382–399.
Tann, K. (2017). "Context and meaning in the Sydney architecture of systemic functional linguistics." In T. Bartlett and G. O'Grady (Eds.), *The Routledge Handbook of Systemic Functional Linguistics*. London: Routledge, 438–56.
Tann, K., and O.B. Ayoko. (2020). "A social semiotic approach to the physical work environment." In O.B. Ayoko and N.M. Ashkanasy (Eds.), *Organizational Behaviour and the Physical Environment*. London: Routledge, 214–231.
Van Leeuwen, T. (2005). *Introducing Social Semiotics*. London & New York: Routledge.
Van Leeuwen, T., K. Tann, and S. Benn. (2016). "The language of collaboration: NGOs and corporations working together." In H. de Silva Joyce (Ed.), *Language at Work: Analysing Language Use in Work, Education, Medical and Museum Contexts*. New Castle, UK: Cambridge Scholars, 45–66.
Van Marrewijk, A. (2009). "Corporate headquarters as physical embodiments of organizational change." *Journal of Organizational Change Management* 22(3): 290–306.
Van Marrewijk, A., and Yanow, D. (Eds.). (2010). *Organizational spaces: Rematerializing the workaday world*. Cheltenham, UK & Massachusetts, US: Edward Elgar Publishing.
Wakabayashi, D. (2021). "Google's plan for the future of work: Privacy robots and balloon walls." *The New York Times*, 30 April 2021. https://www.nytimes.com/2021/04/30/technology/google-back-to-office-workers.html
Wallace, A. (2020). "The death of the open-plan office? Not quite, but a revolution is in the air." *The Conversation*, 22 June 2020. https://theconversation.com/the-death-of-the-open-plan-office-not-quite-but-a-revolution-is-in-the-air-140724
Wells, M. (2000). "Office clutter or meaningful personal displays: The role of office personalization in employee and organizational wellbeing." *Journal of Environmental Psychology* 20: 239–255.
Westfall, C. (2020). "Mental health and remote work: Survey reveals 80% of workers would quit their jobs for this." *Forbes*, 8 October, 2020. https://www.forbes.com/sites/chriswestfall/2020/10/08/mental-health-leadership-survey-reveals-80-of-remote-workers-would-quit-their-jobs-for-this/?sh=60ceed4c3a0f
Xiao, Y., B. Becerik-Gerber, G. Lucas, and S.C. Roll. (2021). "Impacts of working from home during COVID-19 pandemic on physical and mental well-being of

office workstation users." *Journal of Occupational and Environmental Medicine* 63(3): 181–190.

Yang, H., M. Tang, X. Chao, and P. Li. (2021). "Organisational resilience in the COVID-19: A case study from China." *Journal of Management & Organization* 27(6): 1–19.

Yates, J., and W.J. Orlikowski. (1992). "Genres of organizational communication: A structurational approach to studying communication and media." *The Academy of Management Review* 17(2): 299–326.

Zilber, T.B. (2018). "A call for "strong" multimodal research in institutional theory." In M.A. Höllerer, T. Daudigeos, and D. Jancsary (Eds.), *Multimodality, Meaning, and Institutions (Research in the Sociology of Organizations, Vol. 54B)*. Bingley, UK: Emerald Publishing Ltd, 63–84.

7 Redesigning organizations through the built environment
Changes at a university campus

Louise Ravelli

Introduction

The intricate relationship between organizations and their built environment has been widely observed and discussed (e.g., Boxenbaum et al. 2018; Carvallho, Goodyear, and de Laat 2017; Rafaelli and Pratt 2006; Ravelli and McMurtrie 2016). Boxenbaum and colleagues (2018, 598) note that 'organizations shape employee interactions with things and one another *through workspace and building designs*' (emphasis added) and that there is a critical gap in current knowledge 'in detailing how the social realm and the material realm become intertwined, and what effects these processes have on organizational practice' (601). It is this intersection of the social realm with the material, through the built environment, that is the focus of this chapter. Not all organizations are able to choose or significantly adapt the built environment they occupy, but the built environment, nevertheless, makes a crucial contribution to the nature of organizations: what they are, how they operate, and the relations between interactants.

This chapter demonstrates how a social semiotic approach to the built environment can be developed with a framework called *Spatial Discourse Analysis* (Ravelli and McMurtrie 2016), an extension of multimodal discourse analysis. The chapter focuses on institutions of higher education – universities – as complex organizational sites where the built environment plays a critical role. While some universities may adapt pre-existing spaces to suit new purposes, the majority have been purpose-built, either commencing long ago (e.g., Bologna, Oxford, Cambridge, each nearly 1,000 years old) or more recently (e.g., Birmingham UK, founded 1900; University of Wollongong, Australia, founded 1975; National University of Singapore, founded 1980, merging Nanyang University with the University of Singapore). All must expend substantial sums on upkeep and maintenance, and at different periods, all will expend further on repurposing, improving, and/or expanding their built environment. The university in focus in this chapter is the University of New South Wales in Sydney, Australia (UNSW), which has recently invested in the redesign of informal, outdoor learning spaces. This follows several prior waves of change that have seen massive

DOI: 10.4324/9781003049920-7

investment in renovation of the main campus, as reported elsewhere (Ravelli 2018; Ravelli and McMurtrie 2017; Ravelli and Stenglin 2008). While all these changes contribute to factors such as organizational identity, renovation of the outdoor learning spaces is particularly pertinent to issues of university/ student relations, new pedagogical practices, and contemporary student life.

The chapter begins with an overview of the spatial discourse analysis framework that underpins the study of the built environment at UNSW. Then, UNSW, as an organization, will be introduced along with the specific spaces to be analysed, namely informal outdoor learning spaces. The analysis of these spaces is followed by an evaluation in relation to their positive and negative contributions to organizational issues, for the university, its staff, and its students. The chapter concludes with suggestions for extending Spatial Discourse Analysis to other organizational sites.

Approach and theoretical framework

As indicated in Chapter 1, a social semiotic approach is one that situates meaning-making practices within their social context, interpreting textual resources in relation to cultural processes and seeing these two aspects as being mutually informing rather than deterministic in either direction. Underpinned by work in linguistics and semiotics by Halliday (1978, 1994), further work influenced by Kress and van Leeuwen (2001, 2020) has extended this approach to a range of modes and media, including moving and still images (Bateman and Wildfeuer 2016; Kress and van Leeuwen 2020), hairstyles (McMurtrie 2010), and the built environment (McMurtrie 2017; Ravelli and McMurtrie 2016; Stenglin 2004) to indicate just a few examples.

Core to this approach is the understanding that meaning goes well beyond representational (content) senses to include both interpersonal (social, attitudinal) and textual (compositional) meanings and are interpreted in connection with explicit textual evidence.

Ravelli and McMurtrie (2016) refer to the application of such an approach to the built environment as *Spatial Discourse Analysis*. It is taken as given that the built environment communicates to those who move in, through, and around it as innumerable architects and scholars of architecture, history, and sociology, *inter alia*, have enumerated. McMurtrie (2017, 16), referring to Preziosi (1979, 4) states: 'Every society communicates through its buildings, its architecture.' For Ravelli and McMurtrie (2016, 12), spatial texts are not just buildings but:

> ...more fully the synthesis of building, space, content and user. ... We examine both the built structure, its overall form and space, what is put inside and outside the building, and how it is used by people. The aim is to understand how spatial texts make meaning and contribute to socially-constructed knowledges.

A number of further points about this approach are pertinent. When considering aspects of the built environment as a communicative text, it is important to differentiate the perspectives of 'looking at' a building (as if it is a static two-dimensional image) vs 'being in'/'moving through' a space, in its three-dimensionality. As McMurtrie explains (2017, 173), space can be experienced in two fundamental ways: serially or configurationally.

Additionally, what a spatial text means and what it says depends fundamentally on two further factors. First, contextual location is crucial: historically, socially, and culturally, in terms of the spatial text itself (When was it built? For what purpose? By whom?) and in terms of the 'viewing location' (From which [metaphorical] standpoint is it viewed? As a historical artefact? As part of the contemporary environment? What purpose does the building serve now? etc.; see van Leeuwen 2018, 239). Second, the 'size of frame' through which the text is viewed or experienced is also crucial. It may be that a whole building is under analysis or perhaps just one floor or one room on one floor, and so on. Formally, in terms of systemic-functional linguistics, this is referred to as a 'rank' based approach (McMurtrie 2015), and it is usually necessary to move back and forth between ranks theoretically, just as one does in actual life. That is, a floor is understood in relation to the rooms within it as well as the building it sits within, and so on.

Extending the Hallidayan metafunctional approach, via Kress and van Leeuwen's visual grammar, produces the metafunctional terms of *representational, interactional,* and *compositional* meaning.[1] Additionally, Ravelli and McMurtrie (2016) extend Halliday's *logical* metafunction for language to include *relational* meaning in spatial texts. These terms are illustrated in Table 7.1.

The analytical framework for each of the metafunctions is described briefly here (and see Ravelli and McMurtrie 2016). *Representational meaning* is concerned with aspects of the built environment that 'build a sense of the world around us, what it consists of, and how users might participate in it' (Ravelli and McMurtrie 2016, 6). It leads to specific questions about spatial texts, such as what a space 'is'; what functions are indicated and

Table 7.1 Metafunctional terminology across language, image, and the built environment

Language Halliday (1994)	Image Kress and van Leeuwen (2020)	Built environment Ravelli and McMurtrie (2016)
Ideational (experiential + logical)	Representational	Representational Relational
Interpersonal	Interpersonal	Interactional
Textual	Compositional	Compositional (/organizational; see endnote 1)

Table 7.2 Key analytical questions for each metafunction (relevant to current analysis)

Representational meanings	Interactional meanings	Compositional meanings	Relational meanings
• What is the space 'for'? • What functions/uses are indicated? • What actions are enabled for users? (e.g., sitting, moving); can all users act in the same way?	• Does the institution manifest its power and/or enable power for users? • Is the control of movement regulated or free? • How are participants positioned to interact with each other? • Can users bind with the space? • Can users bond with the space?	• How are the parts brought together to make a meaningful whole? • What stands out – what is backgrounded? • Are component parts clearly segregated or seamlessly integrated? • What movement patterns are enabled through the space?	• Are components dependent or independent of each other? • Are they the same or different in metafunctional terms?

what activities are enabled for users (Table 7.2). In a university, a large room with raked, fixed seats and a podium at the front suggests a 'lecture'; a small room with flat, moveable seating and a desk at the front suggests a 'tutorial'. Such features do not define the representational function of the space – a lecture theatre can be used to give a tutorial, show a film, or host a party, but it does suggest what is most likely to occur there.

The identification of actions enabled for users derives from a description of process (verb) types in language (Halliday 1994), adapted for visual images by Kress and van Leeuwen (2020). Kress and van Leeuwen posit a fundamental split between *narrative* (dynamic) and *conceptual* (static) process types; this basic split is also relevant to an analysis of spatial texts (Ravelli and McMurtrie 2016). Narrative processes may also be *transactional*, in which the action is extended from one user to something or someone else (e.g., *eating a sandwich*), or *non-transactional*, in which there is no such extension (e.g., *working*). Conceptual processes may also have subtypes, though these will not be explored in the analysis below. Spatial design can enable hybridisation (Stenglin 2004) – that is, multiple activities to take place simultaneously, for example, *eating* and *working*.

Interactional meanings create 'ways of relating to each other' (Ravelli and McMurtrie 2016, 6), both within, because of, and with the built environment. That is, interactional meanings are concerned with how users behave in relation to the spatial text, as well as with each other, how spatial design contributes to emotional responses within and to spatial texts, and how such choices can construct a 'persona' for a spatial text. There are a number of systems that contribute to the analysis of interactional meaning, but only those directly relevant to the analysis below are elaborated here. First, the institution can construe its relation to users via systems of *Power*, realised, primarily, by the manifestation of institutional presence, e.g., through great height, volume, or mass or, perhaps, through the quality and finish of the materials used and the inclusions. This is often seen in contemporary universities through the use of iconic buildings to indicate their status. *Control* is concerned with the extent to which movement within the space, and with objects or inclusions within the space, is regulated or free, realised by features such as barriers/gateways, and so on. This might be explicit, for example, requiring a pass to enter the library, or implicit, with the expectation that only enrolled students attend a particular class. Relations between interactants can be described in terms of *social geometries*, as enabled by the placement of seating, for example, where placement may enable *individual* (solo), *collaborative* (side by side), *conversing/confronting* (opposite), or *social* (around) settings (McMurtrie 2017).

Whether users feel anchored within a space can be realised by elements of *Binding* (Stenglin 2004), such as a lowered ceiling that makes a space feel cosier, a seat that encourages a user to stay, or practices such as looking at a screen that enable *self-binding* (Ravelli and McMurtrie 2016). At the same time, *Bonding* (Stenglin 2004) refers to the extent to which a user feels a sense of identification with a space and what it stands for, for example, by aligning with values expressed through symbols, such as a flag, a logo, or a particular colour that is associated with a place or an institution.

Compositional meanings

> bring the disparate components of a text together to make something unified and whole ... (it is) an intrinsic part of meaning-making: a house can have the same set of rooms, but arranging them in a different way creates a different house.
>
> (Ravelli and McMurtrie 2016, 7)

Architectural studies scholars make the same point; Moore et al., (1974, quoted in Ching 2007) say that:

> A good house is a single thing, as well as a collection of many, and to make it requires a conceptual leap from the individual components to a vision of the whole. The choices... represent ways of assembling the parts.

Key questions and systems here include how the parts are brought together to make a meaningful whole (*information values*); what stands out – what is backgrounded (*salience)*; whether component parts are clearly segregated or seamlessly integrated (*framing*); and what movement patterns are enabled through the space (*navigation paths*). Information values can be *integrated*, in which elements in the Margins relate equally to a Center, or *polarised*, with differential weighting of elements either on the vertical axis (*Ideal/Real*), the horizontal axis (*Given/New*), or along a temporal dimension (*Before/After*). For example, it may be that one part of a university campus is perceived as the 'main' building and others are subsidiary to that. It, thus, becomes the Center for the others as Margins to it. *Salience* for one particular element among others can be achieved through a range of factors, including larger size, contrasting colour or material, placement in relation to information values (e.g., as Center), or symbolic values. Iconic buildings are often salient because of their architectural difference from surrounding buildings. *Framing* in the built environment is concerned with the *permeable* or *sealed* nature of relations between elements in terms of movement in both visual and auditory channels (Boeriis and Nøorgard 2013, 77). Thus, two classrooms might be separated by a solid wall, so they are strongly framed as different or by a wall that can be folded back to allow permeability between the rooms. *Navigation* refers to the pathways available for users and is tracked along *promenades* (McMurtrie 2017) – that is, movement between points of stasis. This might be along internal corridors between classrooms, an outdoor walkway, and so on.

Relational meanings are concerned not just with *where* elements might be placed but also how that placement construes dependency between them as well as the semantics of that connection. In spatial texts, different components may be *paratactically related*; that is, they are relatively independent, such that one can move from one component to the next without backtracking – for example, moving directly from a lecture to a tutorial room. For *hypotactic* relations, some elements may be dependent on another, such that backtracking is required to move between spaces – for example, needing to go through one building to get to another. Semantically, relations between components may be the *same* or *different*, across each of the other metafunctions – that is, representationally, interactionally, or compositionally. A student moving from one tutorial to the next might be changing subjects (topics), but representationally, the function is largely the same (teaching and learning) as would be the interactional and compositional meanings. Moving from a lecture to a café, however, would likely be different across all the metafunctions.

Some of the key analytical questions relevant to each metafunction are illustrated in Table 7.2.

The above discussion illustrates some of the background of spatial discourse analysis. Analyzing spatial texts in this way begins to reveal how the design of the built environment manifests many aspects of the institution as an organization: how it uses spatial design to reflect its philosophies of education and how design construes roles for its users. It is important to emphasise that these are *semiotic* constructs: users are at liberty to reconstrue these spaces, not perhaps with unlimited freedom but, nevertheless, potentially at cross-purposes with the design (for example, a seat designed for *sitting* may be used as a place to sleep or to jump up and down on).

Contextual background

What is UNSW as an organization? It has a campus, designated staff and enrolled students, and a website presence, but this does not capture what it is as an organization. As an organization, it is all these things, and much more. It is its physical structures, the staff it employs, their hierarchy, and the roles allocated to them; it is the students and their different types and interests; it is the many policies, processes, and practices implemented every day; it is its branding and marketing and also the lived experience of working and studying there (which may or may not align with the branding and marketing); it is the regulations of government that the university operates within; it is everything from the major vision statements of the vice chancellor to the micro-moments of filling in a form to apply for leave, not to mention the fundamental activities of research and learning that take place there.

Certainly, within all this, the physical and material fabric of the campus plays a critical role. Universities and their architectural fabric are inherently intertwined. Edwards (2000) identifies at least nine types of university master plans, including the 'collegiate' (e.g., Oxford, Cambridge, UK), the 'linear/megastructure' (e.g., Simon Fraser, Canada), and the 'place-making' (e.g., University of Birmingham, UK). Stern (2010) notes that the University of Virginia, founded by Thomas Jefferson in 1817, saw the implementation of the 'academical village', 'a new conception of higher education' that was shaped ' as a learning environment unlike any before' (17). As Boeriis and Nørgaard (2013) have shown in their study of the built environment at Southern Denmark University (SDU), 'the very university buildings may realise discourses about university education, and more generally about the university system itself'. Importantly, as Ellis and Goodyear (2016, 149) note: 'Many billions of dollars are spent every year on building and maintenance and [that] buildings have long played significant practical, emotional and symbolic roles in university life.'

Founded in 1949, UNSW is a relatively young university, with its first permanent building opened in 1955 (UNSW Archives (a) n.d.; UNSW Archives (b) n.d.). It is considered one of the eight leading universities in Australia, with nearly 8,000 students and 22,000 academic and professional staff (UNSW n.d.). Originally with a focus on science and engineering, it now has seven faculties across two campuses in Sydney and one campus in Canberra. Since its inception, there have been a number of waves of renewal and renovation of the campus. Notably, the 1990s saw a vigorous wave of campus renewal, which succeeded in giving the university a wholistic identity and visual appeal that it did not previously have (UNSW Archives (a) n.d.). This was achieved through multiple strategies, including relocation of car parks, articulation of covered pathways to link otherwise disparate areas of the campus, and creation of a unifying walkway leading to (and from) a strategically placed 'iconic' building (Ravelli and Stenglin 2008).[2]

The 2000s have seen – and continue to see – the renovation and/or replacement of entire faculty buildings, mostly within the existing campus structure, although some entirely new buildings have also been added. This has succeeded in bringing teaching and research facilities up to 'world class' standards (UNSW Learning Environments n.d.) and has included the sophisticated incorporation of both networked and wireless technology across the campus. An important element of this phase of change was the substantial refurbishment of the university library. Prior to renovation, the key areas students used were like many conventional libraries – rows of bookshelves and minimal accommodation for students to study, mostly in single-person carrels, with a small number of group-study rooms available. The renovation saw the reconceptualisation of these spaces to reduce the space allocated to books and expand both the quantity and variety of spaces available for students, from quiet single-study and group-study options to informal small group options and casual spaces for relaxing and chatting. This has resulted in a congenial, multipurpose space that students use extensively (Ravelli 2018; Ravelli and McMurtrie 2016, 2017).

Since 2016, another notable wave of change can be seen in the conversion of general-purpose classrooms to what is designated (by the university) as 'active learning spaces' (ALS). These are tutorial-style classrooms (as opposed to large lecture theatres) that have been reconfigured from rooms with fixed or minimally moveable seating and a teacher-centric focus for the provision of technology (whiteboard, projector, etc.) to rooms that have easily-reconfigured furniture and a student-centric provision of technology (multiple whiteboards, and projectors around the room that students can operate). These physical changes align with higher education trends toward more student-centred pedagogies (Ravelli 2018; Wu 2022).

Large-scale transformation continues to take place at UNSW, and another notable development on campus is the upgrading of 'informal outdoor learning spaces'. These are the focus of the next section.

Informal outdoor learning spaces

A recent phase of redevelopment at UNSW has been the upgrading of informal outdoor spaces to allow for more seating and better provision for students using their electronic devices. While there are many parts of the campus experiencing these transformations, a clear illustration is provided in 'the Quadrangle' (the Quad). The Quad is a key (but not the sole) gathering place for students at the university. It is located, more or less, at the physical center of the campus, being about half-way between what are referred to as 'upper' and 'lower' campus (see Figure 7.1).[3] The Quad has two-story buildings on three sides, including tutorial rooms as well as some offices and other functional spaces, such as a pharmacy, medical center, café, and travel agent. The fourth 'side' of the Quad is open.

The Quad was completed in three stages between 1993 and 1995, during the busy construction period of the 1990s, and was designed by architects Peddle, Thorp, and Walker (Luscombe 2001). The open space within the Quad consists of lawns, with two diagonal paths intersecting in the middle. The blonde-brick construction is typical of the era, with colonnades around the three built sides, forming covered walkways that give shade from the sun and protection from rain. The only fixed decoration is a large sundial (the Millenial Sundial) placed above the second level of the southern side, which was added to the Quad in 2001 (UNSW Archives (a); see Figure 7.2, left). Luscombe further notes (2001, 29) that 'the external circulation spaces on the ground floor and first floor provide a place for staff and student interaction while also forming part of the covered *University Walk*'.

The Quad is an important transitional space on the campus; that is, it is a place where multiple paths cross in terms of students and staff moving between classes and in terms of people moving between the 'upper' and 'lower' parts of the campus, with the Quad located more or less at the half-way point. Luscombe (2001, 40) notes that the spaces of the Quad are part of a designated 'University Walk', which 'serves to unify and integrate the campus', adding that 'it is in a sense the life-blood of the university'.

As a gathering place, the Quad is an area where students can come together. It is a focus for specific events hosted by student organizations, such as 'Wellbeing Week' and 'Pride Week', with stalls and activities around such themes located on the open lawns. Throughout the year, students play organised and informal games or lounge around on the grass, talking and relaxing. It is, of course, important to note that, being located in Sydney, Australia, the weather is mostly conducive to outdoor life, and while indoor facilities for eating and relaxing are certainly provided, this is to a much lesser extent than might be found in universities located in other climates.

Prior to recent renovations, the walkways around the edges of the Quad were largely empty of furniture or decoration, with only the occasional wooden bench seat placed against the bare brick walls to provide a small amount of seating (Figure 7.2, right). These walkways have now been filled with a variety of furniture, including long benches with laptop worktables; double-sided working booths, with seat-level benches or high barstool-style seating; vertical, open, wooden screens to partition spaces; and decorative frames overarching some of the seating. Electric power points are available throughout (Figure 7.3). Clearly, all this provides much more seating for students than was previously available, as well as different kinds of spaces, allowing individual and collaborative use, the chance to power up electronic devices, and tables to rest computers, books, or food on. Such

152 Louise Ravelli

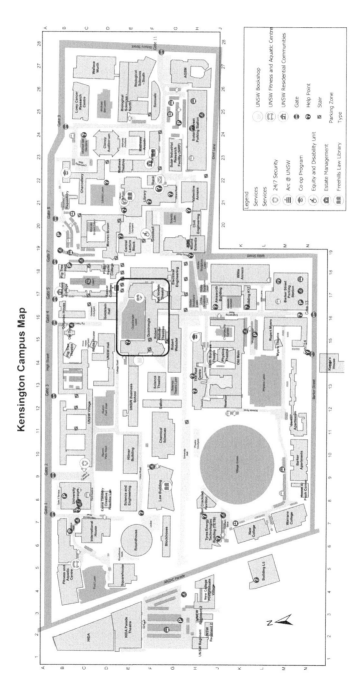

Figure 7.1 Campus map, with Quadrangle highlighted (Source: https://www.estate.unsw.eAcdu.au/getting-here/maps; accessed July, 2021)

Redesigning organizations through the built environment 153

Figure 7.2 Overview of the Quad (left) and walkways prior to renovation (middle and right) (Photograph by the author)

Figure 7.3 UNSW walkways in the Quad following renovation (Photograph by the author)

changes are not unique to the university but draw on well-established practices and quasi-institutionalised templates in corporate and other workplaces where varied and co-working environments have become the 'new norm' for many organizations (Dale and Burrell 2010; see also Shortt 2015). As van Leeuwen and Zonjic say (Chapter 3), 'organizational semiotic resources often spread beyond the context in which they originated'.

These now archetypal configurations are sometimes referred to as 'elevated' workplaces, which boost a sense of corporate identity through sophisticated design choices (McWhirter 2019), or as 'responsive' workplaces (Openshaw 2017), which cater for different personality types through multiple spatial configurations (Smollen and Morrison 2019). The most well-known early exponent of this practice is Google, which redefined their working practices through the design of their corporate headquarters, Googleplex, in 2003 (Wakabayashi 2021). UNSW, with its emphasis on outdoor working places, now finds itself in a curious synergy with Google, which because of the pandemic, is now seeking to maximise the potential of working outdoors.

These newly furnished spaces are now heavily used throughout the day, and anecdotal evidence suggests that students are very positive about the facilities. It is obvious that these facilities afford greater comfort and greater opportunity for a variety of activities (eating and working, for example) than was the case before. However, a more comprehensive metafunctional analysis points to other implications of these spaces beyond comfort and multifunctionality, which may or may not be viewed positively. Analysis of representational, interactional, compositional, and relational meanings will reveal additional nuances that demand critical evaluation. As Smollen and Morrison say (2019, 427), referring to Kornberger and Clegg (2004), 'Workspaces are created through human interaction by architects and designers with guidance or direction from owners and managers. These workspaces then shape human interaction and influence behaviour and job satisfaction.' That is, the facilities provided are not just 'facilities', but a way of both reflecting and constituting organizational culture – that is, 'the tacit social order of the organization' (Groysberg et al. 2018, 46, cited in Smollen and Morrison 2019, 428). The focus for this analysis is particularly on the facilities provided in the colonnades as opposed to the open grass in the center.

Representational meaning

As noted above, representational meaning in spatial design is concerned with the functions, uses, and processes facilitated by that design, and the roles enabled for users in relation to those processes. The colonnades of the Quad no longer seem to be just walkways to enable transition between classes or between different parts of the campus, nor are they just spaces that provide a little shelter should it be raining or a place just for sitting or eating lunch. The provision of laptop tables, power points, and collaborative seating more clearly enables processes of studying/working and of using electronic devices. These facilities encourage students to actually stop in the Quad and engage in either social or learning processes. That is, it becomes the location for specific activities and, thus, a destination point in itself.

More formally, the earlier version of the Quad promoted non-transactional processes of *walking/moving through*, with minimal provision for transactional processes such as *eating* and *reading*, and no overt provision for processes that would include socialisation or collaboration with other users (within the space of the colonnades, that is; the lawns were and are still open and available). The current version of the Quad still facilitates the non-transactional processes of *walking/moving through* (although arguably slightly less efficiently than before, as discussed below) and overtly promotes processes of *eating, using laptops,* and *collaborating with others.* Student experience is not required to be social or collaborative, but it is assumed that it can be.

With the formerly, more or less, 'empty' walkways, students would have to adapt these spaces themselves, for example, sitting on the ground if the few bench seats were full, perching their computers on their laps. But that left the range of possible activities open and undefined. In other words, students' Agency as social actors (van Leeuwen 2008) was not enabled in any specific way, but nor was it delimited. While there are now greater facilities, it also means that the range of possible activities is, in some ways, more circumscribed. Students can, of course, still use any space in resistant or subversive ways, but curiously, it seems to result in something akin to what Dale and Burrell (2010) describe in terms of the 'aestheticisation' of the workplace. They observe that organizational workplaces such as *National@ Docklands* and *Interpolis* in the UK have been redesigned almost 'as homes', with kitchens, recreation rooms, and so on. This aestheticisation, they write, 'is combined, almost ironically, with the disappearance of the workplace itself *as a workplace*' (20, emphasis added; see also Burrell and Dale 2014). A similar analogy can be found in Adami's (2018) analysis of the renovation of the Kirkgate Market in Leeds, which introduced new features but also eliminated many former practices, resulting in a kind of 'endangered semiotic diversity' (20). In the Quad at UNSW, the aestheticisation and renovation of the walkways coincides with an apparent increase in the variety of activities that are enabled by the design; at the same time, this variety is circumscribed by the design itself. As the vernacular disappears, homogenisation replaces it (see also Aiello and Dickinson 2014; Crosby and Seale 2018).

The redesign of the Quad, thus, raises questions of users' (students') Agency in relation to the processes with which they engage. Students have Agency in terms of moving through or stopping in the Quad and Agency in terms of where they stop and what activity they take up. However, as the new facilities are largely fixed in place (for example, chairs cannot be moved), Agency is largely removed in terms of how, or if, these spaces can be reconfigured. This contrasts with other aspects of recent redesigns at the university, for example, in new classrooms and in the renovated library, where much of the seating can be easily moved and reconfigured (Ravelli 2018; Ravelli and McMurtrie 2017). Burrell and Dale (2014) refer to an extreme example of the delimitation of Agency in the work of Wasserman (2012). Wasserman (2012, 17) describes an open-plan office in which every element of the design is pre-determined and fixed, producing a kind of 'physiological uniformity' in its subjects. In such ways, Agency, in terms of representational meaning, overlaps with aspects of Power in terms of

156 *Louise Ravelli*

interactional meaning; that is, in the Quad, the institution largely retains Power over the provision of facilities. Burrell and Dale (2014, 5) make the same point, noting that particular 'spatial narratives' result in 'affective ties', and that space 'is intimately connected with power relations' (6).

Interactional meanings

Interactional meanings in spatial design are concerned with how relations between users are constructed (for example, student to student, and institution to student) and how users are made to feel in terms of security and belonging in the space.

The new seating provided in the Quad facilitates two key forms of social interaction. The long seats with laptop tables and the high benches with power points (Figure 7.3) suggest either individual usage or collaborative usage with students side by side (McMurtrie 2017). The tables with seating on both sides and soft bench seats suggest collaborative and social usage (Figure 7.3). In the previous iteration of the Quad, as already noted, the few simple benches provided only minimal opportunity for individual seating and possibly some collaboration with individuals side by side. Thus, the new version of the Quad greatly increases both the opportunity for social interaction and the variety of possible interactive forms.

As always, however, design and use can vary, and students' social interactions are in no way defined solely by the seating forms. In collaborative spaces, students can choose to self-bind by focusing on a screen or book and/or by wearing headphones (Figure 7.4, left). In otherwise individual spaces, students can use proximity and social geometry of their bodies to transform these into collaborative ones (Figure 7.4, right, couple chatting).

As noted above, changes in the Quad also impact questions of Power and Control, closely related to the dimension of Agency in representational

Figure 7.4 Self-binding (left); collaboration (right) (Photograph by the author)

meaning. Movement through the walkways and use or not of the facilities remains free and unrestricted; there is no institutional requirement to move in a particular direction, to pass through barriers, or to sit in particular places. However, as the new facilities are largely fixed in place (except for some of the chairs at the high benchtop tables), the institution retains Power and Control over these. The new facilities also implicitly assert the Power of the institution, as it is expensive to provide and maintain them.

Aesthetic aspects of the new facilities have additional implications for interactional meanings. Multiple framing devices, such as the decorative archways above some of the seats (Figure 7.4, left) and vertical slatted screens between some of the seating sections, greatly increase the effect of Binding (Stenglin 2004). That is, such devices help to define and close in otherwise large and open spaces, adding a sense of comfort and belonging for users, encouraging them to stay rather than simply move through. Similarly, the repeated use of the university's key branding colour, a bright, saturated yellow (used especially in the upholstery) increases the effect of Bonding (Stenglin 2004), or 'a sense of cohesion and belonging' (Burrell and Dale 2014, 5). The saturated yellow is used consistently through the University, on the website, in corporate materials, and in decoration, as a 'bondicon' (Stenglin 2004). This simple design choice reminds users that this is not just any space but a space belonging to UNSW (and see Laba, Chapter 4).

In many ways, then, these new provisions enable new forms of 'community' to be articulated, both among students (through social geometries) and between students and the university (through Binding and Bonding). As Dale and Burrell (2010, 24) say:

> 'Community' works as a spatial organizing principle, and it does so in a diffuse way. Regardless of the experience one might have of any particular community, the idea in itself provokes almost Garden of Eden images of harmony, belonging and cohesion. In this way, the use of 'community' in the reshaping of organizations has much to do with cultural and emotional management.

The changes in the Quad *do* create and enable new forms of community – students are not just passing through but now stopping, working, and socialising, all bound not only to this space but to a greater sense of the university as a whole.

Compositional meanings

Compositional meanings in spatial design are concerned with how the parts are brought together to make a whole. As discussed above, framing is one of the resources that indicates the separation or integration of spaces and may be strong (e.g., solid walls) or weak (e.g., no walls between functionally separate areas). In the Quad, predominantly weak framing is used to suggest distinct but, nevertheless, connected spaces. For example, slatted screens define separate spaces but allow air, light, and noise to permeate (Figure 7.3; see Boeriis and Nøorgard 2013). Framing is also achieved by changes in the forms and decoration of seating (see previous images), albeit within a limited range. At the same time, the limitation on variation, resulting in repetition of forms, materials, and colours, creates a rhyme (Kress and van Leeuwen 2020) that ensures that the different areas of the Quad cohere with each other as well as with the institution as a whole. Through such resources, the colonnades of the Quad are both 'one' place (seen as a whole) and 'many' (seen individually). It is interesting that none of the differentiated areas have been made particularly salient – that is, no one of the spaces within the Quad is larger, differently designed, or more strongly framed than any other. Thus, all the variety of spaces within the Quad are given equal value. As always, such values can be changed by actual use, so for a particular student or students, one area may have greater salience than another for their own personal, social, or cultural reasons. Also notable is that the classrooms themselves are strongly framed in comparison with the open spaces of the Quad, through separation by walls and a door and a strongly contrasting design aesthetic.

The changes already described for representational meaning and interactional meaning have a deep impact on compositional meaning also. In compositional terms, because the fundamental functionality of the Quad has changed, and because it has an entirely new potential for Binding, the Quad is no longer just a useful shelter from the rain nor a transitional point between classes, but it is a destination in and of itself. In terms of information values, the classrooms previously had the (symbolic) information value of Center, with the spaces in the colonnades functioning very much as Margins to the classrooms. Now, the spaces in the Quad could be said to function as (symbolic) Center, with formal learning activities (classes, going to the library) at the Margins.

As a transitional space, the Quad is now somewhat less successful, both because users do actually stop here rather than just transition through, and because the available space for moving is narrower, so the colonnades become more congested as students move between classes. As McMurtrie (2013, 2017) says, a *promenade* – the point between movement and stasis – is the fundamental unit of analysis in the built environment. Here, where previously there were virtually no points of stasis so that there was only movement (between classes, between parts of the campus), now the points of stasis have been not only created but also given an entirely new value of their own. These values are intertwined with changes in relational meanings, as discussed below.

Relational meanings

Relational meaning (Ravelli and McMurtrie 2016) is an adaptation of Halliday's logical metafunction for language to the relation of spaces to each other. An understanding of relational meanings in the Quad is key to articulating the significance of the overall changes. In relational terms, both the taxis (dependency) of the connections between spaces has changed and so, too, has the logico-semantic value (meaning) of those connections.

Prior to the redesign, movement for students within the Quad could be said to be from classroom to classroom or from classroom to another part and function of the campus (lecture theatre, library, food outlet). The key points of stasis were the classrooms themselves; the Quad was a connecting device and not (generally) a place for stopping. In semantic terms, the classrooms 'added' to each other: one class is followed by another, and so on. While the topic and content of the class (course, subject) may change, functionally, each classroom is, more or less, the same in terms of representational, interactional, and compositional meanings. That is, each classroom serves to hold a class, enables particular relations between teachers and students, and has similar information values, framing, and salience.

Following the redesign, the Quad becomes a point of stasis in itself; thus, students move from the Quad to the classroom and back to the Quad. In other words, students are consistently moving back to the Quad as a starting point. The semantic relation then is one of 'enhancing' (changing) the experience, as metafunctional meanings across the two places are different. Interestingly, representational meanings remain predominantly the same; that is, both the classroom and the Quad now function as places to 'work' (study, learn), although the Quad accommodates other functions as well, such as socialising and eating. Interactionally, the Quad enables multiple forms of social geometries, minimises the visible Power of the institution, and promotes higher affiliation with the space and the institution. Compositionally, it is now the Quad that is informationally central rather than the classrooms. Further, the open framing of the Quad is now strongly contrasted with strong framing in relation to the classrooms, which are different in terms of design, function, and access. The overall shifts in relational meanings are summarised in Table 7.3.

Discussion

Observing such differences is one matter; evaluating them is another. From a positive point of view, it is clear that these spaces are being used extensively and are, more or less, constantly filled with students, which suggests students' positive orientation to the Quad's redesign. As Ellis and Goodyear note, in relation to the impact of technology on students' lives (2016, 149):

> The 'boundaries' between the physical and the virtual are becoming less clear and more permeable. This permits and promotes redistributions of

Table 7.3 Relational meanings of the walkways in the Quad, pre-, and post- design changes

Relational meanings	PRE – *design changes*	POST – *design changes*
Dependency	Quad = connection between classrooms, hence relation of classrooms to each other is paratactic (class + class + class …)	Quad = starting and return point, hence relation of Quad to classrooms is hypotactic (Quad × class × Quad × class …)
Semantics: Representational	Quad = place to transition between classrooms	Quad = place to work/study and/or socialise
Semantics: Interactional	The Quad is functional only; no explicit manifestation of Power of institution and no explicit manifestation of Binding or Bonding devices	The Quad manifests Power of the institution; both enables and restricts Agency; binds students to the Quad as a place; bonds students to identify with the university
Semantics: Compositional	Quad is Marginal to classrooms as Center	Quad is Center, with classrooms as Marginal

study activity in space and time, with many students demanding greater flexibility in order to fit study around other aspects of their lives, including paid work and caring for others.

The redesign of the Quad supports these new conditions and could even be said to help students prepare for the types of workplaces they are likely to face – that is, ones that can be fragmented as well as ones that encourage collaboration. Van Leeuwen and Zonjic (Chapter 3) note that the spread of semiotic resources from one context to another 'spread(s) the cultural values of the organizations in which and for which they originated'. The changes are, perhaps, also a manifestation of what Boeriis and Nøorgard (2013, 87) identify as the ideal of 'freedom with responsibility … that has gained ground in many segments of contemporary society, including education'. That is, students are free to use these spaces or not, but they are responsible for taking charge of their learning by deciding where, when, and with whom they learn.

The redesign of the university spaces also has a strong parallel with the redesign of offices toward notions of 'home', that is, working spaces that accommodate 'lounges, designer kitchens, and comfortable "break out" spaces, which appeal to the freedom of domesticity' (Burrell and Dale 2014, 5). This is a way 'to break down the barriers between public and private life so that people identify more closely with the organization in a positive way' (Burrell and Dale 2014, 5; see also Ravelli and McMurtrie 2016, 87). However, less positively, the changes can be viewed in other ways. It could be argued that these changes say to students 'You should always be working', or 'You should be doing your work everywhere'. Representationally, the functionality of the design supports learning processes (working on your computer); interactionally, it says you can stop here but only in the way/s we have pre-defined; and compositionally, it says that informal learning – in the actual in-between spaces of more formal learning environments (the classroom) – is the anchor point of study, and other activities are ancillary rather than vice-versa. As Ellis and Goodyear (2016, 149) add: '[Such] flexibility is accompanied by dangers of fragmentation, as learning experiences become spread across fragments of time and different locations, as well as across multiple devices and media, and in interactions with different groups of people.'

The changes also say something about the responsibility the university takes up as an organization and the expectations users have for organizations in terms of who provides facilities. The abundance of facilities here says, 'we are trying to cater to everyone', and conversely, 'everyone should be catered to', or perhaps, 'everyone deserves to be catered to'. At the same time, students may not be aware that the university has taken funds from elsewhere, such as administration, to enable these changes. The contrasts in positive and negative evaluations of the redesigned Quad are summarised in Table 7.4.

Conclusion

At UNSW, significant investment in new and renovated built spaces demonstrates the university's commitment to ongoing adjustment of its identity, both responding to and impacting upon student demand and expectations, changes in the higher education landscape, and altered practices of teaching and learning, not to mention changes in ways of 'being' a student. It could be dismissed as nothing more than the provision of nice, yellow chairs and more power points, but an examination of the sociomateriality of these spaces reveals that it is much more than

Table 7.4 Contrasting positive and negative evaluations of the Quad

Positive evaluation	Negative evaluation
Student experience is more flexible	Student experience is more fragmented
Students can work anywhere and can relax as if at home	Students should always be working, and there is no distinction between work and home
The institution provides well for students	The institution has diverted resources from elsewhere
Classes are only one part of learning, and learning can take place anywhere	Classes do not really matter

that. As Fenwick notes (2010, 107), 'sociomaterial accounts ... claim that matter is a critical force in the constitution and recognition of all entities, their relations, and the ways they change (or "learn")'. They add that work life – and by extension, I would say, university life – is 'fully entangled with material practice' (105).

The built spaces of work and learning are integral to everyday life; the built environment manifests the social values of institutions – as organizations – and scaffolds the social practices of its users, even if never fully determining them. As Boxenbaum et al. say (2018, 601): 'An empirical research frontier lies in detailing how the social realm and the material realm become intertwined, and what effects these processes have on organizational practice.' This metafunctional analysis of the design changes in the Quad at UNSW demonstrates how material resources can shape meanings – about the institution, its relations with and between students, and the very nature of learning in the contemporary context. The design changes arise in response to current sociohistorical conditions, but also feed back into them, constituting the process of change itself, demonstrating that 'space itself is productive of social and organizational life' (Burrell and Dale 2014, 22).

Changes to the materiality of the Quad at UNSW are just one further phase of the university's constant development, which can also be seen in other changes manifested in the university's library and classrooms, albeit inflected in different ways (see Ravelli 2018; Ravelli and McMurtrie 2016, 2017). The provision of various forms of seating in the Quad, along with tables, connectivity, and specific design aesthetics, fundamentally changes what these spaces 'say' about, and for, the university and its users, primarily students. As Smollen and Morrison say (2019, 427), referring to Kornberger and Clegg (2004), 'Workspaces are created through human interaction by architects and designers with guidance or direction from owners and managers. These workspaces then shape human interaction and influence behavior and job satisfaction.' Representationally, the nature of users' activities is now different – students can work and socialise here rather than just pass through. Interactionally, multiple forms of students' interaction with each other are enabled, and a stronger affiliation with the university is supported. Compositionally and relationally, what it means to 'be' in the Quad, as opposed to a classroom, has been altered. An examination of spatial design after the fact is not able to effect much change in that environment; such changes are costly, and only rarely undertaken, especially on a large scale. But examination of what has been achieved, intentionally or otherwise, provides an opportunity for critical engagement and reflection, a recognition that, along with the positives, there is the potential for a 'dark side' (Taskin, Parmentier, and Stinglhamber 2019, 262). As Burrell and Dale conclude (2014, 22), '" knowing your place" does not mean "accepting your place"'. The reshaping of the university directly impacts its students, and the potentially negative implications need to be made explicit, alongside celebrating its positives.

Notes

1 Ravelli and McMurtrie (2017) use 'organizational' for spatial discourse analysis rather than 'compositional'. The latter is preferred here, to avoid confusion with 'organization studies'.
2 A promotional video from the university that presents some of the campus changes can be accessed at https://www.youtube.com/watch?time_continue=79 &v=B4tutpgDewE (accessed July 2021).
3 The footprint of the university is, more or less, rectilinear. From Anzac Parade at the 'bottom' (left side of the map), it is indeed an uphill walk to get to Botany St at the 'top' (right side of the map).

References

Adami, E. (2018). "Shaping public spaces from below: The vernacular semiotics of Leeds Kirkgate Market." *Social Semiotics*. https://doi.org/10.1080/10350330.2018.1531515.
Aiello, G., and G. Dickinson. (2014). "Beyond authenticity: A visual-material analysis of locality in the global redesign of Starbucks stores." *Visual Communication* 13(3): 303–321.
Bateman, J., and Wildfeuer, J (Eds.). (2016). *Film Text Analysis: New Perspectives on the Analysis of Filmic Meaning*. New York: Routledge.
Boeriis, M., and N. Nørgaard. (2013). "Architectural discourse: The material realization of framing and discourse in a university building." *RASK* 38: 71–100.
Boxenbaum, E., C. Jones, R.E. Meyer, and S. Svejenova. (2018). "Towards an Articulation of the Material and Visual Turn in Organization Studies." *Organization Studies* 39(5–6): 597–616.
Burrell, G., and K. Dale. (2014). "Space and organization studies." In P. Adler, P. du Gay, G. Morgan, and M. Reed (Eds.), *The Oxford Handbook of Sociology, Social Theory and Organization Studies: Contemporary Currents*. Oxford: Oxford University Press, 684–706.
Carvalho, L., P. Goodyear, M. de Laat (Eds.). (2017). *Place-based Spaces for Networked Learning*. New York: Routledge.
Ching, F. (2007). *Architecture: Form, Space and Order*. New Jersey: John Wiley and Sons.
Crosby, A., and K. Seale. (2018). "Counting on carrington road: Street numbers as metonyms of the urban." *Visual Communication* 17(4): 433–450.
Dale, K., and G. Burrell. (2010). "'All together, altogether better': The ideal of 'community' in the spatial reorganization of the workplace." In A. von Marrewijk and D. Yanow (Eds.), *Organizational Spaces: Rematerializing the Workaday World*. Cheltenham, UK; Northhampton, MA.: Edward Elgar Publishing, 19–40.
Edwards, B. (2000). *University Architecture*. London and New York: Routledge.
Ellis, R., and Goodyear, P. (2016). Models of learning space: Integrating research on space, place and learning in higher education. *Review of Education* 4(2), 149–191.
Fenwick, T. (2010). "Re-thinking the "thing": Sociomaterial approaches to understanding and researching learning in work." *Journal of Workplace Learning* 22(1/2): 104–116.
Groysberg, B., H. Lee, J. Price, and J. Y-J. Cheng. (2018). "The leader's guide to corporate culture." *Harvard Business Review* 96(1): 44–52.

Halliday, M.A.K. (1978). *Language as Social Semiotic*. London: Edward Arnold.
Halliday, M.A.K. (1994). *An Introduction to Functional Grammar*. London: Edward Arnold.
Kornberger, M., and S.R. Clegg. (2004), "Bringing space back in: Organizing the generative building." *Organization Studies* 25(7): 1095–1114.
Kress, G., and T. van Leeuwen (2001). *Multimodal Discourse: The Modes and Media of Contemporary Communication*. London: Arnold.
Kress, G., and T. van Leeuwen. (2020). *Reading Images: The Grammar of Visual Design*. 3rd edition. London and New York: Routledge.
Luscombe, D. (2001). *UNSW Campus: A Guide to its Architecture, Landscape and Public Art*. Sydney: UNSW Press.
McMurtrie, R. (2010). "Bobbing for power: An exploration into the modality of hair." *Visual Communication* 9(4): 399–424.
McMurtrie, R. (2015). "Towards a grammar of system networks." In A. Archer and E. Breuer (Eds.), *Multimodality in Writing: The State of the Art in Theory, Methodology and Pedagogy*. Leiden and Boston: Brill, 86–115.
McMurtrie, R. (2013) "Spatiogrammatics: a social semiotic perspective on moving bodies transforming the meaning potential of space." PhD Thesis, School of the Arts and Media, Faculty of Arts and Social Sciences, University of New South Wales.
McMurtrie, R. (2017). *The Semiotics of Movement in Space: A User's Perspective*. London: Routledge.
McWhirter, G. (2019). "Stepping it up: A&D firms boost corporate identities with their own elevated workplaces." *Interior Design May*: 194–203.
Moore, C., Allen, G., and Lyndon, D. (1974). *The Place of Houses*. New York: Holt, Rinehardt and Winston.
Openshaw, J. (2017). "The responsive workplace." *Frame* 119: 146–149.
Preziosi, D. (1979). *Architecture, Language and Meaning*. The Hague: Mouton Publishers.
Rafaelli, A., and M. Pratt (Eds.). (2006). *Artifacts and Organizations: Beyond Mere Symbolism*. Mahwah, NJ: Lawrence Earlbaum.
Ravelli, L. (2018). "Towards a social-semiotic topography of learning spaces: Tools to connect use, users and meanings." In R. Ellis and P. Goodyear (Eds.), *Spaces of Teaching and Learning: Integrating Perspectives on Teaching and Research*. Netherlands: Springer, 63–80.
Ravelli, L., and McMurtrie, R. (2016). *Multimodality in the Built Environment: Spatial Discourse Analysis*. London: Routledge.
Ravelli, L., and R. McMurtrie. (2017). "Networked places as a communicative resource: A social-semiotic analysis of a re-designed university library." In L. Carvalho, P. Goodyear, and M. de Laat (Eds.), *Place-based Spaces for Networked Learning*. Routledge: New York, 111–130.
Ravelli, L., and M. Stenglin. (2008). "Feeling space: Interpersonal communication and spatial semiotics." In G. Antos and E. Ventola (Eds.), *Handbook of Interpersonal Communication*. Berlin: Mouton de Gruyter, 355–396.
Shortt, H. (2015). "Liminality, space and the importance of 'transitory dwelling places' at work." *Human Relations* 68(4): 633–658.
Smollen, R., and R. Morrison. (2019). "Office design and organizational change: The influence of communication and organizational culture." *Journal of Organizational Change Management* 32(4): 426–440.

Stenglin, M. (2004). "*Packaging Curiosities: Towards a Grammar of Three Dimensional Space.*" Unpublished PhD Thesis, Department of Linguistics, University of Sydney.

Stern, R.A.M. (2010). *On Campus: Architecture, Identity and Community* (Ed. P. Morris Dixon). New York: The Monacelli Press.

Taskin, L., M. Parmentier, and F. Stinglhamber. (2019). "The dark side of office designs: towards de-humanization." *New Technology, Work and Employment* 34(3): 262–284.

UNSW (n.d.). https://www.unsw.edu.au/about-us/unsw-glance. Accessed July, 2021.

UNSW Archives (n.d.a). "Campus buildings exhibition." University of NSW. Accessed September, 2019. https://www.recordkeeping.unsw.edu.au/university-archives/online-exhibitions/campus-buildings-exhibition.

UNSW Archives (n.d.b). https://www.recordkeeping.unsw.edu.au/university-archives/historical-resources. Accessed July, 2021.

UNSW Learning Environments (n.d.). "Learning environments UNSW Sydney." University of NSW. Accessed July, 2021. https://www.learningenvironments.unsw.edu.au/

Van Leeuwen, T. (2008). *Discourse and Social Practice: New Tools for Critical Discourse Analysis*. Oxford: Oxford University Press.

Van Leeuwen, T. (2018). "Multimodality in organization studies: Afterword." In M.A. Höllerer, T. Daudigeos, and D. Jancsary (Eds.), *Multimodality, Meaning, and Institutions. (Research in the Sociology of Organizations, Vol. 54A)*. Bingley, UK: Emerald Publishing, 235–242.

Wakabayashi, D. (2021). "Google's plan for the future of work: Privacy robots and balloon walls." *New York Times*. April 30, updated October 7, 2021.

Wasserman, V. (2012). "Open spaces, closed boundaries: Transparent workspaces as clerical female Ghettoes." *International Journal of Work Organisation and Emotion* 5(1): 6–25.

Wu, X. (2022). "*Space and Practice: A Multifaceted Understanding of the Designs and Uses of "Active Learning Classrooms.*" Doctoral thesis, School of the Arts and Media, University of New South Wales, Sydney.

8 How multimodal structures constitute organization
The meaning of structure in offline and online shopping environments

Morten Boeriis

Introduction

With the point of departure that 'physical settings provide contexts for behaviour' (Hatch 1987, 387), structural design has been a topic in organization studies for many years. For instance, there has been a focus on organizational space and physical environment (Dale, Kingma, and Wasserman 2018; Elsbach and Pratt 2007; Hatch 2011), materiality in institutions (Vaujany et al. 2019), and organizational aesthetics (Wasserman and Frenkel 2011). Recently, the communication constitutes organization (CCO) literature claims that organizations are the result of communicational actions (see for instance Ashcraft, Kuhn, and Cooren 2009; Brummans et al. 2014; Cooren, Bartels, and Martine 2017; Schoeneborn, Kuhn, and Kärreman 2019; Schoeneborn and Vásquez 2017). The notion that communication constitutes organization is compatible with the social semiotic axiom that social actions and semiotic meaning-making are two sides of the same coin, meaning that all social actions are semiotic, and all semiotic actions are social (Kress and van Leeuwen 2001).

Multimodal social semiotic (MMSS) analysis can provide insights into *how* physical layout provides contexts for behaviour and interaction for both internal and external stakeholders. It is central to multimodal theory that it pays attention to semiotic resources other than language (Baldry and Thibault 2006; Hodge and Kress 1988; Kress and van Leeuwen 2021; O'Toole 1994). It follows from this that, in an organizational context, the designs of different texts play a crucial role in organising and that organizational self-understanding is strongly affected by many sorts of multimodal texts, such as the homepage, the main entrance and the general room layout and decoration, the design of staff uniforms, the web design, and the printed advertising material. MMSS offers a precise analysis of the design of the meaning-making elements in organizations' communications, and by revealing the underlying structures of the designed physical or digital environments, it can shed light on how structure enables specific forms of interaction.

MMSS analyses typically focus on the strategic design of what we can call *the multimodal text in itself* (in a communicational context), whereas

DOI: 10.4324/9781003049920-8

this chapter shifts the focus to *the multimodal text in use* by focusing on the complex interplay of multiple semiotic resources and the actions afforded, instigated, and regulated by these resources in the structural semiotic design. The organizational context is the place where text and user meet – the scene on which the situational and cultural are played out in (inter)action.

What this chapter brings to the fore is a) that structure/structural meaning (the textual metafunction) plays an important role in the organizational communication and b) that the focus on the structural meaning in situational context provides important insights about how organization is constituted by multimodal communication.

The analysis below uncovers the relation between the designed structures and the actions of customers in offline and online shopping instances with a particular focus on search behaviours and search strategies.

Data

The recordings of shopping situations used as data for this study are part of a larger scale study of shopping situations in both online and physical shop environments. In total, it consists of 1,040 minutes of eye-tracking recordings from 64 randomly chosen individual shopping situations. The test subjects in the physical store are wearing eye-tracking glasses, which record what they look at (fixations) and their eye movement (saccades), and a microphone, which records what they say and hear (close distance sound recording). In the online shopping situations, the test subjects were placed in front of a laptop computer with an eye-tracking camera. Both situations were also filmed from a distance of approximately three meters for documentation of actions, body language, interaction, movement, and placement in the shopping situation. In this sense, the data contains both an 'internal' view from the test subjects' point of view and a more external view of the shopping situations.

Theory

Multimodality from a social semiotic perspective

The MMSS approach aims to create an inventory of the semiotic resources available for meaning-making with a given semiotic mode within a cultural community (van Leeuwen 2005, 3). The term 'grammar' is used to describe the conventions of communicative practices. The core social semiotic idea is that, in any instance of text, the distinct meaning of the instantiated choices stem from both the grammatical choice (the 'semiotic address' of the selection in the overall semiotic system) and from the determining context in which it is instantiated. This approach is well suited for analysis in organizational contexts because the text is intended to function in a strategically loaded environment.

Halliday's systemic functional linguistics (e.g., Halliday 1978, 1994) has been the inspiration for MMSS scholars (for instance Hodge and Kress 1988; Kress and van Leeuwen 2001, 2021; O'Toole 1994). In particular, semiotic *metafunctions* has become a central concept. This entails the idea that language and other semiotic modes always create three types of meaning simultaneously: 1) The *ideational metafunction* concerns the representation of the world in the text – it is what the text is about, what is represented, what is going on, how, where, etc. (processes, participants, and circumstances); 2) the *interpersonal metafunction* is the social function of the text – how relations between the text producer and the text consumer are expressed in the text (speech functions, modality); and 3) the *textual metafunction* concerns how words and sentences are organized into a meaningful semiotic artefact/event. This chapter focuses on the latter perspective on multimodal texts, which has, generally, been underrepresented in the MMSS literature so far and provides new insights about the multimodal textual metafunction.

The textual metafunction

The textual metafunction constitutes semiotic elements into a text by weaving them together into an integrated 'meaningful whole' (Kress and van Leeuwen 2021, 179). In any given semiotic mode (or combinations of modes), the textual metafunction provides the 'textness' by means of internal structural logics. The textual systems typically described in relation to language are *thematic structure* (setting the initiating point of departure of a clause) (Halliday and Matthiessen 2004, 58), *information structure* (the relation of already known and new information in a clause) (Halliday and Matthiessen 2004, 89), and *cohesion* (semantic linking in and between clauses) (Halliday and Matthiessen 2004, 87). There are similar functions in play in other semiotic systems, as discussed by Kress and van Leeuwen (2001, 2021) in relation to visual communication, or in relation to sound (van Leeuwen 1999), architecture (e.g., Boeriis and Nørgaard 2013; O'Toole 1994; Ravelli and McMurtrie 2016), and moving images (e.g., Bateman and Schmidt 2012; Boeriis 2009; Kress and van Leeuwen 2021; van Leeuwen 1996; Wildfeuer 2014). The systems of the textual metafunction describe the conventions for making textual meaning in a particular mode.

In this chapter, I depart from the idea that textual interwovenness sets the scene for buying and selling situations, as the shop layout is designed to afford certain 'navigation paths' (Ravelli and McMurtrie 2016, 108). Customers understand the structural meaning of the layout and appreciate how something is foregrounded, backgrounded, grouped together, or separated, etc. but do not necessarily have to navigate the text in any particular order (see also Lemke 2002, 300 on traversals). Some shops are designed for more flexible traversals than others. For instance, IKEA stores are infamous for making customers walk through very long compulsory navigation paths, passing many products on the way. Supermarkets typically have a more open structure but, for many years, have had a practice of placing certain commonly used products in areas furthest away from the cashier, forcing the average customer to walk through more sections of the store to get their typical daily groceries (for instance, dairy products, meat, fruit, and vegetables). To find a particular product, the customer will have to implement the most appropriate search strategy in relation to the shop layout.

Before analysing the structures in digital and physical shops, we shall first elaborate some central textual systems that a MMSS analysis of multimodal structures can draw upon.

Salience

Salience is the function of creating a hierarchy of importance among the elements in the text (Kress and van Leeuwen 2021). Basically, it is the communicative choice of making particular elements stand out relative to other elements in the text – presenting them as 'more worthy of attention than others' (Kress and van Leeuwen 2021, 210). The salience hierarchy can be created by means of contrasting particular elements to the rest of the general text. According to Kress and van Leeuwen, contrast can be achieved through means such as vivid colours, brightness, sharper focus, and relative size (Kress and van Leeuwen 2021, 210). Boeriis (2009, 237) proposes 18 visual contrast forms that are relevant for analysing both web texts and spatial texts (Table 8.1).

Table 8.1 Contrast forms relevant for analysing salience in web texts and spatial texts (from Boeriis 2009, 237)

Contrast type	Characteristics
Colour contrast	Contrast in saturation or hue
Brightness contrast	Figure darker or brighter than ground
Focus contrast	Figure sharper than ground
Contrast of size	Figure bigger or smaller than ground
Placement contrast	Unbalancing element
Perspectival contrast	Figure closer to viewer than ground
Pointing-out contrast	Pointed out, e.g., by lines
Pattern contrast	Syncopation of pattern
Cohesive contrast	Repeats something from earlier
Alternation contrast	Elements that change over time
Synergic contrast	Works together with another element
General cultural contrast	Uncommon or striking in cultural context
Material contrast	Elements involved in physical actions
Existential contrast	Elements seemingly out of context
Relational contrast	Striking groups or striking components
Contact contrast	Figure gazes at viewer
Angle contrast	Figure seen more frontally compared to ground
Modality contrast	Figure has a different visual style than ground

According to Kress and van Leeuwen, the salience hierarchy in two-dimensional visual texts sets up 'the "most plausible" reading path' (1996, 219). However, it has also been established that, even in linear written texts, the eyes do not, in fact, follow a path from the most salient element to the second most salient and so on down the salience hierarchy (Holsanova, Holmquist, and Rahm 2006). Our reading paths seem much more erratic as we shuttle back and forth between elements. Nevertheless, even though the implicitly proposed reading path created by the salience hierarchy is not followed, the viewer can clearly identify the salience hierarchy in the text (Boeriis and Holsanova 2012; Holsanova, Holmquist, and Rahm 2006; O'Toole 1994). Similarly, in spatial texts, such as brick-and-mortar shops, 'salience may or may not initiate a navigation path but will foreground significant points along the way' (Ravelli and McMurtrie 2016, 108). The textual layout of a shop sets up the most plausible path of movement, but the customer may take a completely different route through the store. This discrepancy between design/layout and the (reading) path taken indicates a general understanding of the semiotic conventions that are informing our reading of visual texts, regulating, but not defining, our sensorimotor system actions. Analyzing the relation between the salience hierarchy and the actual navigation provides insights into how stakeholders – in this chapter customers – conceive of the organization and how they implement particular strategies to achieve their goal in the organizational context.

For this chapter, I propose operating with five different but interrelated types of salience that interplay in varying combinations when we experience two-dimensional or spatial-visual communication (Table 8.2). By foregrounding certain elements, the organization signifies that these are more important and worthy of attention than others, which communicates what the organization values and which products it particularly wants to be associated with. Through the arrangement of products, for example, a bookstore may imply that it values 'highbrow' literature more than easily read popular literature or vice versa.

Connecting elements

A key resource for segmenting whole texts into their component parts is *framing*, and Kress emphasizes the importance of this notion with the slogan 'there is *no meaning without framing*' (2010, 10, emphasis in original). Framing is the instantiated concrete demarcation of abstract categories. Strategies of grouping, or separating, elements in texts mark conceptual relations between elements. Framing functions both as a demarcation of the whole text as a semiotic artefact or event from the rest of the world (for instance, the literal frame of a painting) and as a text-internal structuring device in which particular elements are either joined or separated by framing devices (for instance, lines or blank space). 'The more the elements of the spatial composition are connected, the more they are presented as belonging

Table 8.2 Salience types

Salience type	Characteristics
Perceptual salience	Attention toward certain visual stimuli governed by our sensorium's biological predispositions. For instance, the visual sense is especially prone to notice human faces and eyes, strong colours, and larger elements as well as to see movement in the peripheral field of vision and, generally, to notice things that stand out in different ways (Guido 2001).
Semiotic salience	Hierarchisation based on established conventionalized choices for selecting certain elements in a text as more salient, more worthy of attention than others (Kress and van Leeuwen 2006).
Idiosyncratic salience	Individual personal preferences, interests, and goals. *Preferenced idiosyncratic salience* concerns the individual's basic preferences and interests that makes them more likely to notice elements that stimulate those interests. *Self-primed idiosyncratic salience* is when an individual is on the lookout for something particular, such that elements in the environment that fulfill the goal of the search are salient to the individual (Nyström and Holmquist 2008). This is also known as a 'searcher' state of mind (Guido 2001).
Primed salience	Preceding co-textual or contextual stimuli can impact on the way the salience hierarchy is perceived. For instance, if individuals are exposed to salient green elements beforehand, there is a higher tendency to fixate on green elements in a visual text (Theeuwes and Van der Burg 2013). This can also be cross-modal semantic priming; for instance, a written text that says 'bald people have more fun' will make bald people (and smiles) more salient in a proceeding image.
Anti-primed salience (salience blocking)	Conscious or unconscious bypassing of known salient stimuli based on cultural knowledge of typical persuasive strategies in text layouts. Even though individuals perceive, understand, and acknowledge the salience strategy of a text design, it is possible to 'filter out' certain salient stimuli, such as strongly saturated colours or movement in the margins in banner ads on webpages (Holmqvist, Holsanova, and Rahm 2006; Foulsham and Underwood 2007).

together, as a single unit of information' (Kress and van Leeuwen 2021, 206) and, as such, framing both presents the text structure and affects the way text consumers process and interact with the presented information.

Ravelli and McMurtrie (2016) argue that *cohesion* is a connecting system under the textual metafunction in spatial texts that provides structural meaning and helps weave the different elements into a coherent text. Halliday and Matthiessen (2004) describes cohesion in language as a 'resource for making it possible to transcend the boundaries of the clause' (532) by creating links between clauses that indicate 'semantic relationships in the unfolding text' (586), such as conjunction, reference, ellipsis, and lexical organization

(533). According to van Leeuwen, cohesive devices in visual texts are semiotic resources such as rhythm, composition, and information linking (2005, 179). Cohesion works at different rank scale levels (see below), and Ravelli and McMurtrie (2016, 110) argue that 'in order for a spatial text to be cohesive, there must be unity *and* differentiation' and that a key resource for creating cohesion through similarity is that of repetition of colour, style, objects, or shapes.

Boeriis (2012) and Boeriis and Holsanova (2012) present the connecting textual concept *affinity*, which describes degrees of relatedness between elements in a visual design through a number of 'affinity mechanisms' that are related to framing, cohesion, and rank. Boeriis's 14 different types of affinity fall into three categories related to the different metafunctions. These include textual affinities, such as segregation, proximity, rhyme or contrast; interpersonal affinities, such as common viewpoint or shared modality profile; and ideational affinities, such as joined process involvement. These affinity mechanisms are in play across texts and are relevant for analysis of both cohesion and rank. As demonstrated in the analysis below, areas in a store (and on a webpage) may be framed; they may be cohesively linked across different locations (pages) through affinity mechanisms such as repetition of colour, shape, motif, or wording. For instance, there can be affinities between printed design, shop layout, and online search engine designs.

Rank

Inspired by Halliday's segmentation of verbal language into morpheme, word, group, and clause (1994), O'Toole (1994) presents an approach to paintings that describes similar structural levels comprising four rank scale levels. Boeriis (2012) develops this approach to encompass all visual multimodal texts, including composite texts, such as ads, homepages, or other texts, which can include images, text, graphics, etc. Boeriis's (2012) *dynamic rank scale* does not follow O'Toole's (1994) *a priori* focus on human participants and their processual relation but, rather, on how individual texts organize any pictorial elements and their parts in the text whole (see Baldry and Thibault 2006, 26 on multivariable rank). The dynamic rank describes four 'rank scale functions' that function simultaneously in visual text (Table 8.3).

The concept *rank scale zoom* (Boeriis 2012) describes how the four levels of rank can operate at different rank scale levels simultaneously (see also Baldry and Thibault 2006). There can be a full rank scale hierarchy in play at a global text whole level (for instance, a web page layout) and, at the same time, also a full rank scale at a local text whole level (for instance, in a photograph in the web page layout). In other words, we can analyse the whole site structure as a text (termed 'global text whole'), we can analyse the individual pages as texts, we can analyse pictures as texts, and we can analyse verbal text blocks as texts (all termed 'local text wholes'). All textual systems function both locally and globally.

Table 8.3 Rank

Text wholes	The overall textual top-level unit of analysis – the combined elements that compose the text in its totality. Often, the text is composed of elements that can be analysed as local text wholes, i.e., texts in texts; for instance, in composite texts such as an article that includes photographs – each photograph can both be analysed as an element (*Figure*) in the global text and as a local text whole (Boeriis 2012).
Groupings	Clusters of elements that via *affinity mechanisms* (Boeriis 2012) are presented as functioning together as a unified entity in the text whole. This can, for instance, be instantiated by means of presenting elements close to each other (*proximity*), by repetition of colour or shape (*rhyme*), by being involved in a common process (*process involvement*), by being depicted from the same angle (*viewpoint*), etc. (Boeriis and Holsanova 2012, 266).
Figures	Secluded elements that are conceived of as single individual elements in the visual text. This can be simple geometrical or irregular shapes (a triangle or an amorphous blotch of black) or more complex shapes, such as an object, animal, or a human body. Common to elements that function as Figures is that they cannot be divided into smaller parts without becoming incomplete (Boeriis 2012).
Components	Parts of Figures, both in terms of torso or limbs on animal objects, but also in terms of attributes such as colour, and even partial material processes of facial expressions fusing to a joined 'looking happy' process (Boeriis 2009, 189).

When navigating spatial or interactive texts, an individual manages concurrent dynamic rank scale perspectives. The hypothesis in this chapter is that people interacting in and with the structural layout understand the local structures immediately in front of them, such as signs, shelves, and walls while, at the same time, they deduce a conception of higher scale structures of the whole area based on the local cues and prior experiences with similar textual structures. Based on the layout experienced, users develop an expectation of relevant local text levels and, within those, relevant rank scale levels of groupings, figures, and components.

Information structure

Kress and van Leeuwen (2021) divide the canvas of two-dimensional visual text into structural zones, each ascribing different meaning to the elements that are placed in them. Boeriis (2009) proposes a dynamic information structure analysis that is partly based on rank scale logics. Rather than exclusively depending on the placement in the overall frame, this approach also takes into account the placement of elements relative to each other. Consequently, left-right relations, top-bottom relations, and center-margin relations can be described at different rank levels in visual texts (Boeriis 2009). A group of elements may all be placed in the right side of the overall frame ('New' at a global scale level), but within that group, some elements may be to the left of others ('Given-New' at group level). This is related to the linguistic *theme-rheme structure* (Halliday and Matthiessen 2004), as the meaning ascribed to the placement has to do with an ordering, a sense of before and after, or point of departure and follow-up. In the analysis below, it is demonstrated how both the placement of product on shelves and products in online search results can be structured according to the logics of information structure.

Analysis

The focus in this analysis is to reveal how the customer 'reads' and navigates the design of the shop layouts and implements search strategies that they deem appropriate for achieving their goal. The analyses presented are not exhaustive but elucidate systems under the textual metafunction that are involved in both physical and online shopping situations. The two examples were selected because of their comparable search goals.

The primary case is a shopping situation from a medium-size Danish brick-and-mortar bookstore involving a customer, *Test Subject 1* (TS1), lasting 6 minutes and 40 seconds from when he enters the bookstore until he leaves again having ordered a book. TS1 enters with the purpose of purchasing a particular book that he has seen in an advertising leaflet on an earlier occasion. The analysis reveals that, in order to achieve his goal, TS1 utilizes five clearly distinct primary search strategies in order to navigate the structural logics afforded by the store environment.

The second shopping situation takes place online in which a woman, *Test Subject 2* (TS2), is also searching for a particular book for 11 minutes and 22 seconds, from when she starts typing in search words until she closes the window, having purchased the desired book and ordered it for delivery to her address. To achieve her goal, TS2 utilizes five partly intertwined primary search strategies to accommodate the design logics of the sites that she is navigating.

Brick-and-mortar search strategy 1: Global scale affinity search for the relevant department

The combined public area of the bookstore is the global text whole of this analysis, and the overall structure is dominated by a few major pathways between product categories, such as specialist literature, fiction, and stationery, with minor narrow pathways between the shelves within the different categories. The books on the individual shelves are ordered alphabetically following the information structure (Given-New and Ideal-Real), and the books are placed with the spine out for fast searching. A few books on each shelf are singled out as more important by being placed frontally (angle contrast). At the end of each row of bookshelves, there are display stands where selected books are presented as especially interesting by use of contrast of placement, pattern (syncopates the search structure), existence (in the store as such), and perspective (foregrounded).

The open structure of the store affords many possible navigation paths, but the most obvious would be to follow the major pathways to a desired category area and then find the precise location by author name. But TS1's navigation does not follow the logics of the major structures. At first sight, it looks like TS1 is just browsing, as he walks around the store looking at random elements with his hands folded behind his back, which would indicate a perceptual-idiosyncratic based 'surfer state of mind' (Guido 2001) in which he is not searching for anything in particular. However, TS1 is, in fact, on a distinct goal-oriented search in which he employs search strategies that are based on his memory of design elements that he has seen in a leaflet from a household-distributed advertising campaign. TS1 remembers the use of colours and explicit language on the printed leaflet and uses this in his refined search strategy ((*self-*)*primed affinity search*) in the store, as he fixates on signs using the same salient red design (colour contrast) and explicit language (cultural contrast). These reference a campaign that was held by the bookstore chain at the time (cohesive contrast), and the controversial formulation was a way of attracting attention. TS1's first fixation on one of these signs happens in the very beginning of the search (see Figure 8.1). It could seem insignificant, but the fixation actually provides a waypoint to the correct area of the bookstore for conducting a goal-oriented search.

Figure 8.1 Fixating the sign

In that way, remembering the campaign design helps TS1 zoom in from the overall bookstore as a text to a grouping of elements of interest. Because TS1 is unsuccessful in finding the book, he fixates on different versions of the same sign at four later occasions, reassuring himself that he is, in fact, searching in the right area. On his traversal to the targeted campaign area of the store, TS1 lets himself be distracted by quite a few salient elements, which is an indication that he has already implemented search strategy 2.

Brick-and-mortar search strategy 2: Self-primed salience and affinity search at prominent displays

After having zoomed in, found, and delimited his search area, TS1 begins a search period in which his navigation paths and fixation patterns do not seem to follow the logics of the shop layout. He is walking around the area, still with his hands behind his back, on what seems to be an unsystematic navigation path in which he passes the same places several times and sometimes stands still, seemingly without a clear purpose, looking around in all directions. His movements do not adhere to the store's design of information structure or salience hierarchy, and at first glance, he seems to follow quite erratic patterns.

However, if we conflate TS1's navigation paths and patterns of fixation with both the shop layout structure and TS1's search goal, it becomes obvious that he utilizes quite a clear strategy in which salience plays an important role, not as a path defining framework but more as a culturally founded conceptual frame of understanding. It is a *self-primed idiosyncratic and affinity search strategy* that is based on his expectations about the salience structure of the store layout. TS1's expectation is that products that are prominent in the marketing leaflet would also be placed prominently in the shop layout.

TS1 fixates on prominently placed elements (placement contrast, perspectival contrast, frontal angle) and bright book covers (brightness contrast) or on books with a clear division into a bright and a dark area (vertical information structure) (see Figure 8.2). This shows how he utilizes his memory of the book cover layout as seen in the advertising leaflet and that this memory informs his search strategy in the store layout. TS1 manages to make an almost exhaustive search of prominently displayed books in the fiction literature part of the bookstore (global text) with this affinity-borne approach in which he seeks out all book covers with relevant similarities in visual design (bright Ideal, contrasting dark Real etc.). TS1 draws upon his cultural knowledge about common semiotic strategies for highlighting campaign elements in shops in combination with his memory of the book cover layout presented in the advertising leaflet.

TS1's navigation path through the bookstore and his search on shelves is obstructed several times by other customers (see Figure 8.3). He is not traveling along the main paths in a systematic way from A to B, but back

How multimodal structures constitute organization 177

Figure 8.2 TS1 search by salience (circles = fixations; lines = saccades)

and forth, constantly changing direction and looking in different directions than the one he is walking. This makes it difficult for the other customers to predict his movements and act accordingly. The store is clearly designed with different search strategies in mind, as the pathways are designed for faster goal-oriented movement to get to the specialized genre and theme-based sections that are then designed for very slow movement and alphabetical searching.

Brick-and-mortar search strategy 3: Alphabetical search

After 2 minutes' searching, TS1 realizes that his strategy is failing, and he then switches to a *self-primed information structural consultative alphabetical search* that follows the bookstore's internal shelf structure. He moves closer to inspect selected bookshelves and performs a systematic consultative-alphabetical search in which he utilizes the searcher-optimized theme- and genre-borne alphabetical structure offered by the shop layout. When approaching the shelves, he follows the horizontal and vertical information

178 *Morten Boeriis*

Figure 8.3 Traversal hindered by other people

structure that places books alphabetically by author from left to right (Given-New) and top to bottom (Ideal-Real). As he reaches the area where the book should be placed, he finds other books by the same author but cannot find the right one. He fixates several times on the other books in the area and on the area around, and he looks behind a book by the same author placed at the front to see if his book is hiding behind it (See Figure 8.4). This shows that he appreciates the structural logics of the store design and

Figure 8.4 Alphabetical search

How multimodal structures constitute organization 179

expects to find the book in the alphabetical information structure as it was not on salient display. After 50 seconds of unsuccessful searching, he turns away from the shelves and walks to the checkout counter with the purpose of getting help from a salesperson.

Brick-and-mortar search strategy 4: Reaffirming leaflet local text whole search

By the counter TS1 notices a stack of printed advertising leaflets identical to the one he had read beforehand, and he picks up a copy and commences a reassuring memory-based area search (*self-primed idiosyncratic and affinity and information structure search strategy*) where the leaflet becomes the local text whole. He clearly remembers that the picture of the book was placed in the Given zone on one of the first right-hand pages in the leaflet. After flicking back and forth between the first few pages, TS1 quickly finds the book on page 5 where it – as expected – is placed in Given as one of two salient elements on the page. He fixates on the page and then the photo representation of the book cover as a local text whole to confirm that he has recalled the book design correctly. The book cover is bright at the top and darker at the bottom, as were many of the covers he fixated on during his search. He presses the leaflet open firmly, as if he wants to make sure it will not close again, and places three fingers in an affirming manner on the page just below the picture of the book, almost explicitly gesturing that he did remember correctly (see Figure 8.5). TS1 has now confirmed that his search strategy was reasonable and, because he was not successful in finding the book, something else must be wrong. This conclusion is a potential problem

Figure 8.5 Leaflet search and employee-assisted search

for the organization as the customer can become confused and frustrated with the store.

Brick-and-mortar search strategy 5: Employee-assisted search

TS1 stands in a queue for some minutes before asking the salesperson about the book, while holding the leaflet open on the page with the picture of the book (see Figure 8.5). The salesperson confirms that the book is on sale in the store and that it should be on display. The interaction with the salesperson explicitly confirms that TS1 was correct in assuming that the salient position of the book in the leaflet means that it is prominent in the marketing strategy and, consequently, should be on display in salient areas of the store layout. The salesperson leaves the counter to make a search at the display stands, shelves, and window displays but returns with the information that the book is temporarily sold out. TS1 signs up for a copy of the book for pick up the next day and leaves the bookstore. To avoid further costumer frustration, the store should consider setting up a sign explaining that the book is sold out. As shown in the analysis above, it would be a good idea for an image of the book to be incorporated into the design of the sign (to support the *self-primed idiosyncratic and affinity search strategy*) and also place signs both at salient display positions and under the author's name on the shelves.

Online search strategy 1: Global scale Google word search for the right shop

In her search for a particular book online, TS2 implements structural search strategies that are comparable to the strategies implemented by TS1. TS2's strategies commence with a broad Google search for the book in any online shop, which is equivalent to TS1's search strategy 2. Her search process utilizes an approach based on verbal and visual resemblance at several levels, and in implementing this strategy, she seeks out the book by a *goal-oriented self-primed verbal search strategy*. The search for the words in the title is both assisted by the search engine and implemented 'manually' through scanning for the words of the title in the search results list (see Figure 8.6a). Scrolling through the search results list, she also uses visual style cues for singling out the book, as can be seen when she fixates on books with similar graphic styles on the front.

Online search strategy 2: Specific Amazon word search on book title

In a new window, TS2 types 'amazon.de' directly into the top URL bar, which brings her to the German version of the site. At the site, she enters the book title into Amazon's search function, and it appears at the top of the results list. TS2 navigates back and forth between different subpages,

How multimodal structures constitute organization 181

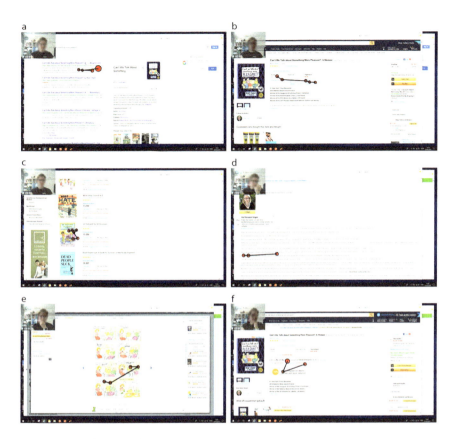

Figure 8.6 Online searching

searching for information about price and binding (see Figure 8.6b). In the Amazon book search (and in other online bookstores), the search results are presented as a vertical list, as on Google, but each individual result in the Amazon search list is organized as a horizontal Given-New structure with a large image of the book in Given and written information in New, and with a local Ideal-Real relation between a salient headline (brightness, size, placement, and perspectival contrast) and supplementing written information (see Figure 8.6c).

Online search strategy 3: Search for better pricing in other online bookstores

TS2 then searches for the book on other Danish online bookstore sites utilising both a *title word search strategy* and a *title word search strategy self-primed affinity search* for the book cover, and she is successful in finding the book in different versions. In both cases, there are quite a number of fixations on the prices of different versions, so it appears she is visiting the sites with a *self-primed strategy* for searching and comparing the different prices. TS2 finds what she is searching for at a good discount on Amazon, but proceeds to search for other purchase options, which suggests that she would rather buy the book in a local Danish online bookstore, but the price difference makes her decide to purchase from Amazon.

Online search strategy 4: Elaborate information search and buy confirmation on Amazon

TS2 makes elaborate use of a *zooming in and out search* in which she moves from the overall site (global text whole) into a part (local text whole) of the site. She navigates back and forth several times to collect detailed information about the book from the site subpages, including price, reviews, and examples (see Figure 8.6d). She clicks and opens a link with examples from the book, where she gets immersed in reading several page examples from the book quite thoroughly for more than 1.5 minutes (see Figure 8.6e). This could indicate that TS2 is having doubts about the purchase, but it could also be the case that she is reaffirming her choice (or 'appreciating the prey after the hunt'). Immediately after, she navigates back to the product presentation page and finds the '*Jetzt kaufen*' ('Buy now' in German) button and begins the checkout procedure, in which she purchases the book for private delivery (see Figure 8.6f).

Online search strategy 5: Scroll searching

When searching through online search results lists in all different search engines, TS2 utilizes subsearch techniques at a more detailed level during the actual scrolling procedure. In the *resting eye scroll search* the eyes do not generate saccades but stay in the same position, fixating on what the scroll movement (in this case, by use of a mouse wheel) brings into view. This 'saccading by scroll' is a very efficient way of scrolling through long lists of search results (similar to swiping through streams of information on social media). Search list searching is a *consultative self-primed salience-based strategy* (only looking for the searched object), and in social media streams, it is a *non-primed idiosyncratic surfer behaviour* (randomly looking for things of interest). The resting eye scroll search seen in TS2's scanning of search results is not a leisurely extensive action but a very quick and efficient way of looking through a longer list of search results. The strategy is comparable to the search strategy of the first two minutes of TS1's search in the brick-and-mortar bookstore.

TS2 also frequently utilises a *dynamic eye scroll search* when going through search results lists, in which the eyes move rapidly with many saccades and fixations forward in the list of search results and in which the scrolling, in combination with zooming and clicking, supports the eye movement by bringing areas of interest into the center of the screen. The dynamic eye scroll search lets the design of the text guide the eye so to speak and, therefore, perhaps lends itself well to more explorative searching approaches. This is based on a *self-primed salience strategy* that is also comparable to the search strategy utilized in the first two minutes of TS1's brick-and-mortar search.

Discussion

When observing customers' actions in shopping situations in physical and online shops, searching may, in some cases, seem like a randomized process, while in other cases, it may seem like a very goal oriented process of navigating straight to the desired product (Hoffman and Novak 1996). Organizations attempt to optimize their shop design for unhindered sale, use, and navigation while at the same time, conveying the best possible image of the organization through the design. Correspondingly, the customers attempt to navigate the shop structure in relation to their individual interests. Analyzing organizations' strategically designed artefacts provides insights into the organization's image and self-understanding, while analysing the actions of stakeholders in relation to these designed artefacts provides insights into how the designed elements are read/received.

The textual weaving of parts into a semiotic whole influences the customers' expectations of the shop, including how they interact with the design and with the employees within the layout. If we take the perspective that an organization is (at least partly) constituted by the actions and practices and symbolic artefacts in it (Schoeneborn, Kuhn, and Kärreman 2019), the layout becomes more than just a matter of marketing or efficient arrangement of the products. The structural logics presented by the textual layout of homepages or physical shops say a lot about the organization, how it sees itself and its employees, and about the assumptions it makes about its customers. The customers' experience with the physical store and the online shop provides a first-hand understanding of 1) how this store is organized for the customers, 2) how the organizations conceptualize their products, and 3) what image or identity of the organization is represented in the layout. This is an area where MMSS has much to contribute with its detailed focus on the resources of meaning-making.

The analysis above provides insights into how individuals understand and appreciate how textual structures enable multiple navigation paths, fixation patterns, and interactions with people and objects. Several quite different search strategies were implemented that related in different yet appropriate ways (Kress 2010) to the shops' inbuilt design structures. We saw how a series of interplays of multimodal stimuli may afford certain search strategies. TS1 based a substantial part of his search on assumptions about the textual design of the shop layout that drew on an earlier reading of the textual choices in a printed leaflet. The book was presented very prominently in the leaflet, which led to a self-primed search pattern that anticipated salience in the store through placement and perspective. With the book being sold out, TS1 had a frustrating customer experience of insecurity about his memory and search strategy and, in that, potential uncertainty about his conception of the organization behind the store layout. In the online search, TS2 could safely assume that if her title search was not successful, then the store did not offer the searched book, and she could quickly put the buying process on hold while visiting alternative online bookstores, which would have been a time-consuming task for TS1 in the brick-and-mortar bookstore.

In a physical shop, choosing a search strategy that is not afforded by the design can pose challenges for the search, as we saw in the case of TS1 above. The physical challenges of navigating around other customers in the bookstore became more pertinent because of distance restrictions during the COVID-19 pandemic. Organizations had to enforce the structural design by implementing strict rules for movement rather than suggested paths for navigation. Under these conditions, customers have to keep a distance and move in predefined directions, and if the pathways are not wide enough, they are prone to be clogged by other customers or employees. Shopping then becomes a complex (and at times awkward) process of navigating around other customers while trying to maintain the obligatory distance. Meanwhile, online shops only had to deal with increased demand for online products and the need to adjust their stocks and distribution accordingly.

Customers do not have a visual overview of the entire shop at any point during the physical or online search, but the analysis demonstrates that the global text whole is inferred through a process of hypothesis testing and adjusting in the navigation of local text wholes (shelf, area, subpage, picture, etc.). TS1's and TS2's navigational actions in a physical shop and an online shop indicate that they deduce the overall site structure from the layout of the individual subarea, and when moving closer to or clicking on something, they are fully aware that they have 'zoomed in' on a part (local text whole) of the overall text (global text whole). At any given point in the navigation through the global text, there is an immediate understanding of perceivable salience, rank structure, information structure, etc. at that particular position (local text whole), and at the same time, this knowledge is utilized to get an abstracted understanding of the overall textual structuring of the entire shop (global text whole) of which the current array is just a subset. If the local or global structural design does not reflect the shop's organizational logics, this may cause confusion for the customer.

The analysis demonstrates how different organizational texts may impact each other intertextually and multimodally in complex ways, in which the combined meaning-making may only be analysed by focusing on the actual use of the texts in the organizational context. In this case, the analysis demonstrates how stakeholders navigate shop structures as a result of knowledge and expectations about the actual text layout from prior experiences. It is clear from the analysis that customers expect that an organizations' communication will be coherent across different texts, in both style and design, as well as contributing to the overall culture and image of the organization. This is more than mere semiotic cohesion but also conceptual and ideological consistency, providing a stable organizational image. This shows the importance of an organization's awareness of its communication at all levels, such as different texts and designs as well as knowledge about how the different parts operate together.

Shop layout is part of an organization's interface to the world around it. The logics of the meaning made in the shop layout sets the scene for how the organization is seen by customers and other external stakeholders and, similarly, internally by employees. It is important that the layout reflects the right image because it can create confusion and misconceptions if the layout does not reflect or support the organization's image and, consequently, customers' expectations. The MMSS approach provides a nuanced understanding of shop layout as a text and offers specialized methods for close analysis that can help the organization optimize the design of shop layouts. But a very detailed and precise semiotic text analysis is not adequate in itself in relation to organizational communication. The social semiotic approach needs to further strengthen its focus on the multimodal interplay of different designs and different modal elements as well as on the actual use and reception of semiotic designs in a specific situational context. This can be achieved by developing analytical methods that incorporate the contextual and social aspects directly and systematically, as was suggested in this chapter.

Conclusion

This chapter demonstrates how communication does, indeed, constitute organization (Ashcraft, Kuhn, and Cooren 2009; Cooren, Bartels, and Martine 2017; Schoeneborn, Kuhn, and Kärreman 2019) and, more specifically, how *multimodal* communication constitutes organization. In this chapter, I argue that a) an MMSS theoretical framework (Kress 2010; Kress and van Leeuwen 2001, 2021) is particularly valuable for rigorous and nuanced analysis of multimodal communicative constitution of organizations and b) that such MMSS analysis can inform strategic decisions regarding organizational design and development.

In particular, the chapter demonstrates how an MMSS approach can be utilized in the analysis of shopping situations with a focus on textual meaning, elucidating the function of multimodal structure in shopping practices both in physical and online shop environments. It exemplifies how the MMSS approach may reveal how a design is read and how the layout of a room is utilized when stakeholders interact with the designed elements. The MMSS approach combines well with eye-tracking and video recordings in an analysis of the actions of actual customers, both in online and physical shops. This analysis can provide deep insights into customers' conceptualisation of the shop layout logic in relation to their navigation and behaviour in the shop. MMSS's descriptive systemic functional approach makes it possible to conduct close analysis of similarities and differences in structures and search patterns, anchoring the discussion in the actual semiotic actions taking place. The analysis can reveal inconsistencies and incoherencies in different formats, media and modalities that might be construed by stakeholders as bad communication or untrustworthiness and, thus, may harm the organization's image.

In MMSS, all social actions are semiotic, and all semiotic actions are social, as two sides of the same meaning-making phenomenon (Kress and van Leeuwen 2001). In organizational contexts, this leads to the notion that organizations are constituted by social semiotic actions (i.e., organizational semiotics). MMSS is an approach that is particularly suited to analysing such organizational semiotics. Just as eye-tracking may be conceived of as 'a window to the mind' (van Gompel et al. 2007), a MMSS analysis that brings together insights from close text analysis with observations of situational use can be a window to both the organization's desired image and to the customers' and other stakeholders' reading of this.

In this chapter, I have demonstrated that organizational multimodal texts are not distinct phenomena but, rather, that any individual text is perceived against the backdrop of a complex and intertwined interplay of texts and actions in the organization. In other words, all multimodal texts within an organization are woven together into a global organizational meaning-making structure, which is, in fact, what constitutes the organization.

Ethics

All test subjects have accepted participation in the project and allowed for research use and publication.

Funding

This work was supported by the Velux Foundation as part of the project *RESEMINA: the digital resemiotisation of buying and selling interaction* [grant number: 00016980] at the Department for Language and Communication, University of Southern Denmark. The funding source has not been involved in the study design; in the collection, analysis, and interpretation of data; in the writing of the report; or in the decision to submit the article for publication.

Declarations of interest

None

Acknowledgements

The author wishes to thank participants in the RESEMINA project for discussions about the data and especially Søren Vigild Poulsen and Julia Rytter Dakwar for their excellent early commentary on the argument of the chapter. Also, thanks to Anne-Christine Rosfeldt Lorentzen for her invaluable contributions to the process of finalising the chapter.

References

Ashcraft, K.L., T.R. Kuhn, and F. Cooren. (2009). "Constitutional amendments: 'Materializing' organizational communication." *Academy of Management Annals* 3(1): 1–64.

Baldry, A., and P.J. Thibault. (2006). *Multimodal Transcription and Text Analysis*. London: Equinox.

Bateman, J., and K.H. Schmidt. (2012). *Multimodal Film Analysis. How Films Mean*. London/New York: Routledge.

Boeriis, M. (2009). *Multimodal Socialsemiotik og Levende Billeder*. PhD thesis. Odense: University of Southern Denmark.

Boeriis, M. (2012). "Tekstzoom: Om en dynamisk funktionel rangstruktur i visuelle tekster." In T.H. Andersen and M. Boeriis (Eds.), *Nordisk Socialsemiotik: Pædagogiske, multimodale og sprogvidenskabelige landvindinger*. Odense: Syddansk Universitetsforlag, 131–153.

Boeriis, M., and J. Holsanova. (2012). "Tracking visual segmentation: Connecting semiotic and recipient perspectives." *Visual Communication* 11(3): 259–281.

Boeriis, M., and N. Nørgaard. (2013). "Architectural discourse: The material realization of framing and discourse in a university building." *RASK – International Journal of Language and Communication* 38: 71–100.

Brummans, B., F. Cooren, D. Robichaud, and J.R. Taylor. (2014). "Approaches to the communicative constitution of organizations." In L.L. Putnam and D.K. Mumby (Eds.), *The Sage Handbook of Organizational Communication*. 3rd edition. Thousand Oaks, CA: SAGE Publications, 173–194.

Cooren, F., G. Bartels, and T. Martine. (2017). "Organizational communication as process." In A. Langley and H. Tsoukas (Eds.), *The Sage Handbook of Process Organization Studies*. London: SAGE Publications, 513–528.

Dale, K., S.F. Kingma, and V. Wasserman. (Eds.). (2018). *Organisational Space and Beyond: The Significance of Henri Lefebvre for Organisation Studies*. London: Routledge.

Elsbach, K.D., and M.G. Pratt. (2007). "The physical environment in organizations." *Academy of Management Annals* 1(1): 181–224.

Foulsham, T., and G. Underwood. (2007). "How does the purpose of inspection influence the potency of visual saliency in scene perception?" *Perception* 36: 1123–38.

Guido, G. (2001). *The Salience of Marketing Stimuli: An Incongruity-salience Hypothesis on Consumer Awareness*. London: Kluwer Academic Publishers.

Halliday, M.A.K. (1978). *Language as Social Semiotics*. London: Edward Arnold

Halliday, M.A.K. (1994). *An Introduction to Functional Grammar*. 2nd edition. London: Edward Arnold.

Halliday, M., and C. Matthiessen. (2004). *An Introduction to Functional Grammar.* 3rd edition. London: Arnold.

Hatch, M. (1987). "Physical barriers, task characteristics, and interaction activity in research and development firms." *Administrative Science Quarterly* 32(3): 387–399.

Hatch, M. (2011). The symbolics of office design: An empirical exploration. In P. Gagliardi (Ed.), *Symbols and Artifacts.* Berlin, New York: De Gruyter, 129–146.

Hodge, R., and G. Kress. (1988) *Social Semiotics.* Cambridge: Polity Press.

Hoffman, D.L., and T.P. Novak. (1996). "Marketing in hypermedia computer-mediated environments: Conceptual foundations." *Journal of Marketing* 60(3): 50–68.

Holmqvist, K., J. Holsanova, and H. Rahm. (2006). "Entry points and reading paths on newspaper spreads: Comparing a semiotic analysis with eye-tracking measurements." *Visual Communication* 5(1): 65–93.

Kress, G. (2010). *Multimodality. A Social Semiotic Approach to Contemporary Communication.* London: Routledge.

Kress, G., and T. Van Leeuwen. (1996). *Reading Images: The Grammar of Visual Design.* 1st edition. London and New York: Routledge.

Kress, G., and T. van Leeuwen. (2001). *Multimodal Discourse. The Modes and Media of Contemporary Communication.* London: Arnold.

Kress, G., and T. Van Leeuwen. (2006). *Reading Images: The Grammar of Visual Design.* 2nd edition. London and New York: Routledge.

Kress, G., and T. Van Leeuwen. (2021). *Reading Images: The Grammar of Visual Design.* 3rd edition. London and New York: Routledge.

Lemke, J. (2002). "Travels in hypermodality." *Visual Communication* 1(3): 299–325.

Nyström, M., and K. Holmqvist. (2008). "Semantic override of low-level features in image viewing: Both Initially and Overall." *Journal of Eye Movement Research* 2(2): 2, 1–11.

O'Toole, M. (1994). *The Language of Displayed Art.* London: Leicester University Press.

Ravelli, L., and R. McMurtrie. (2016). *Multimodality in the Built Environment: Spatial Discourse Analysis.* New York: Routledge.

Schoeneborn, D., and C. Vásquez. (2017). "Communication as constitutive of organization." In C.R. Scott and L.K. Lewis (Eds.), *International Encyclopedia of Organizational Communication.* Hoboken, NJ: Wiley, 367–386.

Schoeneborn, D., T.R. Kuhn, and D. Kärreman. (2019). "Perspectives: The communicative constitution of organization, organizing and organizationality." *Organization Studies* 40(4): 475–496.

Theeuwes, J., and E. Van der Burg. (2013). "Priming makes a stimulus more salient." *Journal of Vision* 13(3): 21, 1–11.

Van Gompel, R.P.G., M.H. Fischer, W.S. Murray, and R.L. Hill. (2007). *Eye Movements: A Window on Mind and Brain.* London: Elsevier.

Van Leeuwen, T. (1996). "Moving English. The visual language of film." In: S. Goodman and D. Graddol (Eds.), *Redesigning English. New Texts, New Identities.* Hove, UK: Psychology Press, 81–103.

Van Leeuwen, T. (1999). *Speech, Music, Sound.* London: Macmillan.

Van Leeuwen, T. (2005). *Introducing Social Semiotics*, London: Routledge.

Vaujany F.-X., A. de Adrot, E. Boxenbaum, and B. Leca. (Eds.). (2019). *Materiality in Institutions: Spaces, Embodiment and Technology in Management and Organization*. New York: Springer.

Wasserman, V., and M. Frenkel. (2011). "Organizational aesthetics: Caught between identity regulation and culture jamming." *Organization Science* 22(2): 503–521.

Wildfeuer, J. (2014). *Film Discourse Interpretation. Towards a New Paradigm for Multimodal Film Analysis*. London: Routledge.

9 'It's not just getting a biopsy'
Transposing 'take-home' messages from the operating theatre to a proforma

Arpan Tahim and Jeff Bezemer

Introduction

This chapter explores how surgical trainees and their supervisors jointly make and remake meaning, first as they engage in clinical work in the multimodal environment of the operating theatre, and second as they complete a written 'workplace-based assessment form' (WBA). It is the first study to explore how the WBA – a key intervention introduced in the United Kingdom (UK) by the royal surgical colleges in 2007 – is put into day-to-day practice.

Using video ethnographic fieldwork and a social semiotic frame, the chapter explores how a surgical trainee and his supervisor[1] jointly construct, reconstruct, and transpose 'take-home' messages as the work unfolds in the operating theatre and, in retrospect, as they complete the WBA form. We adopt the notion of a 'take-home message' from our focal trainee as a shorthand term for meanings that are extracted from ongoing semiosis and transformed and fixed in a way that they can 'travel' to and are relevant for other spatiotemporal contexts and parties. In this way, we contribute to the development of a multimodal notion of 'textual trajectories' (Maybin and Lillis 2017) – i.e., ways of accounting for 'the changes, movements and directionalities of texts – and relationships between these – across social space and time' (409).

Our aim is, first, to explore the construction of messages as the interaction between trainee and supervisor unfolds in the operating theatre. What is it that trainee and supervisor draw attention to as they operate and supervise, respectively, using the semiotic resources available to them? How do they construct messages as the procedure unfolds? To what degree are their orientations and interests aligned? Second, we aim to explore the selection and transformation of messages onto the WBA form. What is included, and what is excluded? How are they rearticulated in writing? What is gained, and what is lost in this process of entextualisation? Third, we suggest factors shaping the (sequential) co-authoring of the messages. What are the conditions under which the forms are completed? What are the trainee's concerns as they complete the form? In so doing, we demonstrate some of the questions that social semiotics asks about (meaning-making in) organizations and the tools it has available to account for them. The questions also illustrate how social semiotics can help address questions from organizational studies, notably in relation to the emergent, unpredictable character of work, communication and learning (Iedema and Bezemer 2021), and organizational interventions (such as proformas) designed to manage these.

Social semiotics has previously highlighted the role of the body in communication in the operating theatre and other clinical environments (see Bezemer 2020 for an overview). As sign-makers, clinicians select and subject to interpretation noticeable material forms and formations in their environment. This includes the sounds that make up speech, for example, or the graphics displayed on a monitor, which stand for numbers indicating the patient's heart rate, as well as bodily forms and formations – postures or movements – produced by colleagues for practical purposes. For example, a scrub nurse routinely establishes when and how to assist a surgeon through ongoing readings of the surgeon's bodily actions, which to them, indicate what instruments the surgeon is likely to need next. In these instances, the communicative and practical functions of the body are inseparable – all the more so as teams work on the tacit agreement that colleagues should anticipate rather than await requests.

Social semiotics ought to also concern itself with the ways in which clinicians (and patients) develop semiotic resources to *read* and communicate the *patient's* body as 'an inextricably complex *text*' (Sebeok 1985, 2, emphasis added). The underlying disposition of clinicians that shapes this 'body text reading' might be described as a 'professional vision' (Goodwin 1994) or, more specifically, as the 'clinical gaze' (Foucault 1994). Of interest to us are 'the terms [...] that physicists [...] have worked out to transpose sign processes of their fields of phenomena into the human language and that can be interpreted as translations' (Jakobson 1971, cited in von Uexküll 1986, 209), though we would replace 'human language' with 'the modes available to them'. These meaning-making practices underpin all clinical action and all expression in response to engagement with a patient body. It includes practices of seeing, touching, and hearing through which the clinician comes to recognise forms as instances ('tokens') of categories ('types') developed and shared within the clinical community and an expressive repertoire that enables them to represent and communicate about these forms.

In the operating theatre, modes of communication provide means for expressing understandings of the patient's condition. This includes possibilities for communicating sensory experiences. As clinicians inspect, palpate, and auscultate, they make meaning; they attach meaning to corporeal forms. Speech, writing, drawing, and other modes of communication are available to articulate the meanings made, enabling them to develop joint accounts of the patient and 'calibrate' (Goodwin 2017) their understandings. Technologies assist health professionals by mediating sensory experiences; in the case we present in this chapter, surgeons use a camera to see inside a patient's throat, with the output rendered on a screen. They need to work to produce a picture of areas of interest, manipulating tools as well as the area of interest before they can enter into discussions about what they see.

Clinical work, including surgery, is routinely reviewed and assessed, and the WBA is a case in point. This process is always mediated by modes and media of communication. For instance, a clinical event may be recorded in written notes or numbers representing judgments along pre-defined categories ('rating'). It may also be automatically recorded, e.g., as video or digital data from equipment, sensors, and so on; all these recordings can be subjected to interpretation. Assessors express their interpretations and build joint accounts of (recollections or recordings of) events using speech, gesture, and so on and may produce an official report, typically in writing. Assessing, then, is an instance of 'resemiotisation' (Iedema 2003), in which meanings are made and remade ('translated') according to specific needs and semiotic structures and possibilities for expression. This comes with a shift in focus from developing (shared) understandings of the patient to developing (shared) understandings of the clinician.

We adopt Kress's (2010) notion of design as the process of making 'selections and arrangements of resources for making a specific message about a particular issue for a particular audience'. Design is the process whereby the meanings of a designer (a teacher, a public speaker, but also, much more humbly and, in a sense, more significantly, participants in everyday interactions) become messages. 'Designs are based on (rhetorical) analyses, on aims and purposes of a rhetor, and they are then implemented through the instantiations of choices of many kinds' (28). This is a prospective notion of design as 'a means of projecting an individual's interest into their world with the intent of effect in the future' (23). This tallies with our focal trainee's notion of the 'take-home' message as that which can be extracted from ongoing practice and ought to be recorded and remembered to support future action.

We develop an analysis of 'intertextual chains, i.e., pairs or series of communicative situations, or texts, in which (in some sense) the "same" content, e.g., the same "case", is treated' (Linell 1998, 149). We explore, first, a WBA form completed by a surgical trainee, and second, a video recording of the happenings in the operating theatre to which the form refers. We also draw on interviews with the trainee, which help us contextualise the forms and understand the ways in which the trainee weaves the WBA into day-to-day practice.

The WBA

The WBA refers to the assessment of a day-to-day activity undertaken in the working environment of a post-graduate surgical learner (Postgraduate Medical Education and Training Board Workplace Based Assessment Subcommittee 2005). In surgery, these activities are diverse. They range from interactions with patients, families, or colleagues in wards or clinics, through to the execution of precise technical skills in the procedural or operative setting. WBAs are one of several elements of a surgeon-in-training's learning portfolio that ought to demonstrate progress and development during the training program. Their progress through their training program is summatively assessed and recorded during formal Annual Review of Competence Progression (ARCP) meetings. An important marker for progress through these meetings is the appropriate completion of a pre-determined quota of WBAs. Although overall requirements differ between region and specialties, a typical trainee is currently expected to complete 40 WBAs each year. This equates to roughly one WBA event every week.

The WBA form reframes a work environment as a learning environment and, in so doing, mediates between two different sets of concerns, each under the primary responsibility of a different organization. In the operating theatre, the orientation of trainee and supervisor shifts between a team's care for a patient (which is the primary responsibility of the hospital trust and regulated by national protocols, guidelines, and so on) and the assessment of the performance of an individual trainee (which is the primary responsibility of the royal colleges, who have set up the Joint Committee of the Surgical Training to manage this). Yet on the WBA form, the assessment of the trainee is the sole focus. Put differently, as they complete a WBA, surgeons shift between being clinician and trainee/supervisor, transposing meaning from one organization – the hospital trust – to another – the Joint Committee.

In the past two decades or so, organizations providing public services in the UK and elsewhere have come under significant pressure to adopt explicit 'standards' of practice and to routinely measure progress and improvement against these standards. The WBA is a manifestation of this trend in surgical education. WBAs were introduced to surgical training pathways in the mid-2000s as part of a large-scale, conceptual shift in medical education toward measuring learner competency in daily practice. Contemporary competency-based models of education now require learners to demonstrate competency in the workplace – namely that they have the knowledge, skills, and attitudes required for independent practice as a specialist within their chosen field (Burg 1982). This means that the previously undefined and 'nebulous' educational activities, practices, and processes now need to be made explicit. Furthermore, these educational activities need to be continually measured and assessed (Frank et al. 2010, Holmboe et al. 2010).

Policies commonly stress that these WBAs have a formative benefit for the learner. However, they also make explicit the use of WBAs in a (potentially high stakes) summative capacity. For example, the curriculum for one surgical specialty describes the purpose of the WBA as follows (ISCP 2018, 172):

- To provide short-loop feedback between a supervisor and the learner.

- To facilitate the provision of formative guidance.
- To encompass the assessment of skills, knowledge, behaviour, and attitudes during day-to-day surgical practice.
- To inform educational supervisor's summative assessment at the completion of the placement.
- To contribute toward a body of evidence held in the trainee's learning portfolio and be made available for the trainee's annual review.

This list starts with a focus on the formative nature of these exercises – each facilitating or stimulating formative guidance and feedback between learner and assessor/supervisor. However, as the list progresses, the rhetoric shifts toward the summative purpose of the WBA, both within particular placements – to decide whether learners have performed appropriately and, perhaps, most significantly for the learner, to contribute toward evidence at a trainee's annual review. This dual functionality has been confusing and controversial for the surgical community (Ali 2013).

Doing a WBA

An example of a WBA form is shown in Figure 9.1. The form asks the authors to name the procedure that they are reporting on and to *give feedback on* and *assess* the performance of the trainee. The WBA shown in Figure 9.1 is an example of a so-called 'procedure-based assessment' (PBA). This is a direct observation of a more advanced surgical procedure or operation, which typically takes place in the operating room. Other WBAs look to examine practice during simpler clinical interventions (for example the 'direct observation of procedural skills' assessment), while other represent observed assessment of a trainee's clinical skills in history taking, examination, or information giving (the 'mini-clinical evaluation exercise') or can represent formal discussion related to an aspect of a patient's care (case-based discussion).

The form shown in Figure 9.1 was completed by a surgical trainee eight weeks after having been involved in a laryngoscopy. This is a diagnostic procedure aimed at examining the inside of a patient's throat to inform decision making about treatment.

One set of comments on this form reads as follows:

(1) Microlaryngoscopy for confirmation of recurrence post Chemoradiotherapy (CRT) of glottis Squamous cell carcinoma (SCC) (General)
(2) Good understanding of the principles of the procedure and fluent in carrying out laryngoscopy confidently. Protects lips/teeth/gums throughout (feedback strengths).
(3) Anticipate next steps in mapping/staging patient and appropriateness for laryngectomy. Inspect subglottis and extend of anterior spread into piriform fossa (feedback development needs).

'It's not just getting a biopsy' 195

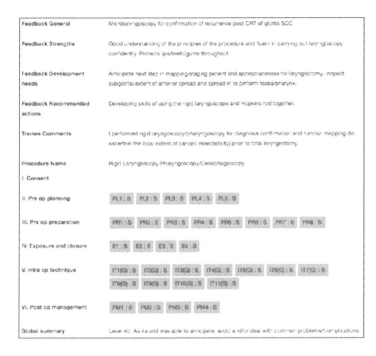

Figure 9.1 The surgical trainee's (T1) completed WBA form

(4) Developing skills of using the rigid laryngoscope and Hopkins rod together (feedback recommended actions).
(5) Level 4b: as 4a and was able to anticipate, avoid, and/or deal with common problems/complication (global rating).

The elliptic, one to two sentence comments are typical of what we found in the ten forms collected. The comments refer to *selected* features of the trainee's 'performance', reducing a series of events and conversations during a 20-minute procedure in the operating theatre (which we will present in detail in the next section) to a handful of sentences. The comments refer to *areas of performance* in *shorthand formulations* (e.g., anticipating next steps, inspecting subglottis, using certain instruments), leaving much of what it means to perform in those areas unarticulated. As we shall show in the remainder of this chapter, these references to selected aspects of surgical work stand for vast bodies of embodied knowledge and semiotic skills.

Crucially, performance in some areas is *evaluated* as 'good', 'fluent', 'confident' (1), and subsumed under the pre-given heading of 'general feedback' (1), 'feedback strength' (2), 'feedback development need' (3), 'feedback recommended actions' (4) and 'global rating' (5). The comments further suggest that *two authors* are involved: through third-person verb forms and use of imperative mood, the author of (2) and (3) positions themselves as a reviewer of another person's performance, while another author writes in the first person, commenting on their own performance:

(6) I performed rigid laryngoscopy/pharyngoscopy for diagnosis and tumour mapping (to ascertain the local extent of cancer/resectability) prior to total laryngectomy. (Trainee comments)

In the other sections of the form, the author is asked to evaluate the performance in different *stages* of the procedure. The available options to select are pre-given by the form. To illustrate using the form above, the pre-operative (pre-op) planning domain is subdivided into five steps (PL 1–5). For each step, the author chooses from the pre-existing options (N = not assessed, D = development required, S = satisfactory). The pre-op preparation stage is subdivided into eight steps (PR 1–8). The next stage, exposure, is made up of four, and so on. In this case, all stages were evaluated as 'satisfactory'. The form needs to be submitted by the trainee to the online platform and then validated on that platform by the assessor who observed the procedure. It is possible to submit, validate, and upload the proforma without entering comments into the free-text spaces (1–4 and 6 above); only the numerical, global ratings (5) are mandatory.

Only in (6) does the form identify the expected author ('Trainee comments'). Sections 1–4 are headed 'feedback' and apparently for the supervisor to complete; all other fields are 'ratings' and are, apparently, also for the supervisor to complete. However, trainees have indicated in interviews that they complete all sections themselves and that supervisors generally expect their trainees to do so. Supervisors still need to sign off or 'validate' the form online and may take a closer look at what the trainee has actually written. Thus, both supervisor and trainee are 'agents of entextualisation' (Park and Bucholtz 2009, 486) in a complex co-authorship. As the trainee completes the supervisor's fields 'on behalf of' the supervisor, the trainee carefully considers the image projected of him or herself and the social implications of 'over or underselling':

> I think I am one of those guys who will always put Level 3, when the boss thinks I am Level 4. It feels a bit awkward if the boss looks at it, and I don't want the boss to feel that he has to downgrade it. So, I rather they upgrade it.
>
> (Interview with surgical trainee)

Trainees generally complete the forms two to eight weeks after the selected episodes took place (which raises interesting questions around the role of memory in the WBA reporting system), often in batches of five or more (this trainee sent off more than 15 forms to his supervisor to be validated in one batch) amidst a generally intense and heavy workload.

Against this brief background sketch of the way WBA forms are completed, it is no surprise that the forms do not simply 'transpose' meaning that was made by supervisors and trainees in the operating theatre. The point that meanings change as discourse is extracted from one context (in our case, the operating theatre) to another (the WBA platform that hosts the trainee's learning portfolio) has been well made. For example, Linell writes:

> In no case are we faced with a true transfer of something; it is never the propagation of a fixed message across representational instances. Rather, it is a complex transformation, involving shifts of meaning and new perspectives, the accentuation of some semantic aspects and the accentuation or total elimination of others. Even what is usually understood as 'quoting" is a complex reconstruction process, which necessitates an analysis of both the quoted context and the quoting context.
> (Linell 1998, 148)

Some of the changes are a direct result of the time that is committed to 'doing the procedure' and 'doing the form'. The procedure that is the focus of the WBA in Figure 9.1 took 20 minutes; in other cases, this could be seven hours or more. In interviews, trainees reported that they typically completed the form in five to ten minutes. This level of commitment alone limits the amount of meaning that can be extracted and represented on the form. The common use of ellipsis (omission of agents, finite verbs) also signals a preference for 'keeping it short'. In practice, this means that the trainee aims to identify a 'take-home message' from each procedure:

> There is a key element: the take-home message from that procedure, which you fill out, which probably is, I put it in recommended actions or development needs. Mapping. That's the learning point from this. OK. All the other stuff, I just fill up with bog standard copy paste stuff.
> (Interview with trainee)

Thus, the trainee does not seek to provide a detailed account of his learning experiences in the operating theatre. It is not merely a retrospective, high-level, subjective summary of learning experiences; rather, trainees select and record what they believe is relevant for future performance, and, as noted above, what they believe supports the image they want to project of themselves as learners to the supervisors and the assessment panel that may get sight of the form.

Other changes are the direct result of the fact that the shorthand references to performance *transcribe* meanings that were originally made in a range of different modes of representation and communication. Conversations between trainee and supervisor involving speech, gesture, facial expression, and so on are reconstituted in writing. In that process, as indeed in any process of 'transcription', one is confronted with challenges that derive from differences between, e.g., speech and writing or gesture and writing, i.e., differences in terms of the way that a mode has come to be structured and organised, to represent the world in specific ways (Kress 2010).

Conversations are not the only source of a WBA form. The WBA form discussed here is a procedure-led one – i.e., focused on work in the theatre, where trainees learn to manipulate tools and patient bodies and learn to see the body in particular ways. As we shall see in the following section, giving feedback on performance in words in this multimodal environment comes with significant losses and some gains. In the WBA form discussed here, reference is made to practical action (e.g., 4) while also including messages that were derived from the spoken interaction (e.g., 3, as we shall see). We note in passing that, were pen and paper used, as is often the case still in hospitals, users could move beyond writing and include, e.g., drawings, even if that is not what the form asks for. Yet the WBA is a digital form, making these kinds of transgressions to accommodate modes other than writing more difficult to achieve.

Video recordings of surgical performance

In the remainder of this chapter, we present video excerpts from the surgical procedure that was documented in the form shown in Figure 9.1. The recordings were made by Tahim, along with recordings of five other participants in the study. In total, he recorded ten sessions that were subsequently recorded on WBA forms. All participants have given consent to be filmed (Tahim 2021).

As with the WBA form, we do not treat the video recordings as 'replicas' of what happened in the operating theatre. Their frame and angle reflect our interest in the surgical team, and they do not record a variety of other factors, such as touch. Yet they do provide a detailed, elaborate registration of the activity that the supervisor and trainee are supposed to review in the WBA form. This enables us to explore the principles by which they reframe/represent theatre happenings to fit the presumed requirements and expectations of the various future readers of the WBA.

The procedure in focus was done under general anaesthetic and involved visualising the vocal cords, using a laryngoscope (referred to in conversation as a 'scope') in order to diagnose a vocal cord cancer. This scope was inserted through the patient's mouth, down behind the tongue allowing the trainee to directly inspect the vocal cord and surrounding areas for lesions. At this point, he was the only person able to look through the scope to see the operative field. However, a pencil-thin camera, placed through the scope allowed the view to be projected onto a monitor for other members of the team to share this view. Similarly, various instruments were placed down the scope at the same time as the camera, allowing for actions to be carried out (for example the suction tube, swabs to wipe, and biopsy forceps). Using

'It's not just getting a biopsy' 199

these instruments, a small sample of tissue from the vocal cord could be taken as a biopsy to be analysed for the presence of cancer.

Importantly for the trainee, this procedure was seen as an essential one for him to master. He had performed it several times before and was familiar with the setup, equipment, and techniques involved. He had also been working in this hospital for several months, so he was familiar with the team and the surgical specialist (who is also his supervisor for the procedure and assessor in the WBA). Later, during an informal discussion with Tahim, he reported that, in preparation for taking part in the study, he and his assessor had spoken prior to the procedure and identified it as one that he could use as a WBA. In this way, his role as the main operator had already been determined. The procedure took approximately 20 minutes.

A first glimpse of the setup can be gleaned from Figure 9.2, highlighting the complex configuration of multiple people with different roles, oriented around a patient, along with different types of equipment – optic and visual equipment of the camera, surgical instruments, and anaesthetic equipment.

We reviewed the 20-minute procedure in detail, identifying 119 microevents – episodes involving sets of participants and oriented to specific areas of action and topics of conversation. They are plotted in a diagram represented in Figure 9.3.

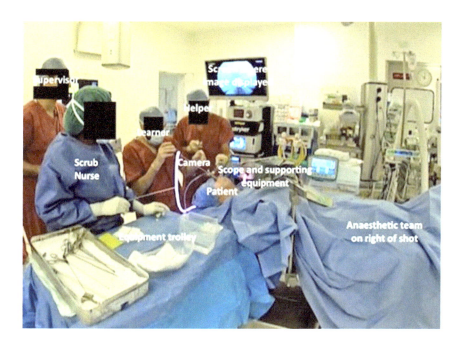

Figure 9.2 Operating theatre environment in which this WBA occurred

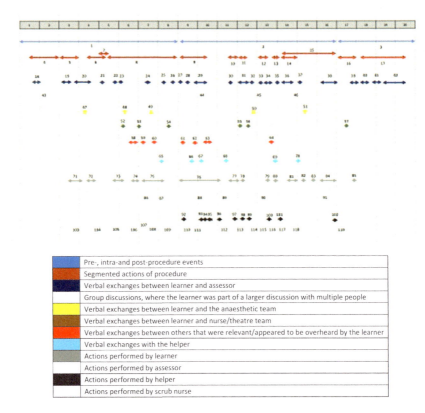

Figure 9.3 Multimodal plot diagram transcribing this clinical activity with colour key

By reviewing descriptions of each micro-event, we identified two meaningful 'threads', i.e., themes that were (re)articulated several times in the course of the procedure, highlighting specific concerns of the participants that they oriented to repeatedly and that would seem possible candidates to become a 'take-home message' on the WBA form. Both illustrate surgeons' ways of embodied and verbal orientation to an area of interest (in or on the patient body) and drawing attention to and naming selected features in that area of interest and considering possibilities for action; they also illustrate the need to facilitate vision, e.g., using optical technologies and by manipulating the area of interest to obtain a view of particular structures (Bezemer, Murtagh, and Cope 2019). The first candidate 'take-home message' that we draw attention to here was the need to get others to provide pressure on the patient's neck to enable the team to properly visualise the tumour and fix the desired view by taking pictures. This concern was not referred to on the WBA form.

The second candidate 'take-home message' was to take advantage of the opportunity of the 'live' examination to see possibilities for future surgical intervention. This, we suggest, was described on the WBA form by the trainee as 'anticipate next steps in mapping/staging'.

The video recordings highlight that the trainee and his supervisor were experiencing the procedure differently. The trainee, as the person who was performing the procedure and advocating for the various steps within it, was focused on handling the scope fluently and getting a biopsy. His supervisor supports him in achieving this but moves beyond these immediate goals by planning (or 'mapping') for the next stage of treatment for this particular patient, establishing the best course of treatment for this patient based not only on getting a biopsy but also on making real-time observations of the surgical field that help to provide insight that could inform his next steps. All the while, the supervisor enacts a pedagogic agenda – not only to guide the trainee through taking the biopsy but also to help him understand the need to plan for the next stage, taking advantage of the possibilities presented by the procedure for examining and recording an area that they may need to operate on in the near future.

'You need to use the people around you as well' (to render objects of interest visible)

The following transcripts show how the supervisor (S) helped the trainee (T1) render the tumour visible by providing so-called 'cricoid' pressure. This leads him to emphasise the need to mobilise assistance. Another trainee (T2) is also present.

In Figure 9.4, Frame A shows the operating trainee using both hands to manage the camera, placing it into the scope and advancing it down the metal tubing of the scope to see the tumour just beyond the end of the scope opening. He is looking at the screen, as is the supervisor. No words are being spoken, as the trainee is trying to manoeuvre into an appropriate position. In Figure 9.4 Frame B, we see the supervisor stepping forward and moving his right hand past the operating trainee's shoulder to touch the patient, getting ready to provide 'cricoid pressure'. Following that, the trainee looks momentarily at the implement and asks T2 to 'assist a bit' (T2 had just offered help). T2 starts making a proposal, but at that point, the supervisor steps in (Figure 9.4, Frame C) and makes an adjustment on the implement (he can reach the scope more easily from where he is), which the trainee's subsequent comments suggest resulted in the desired view of the vocal box.

Figure 9.5 shows what happens some 20 seconds later. The supervisor positions his hand again to provide pressure (Figure 9.5, Frame A). Just at that point the trainee pulls back the scope, and the supervisor withdraws again (it does not look like any pressure was given). Moments later, the trainee asks his helper to provide the pressure.

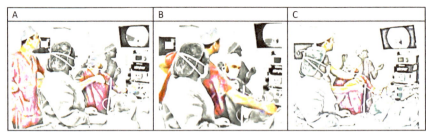

T1:	Drives in scope (Frame A)
T2:	Looks back and forth between monitor and T1
	Shall I focus for you?
S:	Looks at monitor, moves in to give cricoid pressure (Frame B)
T1:	Notices S's hand on patient neck, then gazes from monitor to scope and back to monitor
	Yeah do wanna just assist a bit?
T2:	Gazes from monitor to scope
	Yeah. Should I-
	Reaches out to scope
T1:	Just a little bit on the erm
S:	Yeah
	Reaches out and momentarily gazes at scope
	Let me just do this
T2:	Withdraws hands, looks back at monitor
T1:	It's just a bit tight (Frame C)
	There we go

Figure 9.4 First excerpt showing how trainee and supervisor begin to visualise the tumour

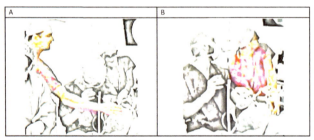

T1:	Do you wanna apply some cricoid?
T2:	Yeah
	Applies cricoid with left hand (Frame B)

Figure 9.5 Further attempts to visualise the tumour

Three-and-a-half minutes later, the trainee is advancing a pair of biopsy forceps down the scope. He is looking at the screen and sees the instrument enter the view and approach the surgical site. We have included a diagrammatic representation of the view on-screen at this point in the transcript (Figure 9.6, Frame A). The tumour (red blur) is at the upper limit of what

'It's not just getting a biopsy' 203

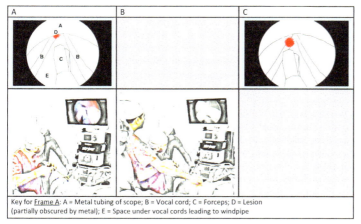

T1:   *Holding scope and forceps, looking at screen* (Frame A)
S: *Starts reaching over T1's shoulder*
      So you need that.
      Hand lands on neck
      Let me try and give you that (Frame B)
View changed (Frame C)
T1:   Thank you
S: And again it's about knowing-
      Withdraws hand
T1:   Yeah
S: You see that? That's representative. But you need to use the people around you as well.

Figure 9.6   The trainee (T1) takes an appropriate biopsy. Key for Frame A: A = metal tubing of scope; B = vocal cord; C = forceps; D = lesion (partially obscured by metal); E = space under vocal cords leading to windpipe

is visible through the scope. The diagram illustrates that about half of the lesion is obscured by the metal of the scope tube. So, while the edge of it is visible, the team cannot see enough of the tumour to take an appropriately sized biopsy.

When the operating trainee has his instrument fully advanced and is trying to get in position to take the biopsy, the supervisor, still closely monitoring the situation, announces that the operating trainee needs something (without saying what). He steps forward to the patient, placing his right hand on the throat of the patient and pushes down applying 'cricoid pressure', stating, 'So you need that' and then 'Let me try and give you that', with 'that' referring to the 'cricoid pressure' (Figure 9.6, Frame B).

The trainee did not communicate a need for help; he did not make a request. Yet the supervisor will have read the picture on the screen (which fails to show the tumour) as a sign that the operating trainee would benefit from facilitation that he, as a supervisor, is in a position to provide. More specifically, the supervisor reads a digitally rendered image of the patient's vocal cords as an artefact of the operating trainee's 'camera work', and, drawing on his understanding of what is to be achieved (i.e., what counts as 'a good picture' in this procedure on this patient), establishes what auxiliary action might enable the operating trainee to achieve that.

The supervisor's facilitation turns out to be effective. The pressure provided on the outside of the neck pushes the lesion inside the throat downward into a better view down the scope, as shown on Figure 9.6, Frame C. The trainee acknowledges the supervisor's help (and the effect it has on the view) by thanking him. He is now about to get into a better position to take a tissue sample. As he manoeuvres, the supervisor begins to make a comment on the learning point that he wants to make ('and, again, it's about knowing') but stops himself as he watches the operating trainee take the biopsy. The supervisor then states he is satisfied that an appropriate biopsy is taken and approves 'yeah, see that's representative', (implying that they may not have been sure to get a 'representative sample' had they tried to perform the biopsy with the previous view, i.e., without 'cricoid pressure'). He then picks up a learning point that he has referred to before ('But you need to use the people around you as well'). Here he is implying that the learner needs to make use of the team to apply 'cricoid pressure', which will make it easier for him to see the tumour and take an appropriate biopsy.

Thus, in the course of this procedure, the supervisor offers to give 'cricoid pressure' four times, and the trainee asks his assistant to provide pressure once. Its value was reiterated several times by the supervisor, and the trainee came to see its benefits firsthand. However, the trainee did not refer to this feedback in the WBA proforma (which was validated by the supervisor). The reasons could be multiple. He may not have considered this feedback at all when writing that statement. He may have interpreted or remembered the situation differently. He may have reasoned that he already knows that one needs to mobilise assistance to obtain a good view. He may also have considered any acknowledgement of this feedback – contrary to the feedback on 'mapping' that we will be discussing in the next section – as not fitting in with the expectations of a trainee's performance at his level of training and experience. For him, at his level of seniority, a fluently performed biopsy – documented and validated – may have been more important than recording feedback that could be seen as an invalidation of having achieved fluency in this procedure.

Although the trainee has not documented this feedback in the WBA proforma, the video record shows that his attention was drawn to its value and use. As the trainee struggled to visualise the tumour, the supervisor offered to perform the manoeuvre twice (in Figure 9.4, Frame B and Figure 9.5, Frame A), although, on both of these occasions, the trainee did not take up these offers. However, despite not taking up these offers, on both occasions, the offers were noted and acknowledged by the trainee (in Figure 9.4, the trainee notices the supervisor attempting to provide 'cricoid pressure', while in Figure 9.5, he asks T2 to replicate the supervisor's actions). In other words, the trainee saw the supervisor offering to perform the manoeuvre, and in doing so, realised it was something this supervisor deemed important and of potential use in this situation. This recognition of its value was then manifested by the trainee's subsequent action as he recruited T2 to apply the manoeuvre instead of his supervisor while he continued the procedure. Through recruiting T2, he demonstrated to his supervisor that he had first recognised the supervisor's efforts to apply the manoeuvre, second that he realised it was a valuable manoeuvre, and third that he was able work independently from the supervisor, using the other team members around him.

The learning experience continued through the action of taking a biopsy, in which the trainee saw the direct consequence, in real working practice, of using this technique. In this example, it allowed him to take a 'representative' biopsy. Figure 9.6 Frame A (top) shows the view that the trainee and his supervisor shared without the application of pressure. When the supervisor pressed down on the neck, the trainee saw explicitly the improved view (Figure 9.6, Frame C (top)), which directly and immediately enabled him to obtain a suitable tissue sample; the effectiveness of the technique was proven. He incorporated this into his subsequent practice, directing his helper once again to apply this pressure. In doing so, he demonstrated his recognition that this remained a useful thing to do and that he was able to apply it correctly and independently of his supervisor's prompts.

In the course of this procedure, the trainee took increasing ownership of the manoeuvre, acting with increasing autonomy, shown by his ever-more explicit directions to T2. Initially the supervisor made the move to apply 'cricoid pressure' with no prompt (Figure 9.4), which the trainee noticed. Later in the procedure, when there was a similar problem, the supervisor again made the move to apply 'cricoid pressure', which the trainee again noticed (not shown). The next time, the trainee asks T2 directly to apply the manoeuvre instead (Figure 9.5).

'It's not just getting a biopsy': Seeing possibilities for future action

The second thread begins with a conversation between the trainee and his supervisor that went on for just under a minute. Prior to the start of the procedure, the supervisor has approached the trainee who is washing his hands. He follows the trainee as he walks over to the operating table, sits down on an operating stool, and highlights to the trainee the purpose of the procedure.

The following excerpts show how the supervisor enacts this lesson of seeing possibilities for future surgical intervention as they jointly examine the operative field.

Somewhat later, the supervisor repeats his point about the laser ('I don't think I can do that with a laser you know 'cause it's just coming in the sub-glottis coming in the sub-glottis'). A little later, he notices that 'the interesting thing is it's a narrow field laryngectomy, which is good'. Later he says 'I'm sure it'll be fine because there's no disease there anyway. 'Cause you gotta remember that you'll enter, won't you, at this point.' As he makes this utterance, he walks over to the screen to point at the reference of 'this point', as illustrated in Figure 9.9.

This collection of segments draws together exchanges that relate to a key point made by the supervisor. He first introduced it to the discussion as an addendum to a previous conversation ('but also, at this stage, you know') while the trainee was in the process of washing his hands. Initially, he was not clear exactly where the supervisor was trying take him, but in the course of that segment, the supervisor probed, asking him what the indication for this procedure was and then guiding him through a process of reframing his thoughts about these reasons (e.g., 'not just concerns'). By the end of Figure 9.7 it appeared that the trainee had come to understand that the assessor was driving him toward an answer related to 'mapping' the next stages of treatment for this patient.

During the conversation that takes place in Figure 9.7, the trainee and his supervisor discussed the 'mapping' principle *in abstracto*, based on predications and guesswork rather than situated in the here-and-now of this patient – what they might find, rather than what they have found. They made few explicit links to the patient who was on the operating table. In the next segments, as the trainee controlled the instruments to allow them to identify the

```
S:    But also at this, at this stage you know, you've got to be thinking why am I doing this procedure. Is that fair?
T1:   Errrr. In that?
S:    W- w- w-
T1:   What's our concern?
S:    Yeah, what, what-
T1:   Well our concern is recurrence
S:    Well not just concern, but thoughts for the future
[...]
S:    So you need to know extent of disease to know what your, what your closure is going to be like
T1:   Yeah yeah
S:    Are you going to need other tissue to close him or not?
T1:   Hmmm
S:    I doubt it
T1:   So we just-
      Judging by what I've got, so far, in the picture in my head [...] That I've seen. But actually, if he had
      lots of piriform fossa going out and lots of posterior pharyngeal wall, that's not just a laryngectomy, is it?
T:    Thank you. Yep
[...]
S:    I'm not doubting he's had radiotherapy and we might have to think about pec major to cover as another layer
T1:   Yeah
S:    But I don't think we'll need pec major at a guess. To be honest I'm guessing. But that's part of the
      assessment today. It's not just getting a biopsy and things like that, is it?
[...]
```

Trainee is now on stool by patient, organising equipment around him. T2 has joined. Another trainee is also present.

```
S:    But actually it's the thought process of the next stage on actually you know to be honest with you.
      Thinking about why I am really doing this yeah I'm getting a biopsy but I'm actually thinking what's my
      resection going to be?
T1:   Yeah yeah.
S:    Where my resection is gonna be – where my cuts are gonna be if I offer this patient a laryngectomy erm in a few weeks' time.
```

Figure 9.7 The supervisor highlights the purpose of the procedure that the trainee (T1) is about to perform

'It's not just getting a biopsy' 207

S:	It does look a bit solid, doesn't it? (Frame A)
T2:	It does. That feels solid to me there, but
S:	*Walks over to monitor and points* (Frame B)
	But it could be fungal
S:	O sorry (*touched T2?*). Coz it's all, it does look- and that's right on the commissure So, okay. Let's take some pictures
	Presses buttons to take pictures
T2:	Look, there's a bit of contact bleeding as well. I think that looks suspicious. Infra-glottically. Sorry
S:	Okay. I've taken a good couple of pictures there
S:	I think we need a good-
T2:	*Points at something on monitor*
S:	I think the problem is, I don't think I can take that with a laser
T1:	Yeah
S:	If that's going sub, you know (quick glance at T1) in the subglottis like that
T1:	Yeah, yeah, yeah I know

Figure 9.8 The trainee and supervisor explore the surgical field and begin to explore the implications for future surgical management

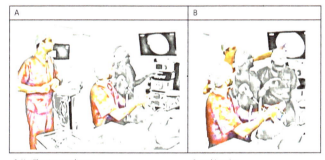

S: You'll enter, won't you   S: at this point

Figure 9.9 Supervisor uses the image on the screen to demonstrate where cuts might be made in a future procedure

presence of a recurrent cancer and to investigate its extent, the supervisor began to emphasise exactly what it was that he saw that was helping him work out a plan for the future and why. In this way, these segments demonstrate how the concept of 'it's not just a biopsy' is put into practice and what it encompasses. The previously discussed 'lesson' highlighted the need to obtain an appropriate picture of the object of interest by adjusting the handheld camera and applying pressure on the patient, which, in turn, demands visual attention to both screen and implement and calls for assistance. The present lesson highlights the semiotic work of drawing a virtual map over the picture thus obtained that highlights destinations and routes that are fit for the implements – vehicles – to be used and fixing the pictorial basis for this map for future reference by taking a 'snapshot' at the right time. Indeed, the metaphor of 'mapping' – building a map – is an apt descriptor of what the supervisor is doing and drawing attention to.

The recording of this message on the WBA proforma is telling for two reasons. First, as a reification of lived experience, it demonstrates how the supervisor's 'take-home message', related to the concept of 'not just a biopsy', gets 'translated' – transformed – by the trainee as 'mapping' and, therefore, becomes personally meaningful to him. It was documented twice in his WBA document (Figure 9.1) as 'Anticipate next step in mapping/staging patient and appropriateness of laryngectomy', and 'I performed rigid laryngoscopy for diagnostic confirmation and tumour mapping'. While the term 'mapping' was not used explicitly by the supervisor during the procedure itself, it appears in line with what the supervisor was drawing attention to during the procedure. Importantly, it also matches his level as an 'ST5' trainee (ISCP 2021, 70). The trainee is aware that, at this level, he needs to demonstrate that he is able to perform this procedure independently, fluently, and effectively. A narrative about 'mapping' the next stage of this patient's management may well have been seen as more favourable to portray in his WBA than one that centred on a technical learning point around applying 'cricoid pressure', which may help explain its inclusion in the WBA form by this trainee.

Discussion and conclusion

Our account has drawn attention to a range of semiotic, embodied practices that surgeons deployed both during and after the operation, including positioning a camera and manipulating its surroundings to obtain a picture that enables exploration of an area of interest; anticipating needs for, and offering and requesting, practical facilitation; interpreting digital renderings and reimagining them as route maps for future interventions; and communicating about selected features to achieve shared understandings. We highlighted the messages that surgeons co-designed as they rendered, read, and recorded digital images of a patient's vocal box and the selective transformation and transposition of these messages – their redesign – onto the WBA form by the trainee. We, thus, portrayed work in a complex organization that is often characterised for its 'technical' demands (such as the notion of a surgeon's dexterity) as *semiotic work* (Kress 2010).

Our account also offers insight into the ways in which a policy intervention is put into practice. The WBA was introduced to standardise and monitor the quality of surgical training. We have shown how a trainee and supervisor adopt and adapt this intervention to fit the demands of the day-to-day routines of surgical trainees and their supervisors and the long-term interests of trainees to complete their training. In so doing, we hope to have clarified some of:

> 'The problems that clinicians have in coordinating complex services that straddle specialities […]; the struggles that result from policy makers seeking to reform hospital organizations and restructure workforce capabilities and rights […], or the organizational-cultural and educational challenges that face health care workers in structuring and integrating their services in ways that benefit the patient.'
> (Iedema 2007, 5–6).

Our account shows that the WBA form must not be treated as a complete record of what was learned or taught. Not all messages emerging from the interaction between trainee and supervisor make it into the WBA form. When using the forms as a basis for further assessment, it should also be borne in mind that they are likely to have been co-authored. Indeed, in our example, it was the trainee who drafted the feedback messages on the form, giving him significant power over the selection and recording process. He indicated that he considers the impression he gives of himself – not wanting to over (or under) sell himself – as he completes parts of the form on behalf of the supervisor, knowing that he needs to sign off on it. We also highlighted that the work of completing forms is usually done in batches, with no more than five minutes spent on each, sometimes several months after the event. These practices do not necessarily 'invalidate' the form. Indeed, while the trainee in our example omitted what appeared to be a recurring message from the supervisor, the feedback he did record on behalf of the supervisor appeared to be in line with the message that emerged in the operating theatre and, crucially, with his level of experience.

We noted that feedback was articulated by the supervisor in different multimodal configurations. As the team is setting up for the operation, the supervisor constructs a monologue about what this type of operation is for, and that it is beyond taking a biopsy. Then, once a picture of the area of interest in the patient had been achieved and all orient to it, he spoke 'to' the picture, verbalising and pointing at the opportunities he saw for future interventions. At this stage, the trainee and supervisor jointly enacted the supervisor's message from just before the start of the procedure. Eight weeks later, as the trainee completed the WBA, he remade the message once again as a generic principle for future action. Each of these configurations enabled trainee and supervisor to make different kinds of statements about the world, ranging from prospectively oriented ones (abstract, elaborate instructions prior to, and abstract, shorthand instructions after the procedure) to instructions focused on the here-and-now of a concrete procedure.

While the WBA is not a complete *record of* learning, it does create *opportunities for* learning at the workplace. In the operating theatre, the trainee was led to perform the procedure while the supervisor provided a running commentary, giving feedback. We noted that the trainee took up some of the feedback in the course of the operation (he started asking his assistant to provide 'cricoid pressure'), while writing up other feedback on the form ('mapping'). The feedback in theatre may have been given even if the trainee had not selected the case for inclusion as a WBA, and the trainee may have reflected on the value of 'mapping' even if he had not completed the form. Yet the WBA helps protect these opportunities in conditions of high workload and pressures, ensuring that trainees do receive feedback on at least some of the cases and that they reflect post-operatively on at least some of the cases, however brief.

We end this chapter with two closing remarks. First, we hope to have shown that social semiotics offers an appropriate means to prize open concrete instances of (technology-enhanced) meaning-making in organizations that advance understanding of professional practices of seeing, manipulating, and communicating about physical-material phenomena; the ways in which 'newcomers' are inducted into these practices; and how their 'performance' is documented and accounted for. Second, we hope to have shown that (health care) organizations offer a prime site for social semiotics to advance its theoretical and methodological apparatus. It is here that we can observe some of the most complex forms of human cooperation and semiosis in action – in our case, oriented to the delivery of services that have an immediate impact on the health and well-being of the public. As *social* semioticians, that environment will remain a go-to site for further research.

Note

1 In the case presented here, both the trainee and supervisor are male.

References

Ali, J.M. (2013). "Getting lost in translation? Workplace based assessments in surgical training." *Surgeon* 11(5): 286–289.

Bezemer, J. (2020). "Social semiotics: Theorising meaning making." In D. Nestel, and G. Greedy (Eds.), *Clinical Education for the Health Professions: Theory and Practice*. New York: Springer.

Bezemer, J, G. Murtagh, and A. Cope. (2019). "Inspecting objects: Visibility Manoeuvres in laparoscopic surgery." In E. Reber, and C. Gerhardt (Eds.), *Embodied Activities in Face-to-Face and Mediated Settings*. London: Palgrave, 107–135.

Burg, F.D., J.S. Lloyd, and B. Templeton. (1982). "Competence in medicine." *Medical Teacher* 4(2): 60–64.

Foucault, M. (1994). *The Birth of the Clinic: An Archaeology of Medical Perception*. Translated from the French by A.M. Sheridan Smith. New York: Vintage Books.

Frank, J.R., L.S. Snell, O.T. Cate, E.S. Holmboe, C. Carraccio, S.R. Swing, P. Harris, N.J. Glasgow, C. Campbell, D. Dath, R.M. Harden, W. Iobst, D.M. Long, R. Mungroo, D.L. Richardson, J. Sherbino, I. Silver, S. Taber, M. Talbot, and K.A. Harris. (2010). "Competency-based medical education: Theory to practice." *Medical Teacher* 32(8): 638–645.

Goodwin, C. (1994). "Professional vision." *American Anthropologist* 96(3): 606–633.

Goodwin, C. (2017). *Co-Operative Action (Learning in Doing: Social, Cognitive and Computational Perspectives)*. Cambridge: Cambridge University Press. doi:10.1017/9781139016735

Holmboe, E.S., J. Sherbino, D.M. Long, S.R. Swing, and J.R. Frank. (2010). "The role of assessment in competency-based medical education." *Medical Teacher* 32(8): 676–682.

Iedema, R. (2003). "Multimodality, resemiotization: Extending the analysis of discourse as multi-semiotic practice." *Visual Communication* 1(2): 29–57.

Iedema, R. (2007). "Communicating hospital work." In R. Iedema (Ed.), *The Discourse of Hospital Communication. Tracing Complexities in Contemporary Health Organisations*. London: Palgrave.

Iedema, R., and J. Bezemer. (2021). "Video-ethnography and video-reflexive ethnography: Investigating and expanding learning about complex realities." In S. Grosjean and F. Matte (Eds.), *Organizational Video-Ethnography Revisited. Making Visible Material, Embodied and Sensory Practices*. Cham: Palgrave MacMillan, 15–32.

ISCP (Intercollegiate Surgical Curriculum Programme) (2018). *OMFS Surgical Curriculum*. www.iscp.ac.uk

ISCP (2021). *Otolaryngology Curriculum*. https://www.iscp.ac.uk/media/1106/otolaryngology-curriculum-aug-2021-approved-oct-20.pdf.

Jakobson, R. (1971). "Language in relation to other communication systems." In *Volume II Word and Language*. Originally Published 1971 edition. Berlin, New York: DE GRUYTER MOUTON, 697–708.

Kress, G. (2010). *Multimodality. A Social Semiotic Theory of Communication*. London: Routledge.

Linell, P. (1998). "Discourse across boundaries: On recontextualizations and the blending of voices in Professional discourse." *Text* 18(2): 143–158.

Maybin, J., and T. Lillis. (2017). "Introduction: The dynamics of textual trajectories in professional and workplace practice." *Text and Talk* 37(4): 409–414.

Park, J.S.Y., and M. Bucholtz. (2009). "Introduction; Public transcripts: Entextualization and linguistic representation in institutional contexts." *Text and Talk*, 29(5): 485–502.

Postgraduate Medical Education and Training Board Workplace Based Assessment Subcommittee (2005). *Workplace Based Assessment*. Postgraduate Medical Education and Training Board.

Sebeok, T. (1985). "Vital signs." *The American Journal of Semiotics* 3(3): 1–27.

Tahim, A. (2021). *How do postgraduate surgeons-in-training learn through workplace-based assessments?* Unpublished doctoral dissertation, University College London.

Von Uexküll, T. (1986). "Medicine and semiotics." *Semiotica* 61(3): 201–218.

10 Texture and texturization in organizational identity design and legitimacy work

Giorgia Aiello

Introduction

In recent years, organizational scholars have become increasingly interested in how contemporary organizations use 'images, logos, videos, building materials, graphic and product design, and a range of other material and visual tools and expressions to compete, communicate, form identity and organize their activities' (Boxenbaum et al. 2018, 598). A versatile semiotic resource that can be used across these communication tools and expressive forms is texture, a resource that is situated at the crossroads of visuality and materiality. Most importantly, texture has become an especially prized semiotic resource for organizations thanks to its ability to convey meaning potentials of authenticity and credibility and, in this way, also communicate them as legitimate in the eyes of the public (Höllerer et al. 2018). Organizations employ a variety of means to show the congruence of their identities with societal values and their status as 'good citizens'. This legitimacy work largely entails the deployment of multimodal messages aimed at promoting an organization as proper and desirable (Lefsrud, Graves, and Phillips 2020). In the wake of the so-called lifestyle economy and of what van Leeuwen (2022) has defined as 'identity design', or the increasing importance of communicating distinctive identities through styles defined by specific combinations of semiotic resources, texture is now widely used to signal a move away from standardisation to appeal to the senses and, ultimately, to also prove that an organization is 'for real'.

In this chapter, I focus on how texture is mobilised to meet key semiotic demands of contemporary capitalism, such as the need to communicate distinctive identities within generic formats, like those that are typically used in corporate branding and media. In other words, texture is often used to foreground specificity (for example, in the guise of locality or diversity) within otherwise standardised communication practices. In doing so, texture also contributes to linking organizational identity design with the promotion of particular experiential meanings and types of provenance, which, in turn, foster concrete forms of attachment to different values. As van Leeuwen (2022) demonstrates, identity design is the bread and butter of contemporary communication, insofar as style, beyond function, has become a fundamental means for defining what is subsequently perceived as the core 'essence' of a product, brand, or organization. Among others, the resources that are most widely used in identity design are colour, shape, movement, and, of course, texture. Here, I am going to examine some of the ways in which different kinds of texture, both visual and material, are mobilised in two sites of semiotic production that are emblematic of global(ist), corporate organizational identities. These are the Starbucks brand and stock photographs from Getty Images. I am choosing Starbucks and Getty Images as my two key examples here because they are both large global corporations that, for over a decade now, have actively mobilised texture as a major semiotic resource in an attempt to address ongoing criticisms and to move away from widespread associations with extreme product standardisation, cultural homogenisation, and consumerism. Taken together, these two examples offer insights on the role of multimodality and visual communication in legitimacy work aimed at connecting the lived experiences of globalising publics to the values promoted by particular organizations through their brand identities. Both examples also illustrate the importance of semiotic change for organizations to keep functioning, if not thriving, amidst uncertainty. Ultimately, texture is a fundamental semiotic resource for organizations, as it contributes to grounding organizational identity in lived experience and embodied knowledge (van Leeuwen 2022).

Before I turn to my analysis of the Starbucks and Getty Images examples, in the next two sections, I discuss social semiotic definitions of texture and the relationship between processes of stylization and what I define as 'texturization'. In doing so, I aim to highlight the importance of looking at texture as a key semiotic resource rather than as a pre-semiotic feature of signs while also pointing to some of the overarching cultural and social processes underlying its mobilisation as a semiotic resource by corporations and other organizations on an increasingly large scale.

A social semiotic approach to texture

Texture is central to a social semiotic approach to materiality and meaning-making because, as van Leeuwen (2022, 96) states, '[t]he meanings of texture derive from our direct, embodied experience of the materiality of objects, from touch and taste'. Art historians and both fine arts and design scholars have long considered texture and materiality more broadly as integral to communicating particular properties and meanings. Overall, however, the study of texture is a relatively new area of interest in semiotics. Traditional semiotics did not concern itself with materiality or with how meaning is made through the concrete, tactile qualities of particular signs (van Leeuwen 2022). In line with their linguistic roots, semioticians have, instead, typically regarded materiality as pre-semiotic while focusing on the formal, symbolic characteristics of signs and texts in their analyses. However, at least since the early 2010s, social semioticians have been at the forefront of research on the meaning-making properties of materiality due to a growing understanding that signs ought to be examined not only in terms of their form and content or more generally in relation to their cultural and social contexts but also in light of the experiential implications of their 'matter' (Björkvall and Karlsson 2011).

Here, I understand texture both as the actual grain of matter and what Djonov and van Leeuwen (2011, 541) have defined as 'an illusion of tangibility', which, as they state, can be achieved 'across different media and can have tactile as well as visual and aural manifestations'. In visual communication in particular, texture is a visual rendition of haptic or tactile features and, more broadly, also of sensorial, indexical features. Regardless of its mode or modes, whether it be colour or shape, for example, and whether one can truly 'touch' it, texture summons us to identify with embodied, experiential meaning potentials rather than simply symbolic ones. Djonov and van Leeuwen (2011) focus on the texture of cashmere as an example of how, depending on the context of interpretation, one's prior experiences with key physical qualities such as softness, warmth, and smoothness may be associated with comfort and luxury or, on the other hand, pretentiousness and a lack of frugality. Likewise, Chen and Machin (2014) examined the progressive integration of Japanese 'Kawaii' culture into the design and redesign of the Chinese women's lifestyle magazine *Rayli*, noting that, in the magazine, 'cuteness' was often associated with the visual representation of textures that implied softness. This was done especially through items of clothing made of fur and flannel but also ruffles and lacy textiles – all textures that point to the delicateness and vulnerability of childhood.

Overall, texture is a semiotic resource whose meaning-making properties depend on the distinctive qualities that it possesses, insofar as these may be associated both with certain types of provenance and experiential meaning potentials. Both Ledin and Machin (2020) and van Leeuwen (2022) have outlined a range of these distinctive qualities, which include but are not limited to density, rigidity, relief, viscosity, and regularity. While none of these qualities can be examined in isolation from one another or from their broader contexts and histories, each quality can also be associated with a range of experiences and values.

An additional point to note is that regularity and especially its counterpart, irregularity, are particularly meaningful in relation to how texture is mobilised in corporate branding and media. In *The Sense of Order*, British art historian E.H. Gombrich (1984) focused on the psychology of decorative art and the cognitive reasons why compositions of basic, regular patterns cater to a universal human impulse to seek order both in space and time. Here, Gombrich made a somewhat poetic statement about the relationship between regularity and texture. He wrote: 'The disturbance of regularity such as a flaw in a smooth fabric can act like a magnet to the eye, and so can an unexpected regularity in a random environment such as the mysterious fairy rings in wild woodlands' (Gombrich 1984, 110). Gombrich's statement points to the importance of our cultural expectations around what kinds of textures we ought to encounter in particular contexts, together with the social values that we may attach to such textures, whether they are regular or irregular. In addition, as Caivano (1990) suggests, textures of all kinds are typically appraised as ordered structures, and it is also for this reason that we may come to assume regularity as a default quality of texture. In this regard, Djonov and van Leeuwen (2011) observe that regular textures may give rise to feelings of predictability and, therefore, also security but also of boredom, overall 'flatness' and a lack of excitement. On the other hand, irregular textures, 'may suggest capriciousness, rebelliousness or unpredictability' (Djonov and van Leeuwen 2011, 551).

However, in an age in which digital reproduction and generic templates have become dominant, irregularity has become an especially meaningful and even prized quality. As Johannessen and van Leeuwen (2018) have pointed out, in graphic communication design there has been a proliferation of irregular or distressed graphics that are clearly produced with computers but that are to be linked with now highly valued experiential meaning potentials, such as 'authentic', 'individual', or 'personal'. As a whole, texture has become an especially important semiotic resource in times in which touch and proximity are, in fact, at a premium and the streamlined, smooth, and ultimately also regular contours of twentieth-century corporate communication have come to be associated with the perils of extreme standardisation and loss of identity. It could even be argued that the importance of texture as a semiotic resource may keep growing in post-pandemic times precisely because of its haptic qualities. To gain a better critical understanding of how this semiotic resource is used in corporate branding and media, I now turn to a discussion of the relationship between stylization and the process of mobilising texture in identity design, which I define as *texturization*.

From stylization to texturization

In previous work on Starbucks and Getty Images, I coined the term 'texturization' to highlight the relationship between texture as a semiotic resource and its active deployment by corporations as a way to gain both symbolic and economic capital or, in other words, to carry out legitimacy work in order to appear as proper and desirable. The notion of texturization describes a process in which material qualities such as graininess, consistency, and concreteness are performatively foregrounded and amplified through visual and multimodal means (Aiello and Pauwels 2014; Aiello and Woodhouse 2016). Texturization is key to a critical understanding of multimodality in contemporary organizational semiotics, but it is helpful to compare it with the notion of 'stylization', which has been at the center of much critical scholarship on the uses of language and other modes of communication in managing, regulating, and ultimately, 'designing' identities. Arguably, stylization, rather than texturization, has long been the main process underlying organizational practices aimed at mobilising semiotic resources in the pursuit of legitimacy.

This is because, as Crispin Thurlow and Adam Jaworski (2006) highlight, stylization is a process in which 'a reflexively managed resource' (104) can be actively used to perform a prized identity. In the pursuit of symbolic capital (Bourdieu 1991), social actors are summoned to perform identities linked to the 'promotion of particular ways of being (or styles) involving language, image, social practice and material culture' (Thurlow and Jaworski 2006, 105). At the same time, the semiotic resources that are performatively used in this process in order to gain symbolic capital are regulated through broader social practices. For example, in her groundbreaking work on linguistic practices in everyday life, Deborah Cameron (1995) highlighted that the regulation of language in contexts such as the teaching of English grammar or the professional application of editorial principles often entails 'verbal hygiene', or a range of actions and rules aimed at 'cleansing' linguistic style from 'inappropriate' characteristics, such as slang or non-standard sentence structures. In other words, verbal hygiene corresponds to the stylization of specific identities for the 'creation and recreation' (Cameron 1995, 17) of normative social structures.

Later, Cameron's work on the hyper-regulation of workers' language in call centres revealed that there was an imposition of a particular, feminised speech style as the standard for these workers' interactions with customers (Cameron 2000). Here, the notion of stylization was connected to the idea that speakers gave a standardised linguistic performance that was scripted from the top down and that this performance was supposed to adhere to corporate norms while also being delivered in ways that made the workers sound both natural and authentic. Through this research, Cameron highlighted the relationship between the intensification of such practices of linguistic regulation and the rise of corporate culture in the so-called 'global economy'. Along the same lines, in her sociological work on consumption and globalisation, Lury (1996, 4) stated that '*a process of stylization is what best defines consumer culture*', insofar as the commodification of objects and identities entails an ongoing tussle between standardisation and variation. And as Thurlow and Jaworski (2006) point out, it is precisely because of their always strategic and often scripted performativity that processes of stylization may be instead mystified as the substantial honouring of specific identities (Thurlow and Jaworski 2006). Overall, corporate branding and media rely heavily on stylization, insofar as specific identity traits are strategically foregrounded by corporations or, on the other hand, contained or even eliminated to achieve discursive ends in line with lifestyle and consumer capitalism.

So, what does texturization have to do with stylization? From a visual and multimodal standpoint, stylization often entails techniques aimed at 'cleansing' images from inappropriate characteristics (Cameron 2000), while texturization deploys cues aimed at invoking the emplaced, embodied, and overall sensorial qualities of semiotic resources (Aiello and Pauwels 2014). However, while texturization might seem to be at odds with stylization, it can be argued that, in fact, the former is an emergent development of the latter. Both stylization and texturization involve the transformation of representational resources for performative reasons and with the aim to craft desirable identities. Both entail agentful interventions on visual substance for the purposes of communication aimed at more or less obvious globalising publics. Ultimately, both stylization and texturization are both vital processes for the generation of meaning potentials catering to organizational identity design and in the service of legitimation.

This said, it is also important to address texturization in its own right, as, in the end, this may be a process that, in fact, exceeds stylization and entails a harder look at the increasing entanglement of top-down and bottom-up aesthetics. To illustrate this dynamic and, more generally, show some of the ways in which texture is used as a semiotic resource in corporate branding and media, I now turn to my two examples, namely Starbucks' (re)branding through its store and logo design and Getty Images' initiatives aimed at 're-picturing' visual clichés about women in stock imagery. I have already written fairly extensively about both examples (Aiello 2018; Aiello and Dickinson 2014; Aiello and Woodhouse 2016), but here I extend some of my previous ideas in this regard to foreground the role of texture as a key semiotic resource in organizational identity design and legitimacy work.

Texture and texturization in the Starbucks brand

Following the 2008 economic crisis, Howard Schultz decided to return as Starbucks' CEO to manage the company's growing financial problems. One of the first things that he did was rehire Arthur Rubinfeld, the creator of the original Starbucks store designs, to help him fix two major issues, namely the coffee chain's 'bloated real estate portfolio and stale store designs' (Schultz with Gordon 2011, 270). Starbucks had increasingly come to be associated with a cookie-cutter aesthetic, mass-produced products, and increasingly mediocre coffee beverages. Arguably, the recession was only the culmination of an ongoing issue with Starbucks' increasing loss of cultural cachet. As a way to revamp Starbucks' brand identity, Schultz and Rubinfeld worked together on a new store design strategy that focused on locality, for example by using repurposed materials and both food products and decorative elements sourced from the local community. Meanwhile, as Starbucks began to devise store designs that 'reflect the character of a store's surrounding neighbourhood and help reduce environmental impacts' (Starbucks Stories & News 2009), the coffee chain proceeded to close hundreds of stores and planned to open significantly fewer stores over time than the corporation had done previously.

The new store design strategy was initially prototyped through a redesign of several stores in Seattle, where the coffee company had its headquarters. Greg Dickinson and I examined the four Seattle stores where the new and, to this day, most recent store design strategy was first tested (Aiello and Dickinson 2014). At the time of our study, the store design strategy emphasised texture through a series of visual-material anchors to the materiality and local provenance of fixtures and furnishings, which were visibly dented, scratched, grooved, and mismatched. The four Seattle stores we examined abounded in reclaimed wood, irregular edges, weathered panelling, and patchy finishes. The dominant colour palette combined the natural browns of wood, with the greys of metal, and, at times, textiles in warm hues. This palette added to the material 'weight' of the store. As a whole, the heterogeneity and irregularity of the visual-material textures of redesigned Starbucks stores contributed to the creation of an ambience that anchored their patrons in the materiality of each store while also highlighting the unpredictability and uniqueness of each locale. This experience of materiality was also linked to meaning potentials regarding the (local) provenance of the materials used for each store's design. On the one hand, this is because texture itself typically foregrounds provenance as a key to its interpretation. As Djonov and van Leeuwen (2011) explain, when we apprehend texture, we automatically generate assumptions and judgments about its physical and cultural sources. For example, a ten-seat communal table in the 15th Avenue East store was made from irregularly shaped and worn-out wood planks that had obviously been salvaged (Figure 10.1). Their shape and texture evoked past uses of a utilitarian and somewhat pre-industrial nature. As a matter of fact, the table's wood planks used to belong to an old boat from the Seattle area. Overall, the store's mix-and-match aesthetic relied on textures that pointed to a do-it-yourself (DIY) and grassroots ethos firmly rooted in the local context.

The appearance of regular Starbucks stores has also changed since 2009, adopting a combination of dark woods, mismatched chairs, and, generally, a more 'material' look and feel. Texture, of course, is also mobilised in the more generic version of the Starbucks store design model. For example, around 2015, the window on the side of the Starbucks store on Mortimer Street in London was covered with a full-length and life-size photograph of burlap sacks, full of what we can only imagine would be coffee beans, that was made to look like these were stacked in the window (Figure 10.2). This fine-grained, high-resolution, blown-up image invited those passing by to linger over the textures of the burlap sacks themselves together with the wooden shelves on which they were stacked. The choice of black and white over colour made these textures 'pop' even more. Overall, the new store design strategy emphasised the actual presence of 'matter' and the ability to experience and linger on its textures, whether visually or haptically.

Around the same time that Starbucks was rolling out its new store design strategy, the logo was also undergoing some important changes for the first

Figure 10.1 A community table made from wood planks from an old boat in the 15th Avenue East Starbucks store in Seattle (Photograph by the author)

time in almost 20 years. The relationship between Starbucks' new store design strategy and the logo is especially interesting because of an apparent contradiction. This is because the history of the Starbucks logo is one of increasing stylization (Aiello 2018). As I mentioned earlier, stylization is a process based on the strategic foregrounding, enhancement, and regulation of particular identity traits at the expense of others, to the extent that this often results in the imposition of a homogenous style as the norm or standard. From a visual and multimodal standpoint, stylization often entails techniques aimed at removing 'inappropriate' characteristics from images and multimodal texts.

Starbucks was born in 1971, with a single store located in Seattle's Pike Place Market, and a logo based on an intricate fifteenth-century Norse woodcut portraying a two-tailed siren, or melusine, with bare breasts, a protruding belly, and a visible genital area. In 1987, the original owners sold Starbucks to Howard Schultz, whom they had originally hired as a marketing manager, a move that corresponded with the coffee company's expansion to other US cities as well as Canada. This is also when the logo had its first major restyling, which entailed the introduction of the now iconic Starbucks colours, but also for the siren's body to be heavily streamlined to

Figure 10.2 A full-length black and white photograph of burlap sacks on the side of the Starbucks store on the corner of Mortimer Street and Regent Street in London (Photograph by the author)

become less sexualised and, therefore, also less 'offensive' for the corporation's expanding market. In the new logo design, the siren's breasts were covered by her wavy long hair, but her navel and body were still visible. When Starbucks went public in 1992, the logo was once again restyled: the overall design remained the same as the 1987 logo, but the siren's body was covered by zooming in on her face. In 2011, the logo was further stylised following Starbucks' expansion to commercial endeavours beyond coffee – such as the introduction, later discontinued, of evening menus including small plates of artisanal food together with wine and craft beer.

Over the years, the logo's graphic features have progressively become more streamlined through the loss of key cues, including the siren's 'bodiness' and, eventually, the logo's linguistic message. In my work on the Starbucks logo, I have argued that the progressive stylization of the logo from its 1971 version up to its 1992 rendition was tied to the strategic deployment and regulation of the siren's feminine appeal (see Phillips and Rippin 2010). This is also true for the 2011 version of the logo, which kept the image of the siren as its central and only motif. I have also argued that, with the loss of the outer circles and lettering from its overall design

Texture and texturization in organizational identity design 221

Figure 10.3 Blown up Starbucks logo on store window by the Old Street tube station in London (Photograph by the author)

and the further streamlining of the siren's features, the Starbucks logo has also become texture in its own right (Aiello 2018). Thanks to its increasing stylization and growing abstraction, the logo has also been progressively woven into the physical and material 'fabric' of Starbucks stores. In Figure 10.3, we can see an example from London, near the Old Street tube station, where the logo is reproduced on one of the windows and covers the entire surface of its several glass panes. Although it can be peeled off the glass to easily modify the window's layout, here the logo looks like a glass serigraphy, or a durable print of the design on the window itself. To apprehend this storefront, we must look 'through' the logo rather than just look 'at' the logo. In other words, here, the logo is mobilised as a texture rather than simply as signage or the symbolic 'face' of the brand. In addition to being placed directly on structural materials such as glass, wood, and other types of panelling, now we often also see off-centre, cropped versions of the logo being reproduced on various store surfaces. Overall, the logo design is no longer simply the face of the Starbucks brand but a textural motif that may be blown up or scaled down and used to 'mark' space and 'make' place through physical rather than just symbolic references to the brand (Aiello 2018).

While they may seem to be quite different from each other, the two approaches to texturization that I have just illustrated do similar legitimacy work for the Starbucks brand. On the one hand, the centrality of visual and material texture in the new store designs contributes to attaching the Starbucks brand to experiential meanings of locality while also evoking related values such as authenticity and environmentalism. On the other hand, the stylised logo has become a textural motif in its own right, thus becoming part and parcel of the built environment and, in this way, of the surrounding urban fabric. In both cases, texture is used as a key semiotic resource for the communication of the Starbucks brand as firmly grounded in the materiality of specific places and, therefore, in the everyday lived experiences of customers. Overall, then, texture and texturization, here, are used to anchor the brand to the material environment in which it is located, working to appeal to our senses and, thus, 'promoting (re)evaluation of the legitimacy' (Lefsrud, Graves, and Phillips 2020, 1056) of Starbucks as a locally meaningful and community-driven organization rather than as a faceless global corporation.

Texture and texturization in 'feminist' stock photography by Getty Images

Not unlike Starbucks, the world-leading image bank, Getty Images, has also turned to texture as a key semiotic resource in an attempt to innovate its product and, in doing so, improve its public image. Stock imagery is most often associated with a very limited aesthetic repertoire of bland and, at times, abstract images with little or no contextual detail (Machin 2004). From a representational standpoint, many of the images that can be licensed through Getty Images and other image banks portray women. This is hardly surprising, given that promotional culture often relies on the commodification and sexualisation of women's bodies while also increasingly integrating feminist claims into media genres such as 'femvertising' (see Gill 2007). This said, stock photos, and generic images of women in particular, are also frequently derided. The internet is replete with humorous collections of images of women laughing alone with salad or digital tablets (Grossman 2014), tongue-in-cheek galleries of ridiculous stock portrayals of feminism, and even videos made with stock footage that poke fun at the polished, idealised, and saccharine portrayals of women that are typical of commercial imagery. In addition to these parodies, bloggers and social media journalists have relished producing scathing critiques of stock imagery at large, decrying its exploitative nature and systematic resort to stereotypes. Overall, throughout the 2010s, it became increasingly clear that image banks, and Getty Images in particular, were not seen as legitimate media organizations, insofar as stock images were overwhelmingly considered poor-quality visuals to be avoided in 'serious' news media or 'high-end' branding and advertising.

Getty Images has addressed the negative feedback received by the industry and the genre both by representing the company in politically conscious terms and by producing and curating visual content that, in the corporation's own words, 'kills the cliché' (Sachs 2014). Typically, the most searched keywords in the Getty Images database are 'woman', 'business', and 'family'. At the 2014 Cannes Lions International Festival of Creativity, Getty Images CEO Jonathan Klein used politicised language to promote Getty's new approach to 'repicturing' these commercially fundamental keywords. He stated:

> Imagery has the power to do more than anything to change people's minds, to galvanize movements, to make governments change direction, to get rid of governments, to show people in power the error of their ways, for the voiceless to get an opportunity to speak.
>
> (Sachs 2014)

As a first major attempt to 'repicture' the world, at the beginning of 2014, Getty Images partnered with Facebook COO Sheryl Sandberg's Lean In Foundation to curate a collection of stock photographs 'devoted to the powerful depiction of women and girls, families of all kinds, and men as caretakers as well as earners' (LeanIn.org/getty). With the motto 'You can't be what you can't see', the stated aim of the images included in the Lean In Collection was to counter negative portrayals and 'shift perceptions, overturn clichés, and incorporate authentic images of women and men into media and advertising' (LeanIn.org/getty). Following some of the key principles of Sandberg's bestselling book, the collection's specific aim was to represent women as both empowered and authentic (see Sandberg 2013). This double aim was made clear across official descriptions of the collection on the Lean In Foundation and Getty Images websites as well as press releases, webinars, and other promotional materials about the collection.

The Lean in Collection by Getty Images was an important move in Getty Images' legitimacy work, as it harnessed feminist theory and feminist politics to create commercial images that, according to the collection's promotional materials, 'flip the script' by representing women as both empowered and authentic. However, the images included in the collection were not only set apart by less conventional ways of representing women's and girls' lives but also by a certain look and feel that, at least until the early 2010s, was not typical of pre-produced commercial imagery (Aiello and Parry 2020). For example, across images in the collection, strategies used include a prevalence of busy, cluttered, or multilayered backgrounds that conferred texture to the image. Likewise, the very texture of photography was foregrounded here as well, with lens flare and other lighting 'glitches' being valorised rather than rejected. Other textural traits pertained to the body, as these photos tended to highlight, rather than airbrush, tattoos, muscles, chest hair, wrinkles, and other visual cues pointing to an individual's physical substance and specificity.

224 *Giorgia Aiello*

Despite the analytical nature of many of these images, ultimately, these were not typical stock images with lowered modality – that is, images that were pereceived as somehow 'less than real' (Kress and van Leeuwen 2006). Instead, they were rich in visual cues pointing to haptic and more broadly sensorial features – that is, they had a high degree of realism from a sensory point of view. This is also something that I have previously argued in relation to Genderblend, a collection of images that originated from the Lean In project and that aimed to portray gender fluid identities in an inclusive manner (Aiello and Woodhouse 2016). Genderblend featured a number of studio shots or close-cropped portraits of androgynous, trans, and more broadly queer individuals. These photographs of individuals 'blurring' gender lines highlighted the bodily textures of these subjects against the decontextualised or muted backgrounds that are typical of 'traditional' stock photography. For example, in a photograph entitled 'Transvestite Asian senior man dancing', the subject was portrayed against a black theatrical backdrop while wearing a red corset, a black split-front skirt, fishnet stockings, high-heeled red shoes, red lipstick, and a choker. The portrayed subject's long white hair, beard, wrinkles and wiry body stood in sharp contrast to these accessories, and these physical characteristics were made more salient through subtle chiaroscuro lighting (Figure 10.4, left). In another studio portrait entitled 'Woman breaking the rules of gender', the portrayed subject was

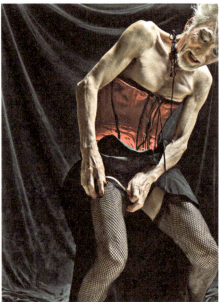 

Figure 10.4 Texturization in stock images: (left) 'Transvestite Asian senior man dancing'; (right) 'Woman breaking the rules of gender' (With permission, Getty Images)

pictured wearing a black tie, a sleeveless white shirt, and white trousers, and both the textures of her full sleeve tattoo and of a mask that looks like a web of black lace around her eyes stood out against the flat dark background and the neutral colours of her clothes (Figure 10.4, right).

In the world of Genderblend, queer and trans identities were foregrounded in relation to individuals' physical attributes, which were highly texturized, and, in this way, they were also made visible but, unlike the women that were portrayed in the Lean In Collection, they were also disconnected from the everyday contexts in which these individuals may in fact live, work, or relate to others (Aiello and Woodhouse 2016; also see Cain Miller 2018). As a whole, however, these stock images that aimed at 're-picturing' women and gender were texturized in ways that subverted the 'rules' of stock photography and were very much in line with trends in digital photography linked to the rise of visual social media in the early 2010s (see Frosh 2013).

In the interviews I conducted with stock photographers that contributed imagery to Getty Images and, in some cases, to the Lean In Collection in particular, there was a general sense that this 'newer' stock photography aesthetic had a lot to do with a demand for intimacy, spontaneity, 'real' happiness that can be 'touched' and the non-staged, but staged, naturalness that is typical of Instagram. The increasing importance of texturizing stock images, as reported by the freelance photographers I interviewed, is also very much because of direct demands by Getty Images as the main worldwide distributor of stock photography. Ultimately, conferring texture to stock images contributes not only to making commercial photographs look more authentic and diverse but also to highlighting both the physical and motivated, rather than conventional and arbitrary, characteristics of portrayed subjects. In turn, this process of texturization has important implications for the ways in which a visual media corporation like Getty Images is 'seen' by the public and also for how it sees itself. Once again, texture was mobilised to '(re)design' Getty Images' organizational identity as socially conscious and grounded in people's lived experience. Getty's legitimacy work, then, ultimately entailed a combination of semiotic claims regarding both the corporation's political values and its stock images' closeness to their portrayed subjects and, as a consequence, to those who may view and/or use them. It can be argued that, as a semiotic resource, texture is particularly important in organizational identity design processes aimed at creating meaningful associations between an organization's 'look' and 'feel' and its broader values and stance in relation to society.

Conclusions

Texture is an especially flexible and versatile semiotic resource for organizational identity design, insofar as it can be rendered both visually and materially as well as through the deployment of reduced representational traits (as in the case of the Starbucks logo) or, conversely, of greater 'fine-grained' detail (as in Getty Images' shift to greater sensory modality in stock imagery).

My research on Starbucks and Getty Images shows how both visual and material texture can be mobilised across different types of 'media' (including, but not limited to store interiors, logos, and photographic imagery) to link an organization's identity to a range of meaning potentials, from authenticity and community to intimacy and diversity, which are, however, also all united by overarching sensory and experiential claims.

Perhaps more importantly, as an overarching strategic meaning-making process, texturization is especially important for organizations that aim to promote themselves as less corporate or more bottom-up than they are in the eyes of the public while also maintaining top-down control over the design of their organizational identity. As explained above, texturization ought to be seen as closely related to stylization, a process aimed at semiotically 'cleansing' an organization's identity from 'inappropriate' traits, often in the pursuit of greater standardisation. However, ultimately, texture is also routinely deployed across organizational contexts in ways that promote concrete forms of attachment to a variety of artefacts, spaces, and media, albeit through top-down choices and practices. For example, in the Starbucks stores that Greg Dickinson and I examined, it was not rudimentary sketches of the local that were 'plugged' into an overarching global format, as often happens in glocalisation. Instead, textures of the actually (rather than virtually) local were materially woven into the making of specific places of globalist consumption. It is important to point out that 'local' Starbucks stores very often rely on local communities and independent businesses not only for their locally sourced furnishings but also for their local offerings in matters of food and beverages (Aiello and Dickinson 2014). Likewise, conferring texture to stock images requires an effort to achieve much greater contextualisation than the typical 'stock photo aesthetic' of blank or blurred backgrounds and neutral or bland colour palettes, for example, through the careful staging of cluttered, layered, or grainy settings and surfaces that are quite often an integral part of everyday life somewhere and for someone. At the same time, these images can be texturized through lighting and photographic effects, thus also bringing the materiality of photography as a creative practice into the picture (Aiello and Woodhouse 2016). It is precisely because of its ability to link bottom-up aesthetics with top-down design that texturization may 'aid legitimacy work by more effectively capturing attention, making a message more intuitively understandable' (Lefsrud, Graves, and Phillips 2020, 1056).

In the wake of the pandemic, the role of texture in organizational identity design may see both Starbucks and Getty Images continue to mobilise texture as a key semiotic resource. As soon as the COVID-19 crisis unfolded, Starbucks made plans to transform its store portfolio to increase the availability of 'drive-thru and curbside pickup options' (Starbucks Stories & News 2020) in which beverages and other products can be pre-ordered through an app. However, the coffee company's 'texturized' approach to store design has remained intact. Along the same lines, the visual aesthetics of stock images from Getty Images (as well as other image banks) have become fully reliant on a more texturized, rather than minimalistic or decontextualised, 'look' and 'feel'.

This said, it is fair to say that the pandemic may eventually lead to a greater degree of reliance on visual rather than tactile texture. While tactile textures entail an engagement with the concrete 'grain' of matter (Conley and Dickinson 2010), visual textures rely on cues that relate to the provenance and experiential qualities of a particular ambience (Djonov and van Leeuwen 2011). As digital technologies enable us to more and more easily replicate 'apparent' material irregularities and patterns pointing to particular haptic qualities on what are inevitably entirely 'smooth' surfaces in space and on screens (Johannessen and van Leeuwen 2018), texture will most likely continue to be mobilised as an important semiotic resource by organizations. Overall, texturization will rely much more extensively and explicitly on new digital technologies of visual production and distribution that can achieve some of the same effects more efficiently. Ultimately, it is most likely that it is ambience evoked through visualisation rather than touch per se that will become increasingly central to how texture is mobilised in organizational identity design.

References

Aiello, G. (2018). "Losing to gain: Balancing style and texture in the Starbucks logo." In C. M. Johannessen and T. van Leeuwen (Eds.), *The Materiality of Writing: A Trace-Making Perspective*. London: Routledge, 195–210.

Aiello, G., and G. Dickinson. (2014). "Beyond authenticity: A visual-material analysis of locality in the global redesign of Starbucks stores." *Visual Communication* 13(3): 303–321.

Aiello, G., and K. Parry. (2020). *Visual Communication: Understanding Images in Media Culture*. London: SAGE.

Aiello, G., and L. Pauwels. (2014). "Special issue: Difference and globalization." *Visual Communication* 13(3): 275–285.

Aiello, G., and A. Woodhouse. (2016). "When corporations come to define the visual politics of gender: The case of Getty Images." *Journal of Language and Politics* 15(3): 352–368.

Björkvall, A., and A-M. Karlsson. (2011). "The materiality of discourses and the semiotics of materials: A social perspective on the meaning potentials of written texts and furniture." *Semiotica* 187(1-4): 141–165.

Bourdieu, P. (1991). *Language and Symbolic Power* (J. B. Thompson Ed.). Cambridge: Harvard University Press.

Boxenbaum, E., C. Jones, R. E. Meyer and S. Svejenova. (2018). "Towards an articulation of the material and visual turn in organization studies." *Organization Studies* 39(5-6): 597–616.

Cain Miller, C. (2018). "What being transgender looks like, according to stock photography." *The New York Times*, 25 October 2018. https://www.nytimes.com/2018/10/25/upshot/what-being-transgender-looks-like-according-to-stock-photography.html

Caivano, J. L. (1990). "Visual texture as a semiotic system." *Semiotica* 80(3/4): 239–252.
Cameron, D. (1995). *Verbal Hygiene*. London: Routledge.
Cameron, D. (2000). "Styling the worker: Gender and the commodification of language in the globalized service economy." *Journal of Sociolinguistics* 4(3): 323–347.
Chen, A., and D. Machin. (2014). "The local and the global in the visual design of a Chinese women's lifestyle magazine: A multimodal critical discourse approach." *Visual Communication* 13(3): 287–301.
Conley, D., and G. Dickinson. (2010). "Textural democracy." *Critical Studies in Media Communication* 27(1): 1–7.
Djonov, E., and T. van Leeuwen. (2011). "The semiotics of texture: From tactile to Visual." *Visual Communication* 10(4): 541–564.
Frosh, P. (2013). "Beyond the image bank: Digital commercial photography." In M. Lister (Ed.), *The Photographic Image in Digital Culture*. 2nd edition. London and New York: Routledge, 131–148.
Gill, R. (2007). *Gender and the Media*. Malden, MA: Polity.
Gombrich, E. H. (1984). *The Sense of Order: A Study in the Psychology of Decorative Art*. London: Phaidon.
Grossman, S. (2014). "'Women laughing alone with tablets' is the new 'women laughing alone with salad'." *TIME.com*, 8 December, 2014. https://time.com/3624276/women-laughing-alone-with-salad-tablets/.
Höllerer, M. A., D. Jancsary, and M. Grafström. (2018). ""A picture is worth a thousand words": Multimodal sensemaking of the global financial crisis." *Organization Studies* 39(5–6): 617–644.
Johannessen, C. M., and T. van Leeuwen. (2018). "(Ir)regularity." In C. Johannessen and T. van Leeuwen (Eds.), *The Materiality of Writing: A Trace-Making Perspective*. London: Routledge, 175–192.
Kress, G., and T. van Leeuwen. (2006). *Reading Images: The Grammar of Visual Design*. 2nd edition. London: Routledge.
Ledin, P., and D. Machin. (2020). *Introduction to Multimodal Analysis*. London: Bloomsbury.
Lefsrud, L., H. Graves, and N. Phillips. (2020). "Giant toxic lakes you can see from space": A theory of multimodal messages and emotion in legitimacy work." *Organization Studies* 41(8): 1055–1078.
Lury, C. (1996). *Consumer Culture*. New Brunswick, NJ: Rutgers University Press.
Machin, D. (2004). "Building the world's visual language: The increasing global importance of image banks in corporate media." *Visual Communication* 3(3), 316–336.
Phillips, M., and A. Rippin. (2010). "Howard and the mermaid: Abjection and the Starbucks' Foundation memoir." *Organization* 17(4): 481–499.
Sachs, M. (2014). "Getty images a cliché-killer at Cannes." Forbes.com, 27 June, 2014. https://www.forbes.com/sites/maryleesachs/2014/06/27/getty-images-a-cliche-killer-at-cannes/?sh=2bdb486d4283
Sandberg, S. (2013). *Lean in: Women, Work and the Will to Lead*. London: WH Allen, Ebury Publishing, Random House.
Schultz, H. (2011). *Onward: How Starbucks Fought for its Life without Losing its Soul (with Joanne Gordon)*. Hoboken, NY: Wiley.
Starbucks Stories & News (2009). "Starbucks Reinvents the store experience to speak to the heart and soul of local communities." 25 June, 2009. https://stories

.starbucks.com/press/2009/starbucks-reinvents-the-store-experience-to-speak-to-the-heart-and-soul-of/
Starbucks Stories & News (2020). "Starbucks to Transform U.S. Store Portfolio by Building on the Strength of Digital Customer Relationships and the Convenience of the Starbucks App." 10 June, 2020. https://stories.starbucks.com/press/2020/starbucks-to-transform-us-store-portfolio-by-building-on-the-strength-of-digital-customer-relationships/
Thurlow, C., and A. Jaworski. (2006). "The alchemy of the upwardly mobile: Symbolic capital and the stylization of elites in frequent-flyer programmes." *Discourse & Society* 17(1): 99–135.
Van Leeuwen, T. (2022). *Multimodality and Identity*. London and New York: Routledge.

Afterword

Theo van Leeuwen and Renate E. Meyer

Recent multidisciplinary work between organization and management studies and social semiotics has been mutually beneficial. It has enhanced the interest in multimodal communication in organization and management studies and extended the understanding of how meaning is constituted, communicated, changed, and stored in and across organizations. It has also advanced the emphasis on the social in social semiotics, through an engagement with issues that are central in organization and management studies and, hence, in contemporary society as a whole, such as innovation, identity, and the legitimation of organizations and their activities and, more generally, with the increasing formalisation of many areas of social life.

This volume contains contributions from social semioticians who have begun to engage with organization and management studies by investigating practices and products of multimodal communication in a variety of organizations: in health-related organizations, including a study of sexual health information produced for diverse audiences in a family planning organization by van Leeuwen and Zonjic (Chapter 3) and a study of the training of surgeons in hospitals by Tahim and Bezemer (Chapter 9); in universities, including a study by Laba of the way university home pages change as they adopt new practices (Chapter 4) and a study by Ravelli of the way a university has changed the layout and furnishing of outdoor spaces to promote team-based learning outside the classroom (Chapter 7); in multinational corporations, through Tann and Ayoko's study of the way spatial arrangements structure relations in an office (Chapter 6) and Aiello's study of rebranding (Chapter 10); in retail environments, through Boeriis's comparison of the way customers navigate brick-and-mortar and online bookshops (Chapter 8); and finally in government, through Björkvall's study of the way Swedish public servants are encouraged to embody the values and culture of the organizations they work in (Chapter 5). The chapters in this volume, thus, cover for-profit, non-profit, and public sector organizations across different sectors and industries.

While, as noted in Chapter 1, earlier semiotic studies often focused on advertising and marketing (with some exceptions, e.g., Iedema 2003), social semioticians have now clearly begun to study a much wider range of organizations and a much wider range of aspects of their internal and external communication practices, and they have also adopted a wider and more diverse range of analytical methods, including not only textual and spatial analysis but also interviews, focus groups, and detailed observation of practices using video and eye-tracking technology. At the same time, organization scholars have embraced a visual and material turn in studying organizational activities and institutionalised practices (e.g., Boxenbaum et al. 2018; Quattrone et al. 2021).

However, the introduction to this volume formulated a more ambitious goal: how might organization studies *change* social semiotics, and how might social semiotics *change* organization studies? How might joint work between the two fields result, not in different perspectives on issues of common interest but in a common perspective, an integration of the two fields of study into what, in the title of this book, we have called 'organizational semiotics'? So, we need to ask to what degree the contributors to this volume have succeeded in working toward that aim. In answering this question, we begin by discussing what organization and management studies can offer to social semiotics and to what degree this potential has been taken up by the contributions to this volume. We also ask the converse question: what can a social semiotic approach to multimodal communication offer to organization and management studies, and to what degree has this potential been realised? It is for this reason that our afterword is jointly written by two authors – one from each of the two disciplines.

To answer the first of these two questions, we need, first of all, to look at the concepts of text and context which are, at least in principle, fundamental to a social semiotic approach to multimodal communication. Semiotics – and social semiotics is no exception here – has traditionally studied 'texts', and, though taking much of its inspiration from linguistics (especially Halliday 1978), it has broadened the notion of texts to include all performances and artefacts that play a role in mediating the communication of meaning and all the different modes of communication that are involved in this. However, the 'social' in social semiotics means that not only texts but also their contexts should be studied. As Halliday put it in relation to language, 'the words that are exchanged get their meaning from the activities in which they are embedded, which again are social activities with social agencies' (Halliday 1985, 5). But, as noted in Chapter 1, while social semiotic theory makes fine distinctions at the level of linguistic structure, it has not provided equally detailed analytical frameworks at the level of context, and, as a result, descriptions of the contexts are often brief and commonsense rather than researched as thoroughly as the texts. Organization and management studies, on the other hand, provide detailed and sociologically well-grounded accounts of a key social context: organization.

What kind of contexts are organizations? In a broad and general definition, they are bounded social entities that are embedded in a certain environment and broader culture and have specific goals, multiple stakeholders, membership rules, and a deliberately designed authority structure, coordination of activities, and communication. Organization studies have focused on the internal workings of such entities – coordination, negotiations, conflicts, hierarchies, leadership, team dynamics, formal and informal structures and processes, meaning-making activities, relations between participants, etc. Research examines these processes in organizations with an eye on the specificities of different organizational forms such as, for instance, public sector bodies or agencies, corporations, partnerships, associations, cooperatives, or, more recently, purpose-driven organizations. Hence, from an organization scholar's perspective, organization as context for text requires specification. However, organization scholars do not only study these entities. They are also interested in organizations as actors engaging with other organizations in networks of organizations and organizational fields, in the doing (organising) in and outside organizations (e.g., social movements, intersectoral collaborations, and collective action), in how the signification of issues that shape the culture in which organizations and organising are embedded (e.g., climate change or vaccination) is contested, and in how organizations, together with other actors, enter into the politics of signification.

Organization and management studies are, therefore, well placed to supplement textual analysis and strengthen our understanding of the relation between text and context. If we take this focus on studying both text and context, both practice and product, as one of the key contributions organization and management studies can make to social semiotics, we will ask below to what degree this has been achieved by the contributors to this volume.

To attend to the second question, namely what can a social semiotic approach to multimodal communication offer to organization and management studies, the easy response would be that social semiotics has enriched empirical studies through new genres of data and more sophisticated analytical tools. While this is clearly the case, it is not the whole story. The potential contribution of social semiotics is much more substantial. Organizational activities are embodied experiences. Organizational activities, practices, organizational boundaries, organising outside and across organizations, and the constitution of organizations as actors are achieved through multimodal communication and meaning-making. In fact, organizations do not exist without them. Multimodal texts in the broad notion above are *constitutive* of organizations and organising. Core concepts in organization and management theory, such as boundaries, identity, purpose and goals, relationships, authority, emotion, space and place, and notions of temporality have to be brought to life through performances and artefacts: texts. A closer engagement with social semiotics will, we argue, not only inspire organization and management research but also impact our knowledge and understanding of core theoretical constructs.

Reviewing the chapters shows that social semiotics has indeed begun to realise the synergy between the two fields. Björkvall, in his chapter on the 'emotional civil servant' (Chapter 5) analyses the 'platform of values' strategies used in the Swedish public service. These seek to foster affect-laden 'core values' that are thought to help achieve organizational goals – values such as 'commitment', 'responsibility', 'cooperation', and 'helpfulness'. Before embarking on a multimodal analysis of the texts that implement this strategy, Björkvall places it in its wider social context as part of a move from rational and rule-driven bureaucracies to affect-driven 'neo-bureaucracies' that seek to shape the identity of civil servants in the way religions seek to shape the identities of their adherents and nation states the identities of their citizens. Boeriis (Chapter 8) introduces Guido's (2001) work on the salience of marketing stimuli, which offers a set of theoretical categories for 'consumer awareness', to then operationalise this with a social semiotic framework for analysing salience and show how consumers actually use salience-based structures to find their way toward the products they seek to buy. Ravelli (Chapter 7) discusses how universities engage in 'consumer-oriented' policies and practices and transform what used to be passageways between classrooms into informal outdoor learning spaces, which she then analyses in detail, using her 'spatial discourse analysis' methodology. Laba (Chapter 4) shows, among other things, how the home pages of university websites have also become more consumer-oriented and, hence, of diminished value for other stakeholders. Tahim and Bezemer's account of apprenticeship training in surgery (Chapter 9) documents the incursion of formalised assessment processes into practices that used to be the province of autonomous professionals (in this case surgeons), traditionally accountable only to their professional ethos and not to managers, and van Leeuwen and Zonjic (Chapter 3) describe how the production of sexual health information in a family planning organization involves teams with different interests, with the result that medical considerations compete with strategies that are influenced by marketing and audience research. They also highlight the importance of cultural literacy and cultural sensitivity in making organizational communication acceptable for the targeted audiences. Tann and Ayoko (Chapter 6) study the elimination of individual 'cells' in the office of a multinational company and the work practices that this affords. Aiello (Chapter 10) discusses how organizations are responding to criticism and moving from profit-driven standardisation and globalisation to increasing localisation and diversification, analysing how Getty Images is 'repicturing' its vast image library in the light of newly emerging values and how Starbucks is rebranding its shops to 'move away from widespread associations with extreme product standardisation, cultural homogenisation, and consumerism'.

Some concepts and topics from the field of organization and management studies resonate in several of the chapters, such as, for instance, the concept of identity: organizational identity (Aiello, Boeriis, Laba, and Ravelli), team identity (Tann and Ayoko), role or professional identity (Björkvall, Tahim and Bezemer), and community identity (van Leeuwen and Zonjic). Design and management of identity have a long tradition in organization studies, and there is considerable potential for mutual inspiration. The studies in this volume give a vivid account of how multiple semiotic modes are mobilised to enact, align with, maintain in the face of challenges, or attempt to change identities at various levels. Embodied practices and relationships also play a role in several of the chapters – in Tahim and Bezemer's chapter (the standardisation and monitoring of surgical training), in van Leeuwen and Zonjic's chapter (the practice of producing communication materials), in Ravelli's chapter (the practice of studying on campus and how the institutionalised relationship between students and lectures is changed through spatial changes), and in Tann and Ayoko's chapter (how space and office layout afford specific work practices while discouraging others). Power, control, and surveillance in organizations are central in different ways in the contributions of, for instance, Aiello (normalised integration of diversity), Tahim and Bezemer (surveillance of a previously autonomous profession), and Tann and Ayoko (control and surveillance through spatial arrangements). Finally, several chapters deal with the way organizations tailor their communication to what they assume will resonate best with different stakeholders. A user perspective is assumed explicitly in the chapter by Boeriis. Ravelli focuses on one stakeholder group (students), Laba shows how the website of a university customises its communication to particular stakeholder groups (potential students and donors), and van Leeuwen and Zonjic show how the producers of text aim to customise their communication to what they assume will resonate with their core audiences.

The authors of the chapters in this volume have engaged with such organizational practices and concepts in a number of ways not only through text analysis but also through archival background research, as in the case of Aiello's research on the history of Starbucks' branding (Chapter 10) or Björkvall's analysis of multimodal documents (Chapter 5). They have also engaged through actually working within and with organizations, using not only interviews and focus groups but also extensive video recordings of organizational practices, as in the case of Tahim and Bezemer's video recordings of surgical procedures (Chapter 9) and Boeriis's eye-tracking and video recordings of customers finding their way in brick-and-mortar and online shops (Chapter 8). In the case of van Leeuwen and Zonjic (Chapter 3), a member of the organization (the manager of the health promotion team whose work they studied) became a co-author, while Tann and Ayoko (Chapter 6), in a somewhat similar way, used the staff member who had designed the office layout they analyse as an informant, thus being able to study not only the 'text' (office layout) but also the intentions behind it and the way it was used by the people working in it. Such strategies not only show, to paraphrase Halliday, how texts get their meaning from the activities in which they are embedded but can also benefit the organizations studied. Tann and Ayoko (Chapter 6) conclude by discussing which of the functions and meanings of the office layout they have analysed will have to change when more and more work will be done away from the office. Van Leeuwen and Zonjic's work (Chapter 3) not only led to the recommendations they list at the end of their chapter but also to workshops with the organization's health promotion team.

There is another key concept in social semiotics to which organization and management studies have much to contribute: the concept of 'cultural context'. As noted in Chapter 1, Halliday argued that social semiotics cannot understand social communication without taking into account not only the micro – 'the immediate sights and sounds surrounding the event' – but also the macro – 'the whole cultural history behind the participants, and behind the kind of practices they are engaging in determining their significance for the culture, whether practical or ritual' (Halliday 1985, 6). In other words, if the social semiotic analysis of multimodal communicative practices and products is to move beyond description, if it is to be able to explain why these practices and products are the way they are or why they are changing in the way they are, the concept of 'cultural context' and the study of cultural histories is indispensable. Organization and management studies have long addressed how some of the cultural changes evidenced in the chapters of this volume impact organizations and processes of organising, and while most contributions to this volume study specific organizations and their structures and processes, each of these organizations represents a specific organizational form. It is, therefore, important to disentangle what is specific for a particular organization, what pertains to an organizational form or a profession, and what reflects broader developments in the sector, field, or the broader culture. Without again discussing each chapter, we can, nevertheless, exemplify how the chapters in this book can throw light on the broader contemporary cultural context in which organizations play such a significant role.

Björkvall's study (Chapter 5) is in line with current research in organization studies that focus on emotionality, not from a psychological or intraorganizational perspective, but as social experience tied to specific role identities – in this case, the ideal emotional costume of the civil servant. Björkvall leaves the boundaries of a particular organization and looks at strategies for construing the role model of an affect-driven civil servant across different public sector organizations. Although his study is located in Sweden, the trends he observes have wider implications not only for the professional identity of civil servants but also for bureaucracy as an organizational form. According to Max Weber's (1921/1972) principles of bureaucracy, civil servants deliver their services '*sine ira et studio*' – that is, without affection or enthusiasm, and after decades of attacks on the Weberian bureaucracy through New Public Management driven reforms, the 'affect-driven civil servant' reveals the direction and the scope of this new strategy. While, as Björkvall discusses, the multimodal portrayal of the affect-driven civil servant is entirely positive, the intended and unintended consequences for the control regime within these organizations and for the impartiality and objectivity of public sector organizations may be less so.

Tahim and Bezemer (Chapter 9) study a typical intra-organizational relationship – the relation between trainee and supervisor – and how the actual learning experience in the operating theatre is translated into a standardised form in order to allow for a formal procedure of assessment. The multimodal lived experiences are transcribed into monomodal verbal text, a transformation that is further amplified by digital forms replacing handwritten notes. However, in order to understand what is going on, it is necessary to leave the concrete organization. The two roles involved belong to a profession that has a long history and is characterised by autonomy, and the formalisation and standardisation observed is part of a struggle to make the profession more 'manageable'. Although not explicitly engaging with related studies in the organization and management domain, this study has great potential to connect to and inform research on expert authority, control, and deprofessionalisation. From an organization scholar's perspective, we would expect resistance that materialises in various ways, for instance, in the development of quite distinct legitimate accounts and a variety of decoupling activities aimed at protecting the inner core of professional autonomy.

Economic and cultural globalisation is the broader backdrop of Aiello's study (Chapter 10), which uses the examples of two corporations that need to comply with cultural notions of diversity and gender equality that are spreading across the globe. The study highlights how, as the cultural expectations to conform to these norms and values intensify, their integration in corporate communication becomes normalised and commodified. This study also links to another important topic in relation to globalisation – the need to anchor the global corporation in a specific location – and shows how this is achieved through the combination of multiple modes.

The interplay between global trends and local instantiations is also a prominent theme in Laba's (Chapter 4) study of a university website. The university is a globally institutionalised type of organization and needs to display adherence to this category but, at the same time, needs to establish its distinctiveness. The study shows how this is achieved through the use of multimodal communication, including name, colour, and images. However, the changes of the website over time not only give insights into the developments of this particular university, but they also reflect a broader trend in the higher education sector that turns students into customers and marketises the relationship between them and faculty. Ravelli's study (Chapter 7) is embedded in the same cultural context. She analyses how the built university campus constitutes not only the social order of the university and its organizational culture but also reflects broader developments in the field of higher education that profoundly redefine the university and its role in society (co-creation of learning, entrepreneurial university, third mission, marketisation of research, and higher education). The new design mimics modern corporations spatially and materialises the diffusion of market and economy rationales into other spheres of society – a trend that has been documented for management tools, terminology, and stakeholder relationships.

In terms of broader embeddedness, Tann and Ayoko's (Chapter 6) study touches many highly relevant topics. The trend to set up shared service centres in large organizations aims to counteract fragmentation but also undermines the autonomy of local units. While accountability and transparency are regarded as features of good governance and have a generally positive connotation, both have dark sides in that accountability leads to stylised reporting schemes that merely hand on responsibility and eventually institutionalise organised irresponsibility, and transparency revives panoptic control fantasies and trigger secrecy. Tann and Ayoko's study can be read as an in-depth, on-the-ground study of how employees deal with such shifts in the regime of corporate control and how they try to restore zones of independence.

To conclude, the papers in this volume have gone a long way toward putting into practice the ambitious agenda we have set for 'organizational semiotics' in the first two chapters. We hope that our book has shown just how many exciting and important projects are possible within this new field. This does not mean that the integration of the two disciplines has now been fully achieved. So, to end this afterword, we offer some suggestions toward the further consolidation and development of our project.

(1) A more detailed agenda needs to be developed to orient social semioticians to issues that are fundamental in organization and management studies, and to the relevant literatures, and to connect organization and management scholars to relevant topics and literatures from social semiotics.
(2) Social semioticians should strive to work with and within organizations so as to research the activities, practices, and institutions in which texts are embedded from their inception to their implementation.
(3) Organization and management scholars should enlarge the repertoire of texts they study and sharpen their analytic capacity to grasp the multimodal nature of all meaning-making in, of, and about organizations within organizations.
(4) The study of digital products and practices and, in particular, the transformations that occur when practices and products are digitised should receive greater attention, as a 'micro' organizational semiotic approach to this issue will be able to reveal much about the 'macro' changes of the social and cultural environment in which we live.
(5) New organizational forms, such as platforms, dual purpose organizations, or decentralised autonomous organizations (DAO) as well as processes of organising outside organizations, such as social movements, and temporary or permanent intersectoral collaborations should be studied from the joint perspective of organizational semiotics by

multidisciplinary teams composed of organization and social semiotics scholars.
(6) Finally, integrating organization and management studies with social semiotic approaches to multimodal communication will greatly benefit from joint research and co-authoring projects between scholars from the two fields, as in the case of Tann and Ayoko in Chapter 6 of this volume as well as between researchers and practitioners, as in the case of van Leeuwen and Zonjic in Chapter 3 of this volume. The discussions and deliberations that are inevitably part of such joint projects will greatly help to bring about the new discipline of organizational semiotics that we have proposed in this book.

References

Boxenbaum, E., C. Jones, R.E. Meyer, and S. Svejenova. (2018). "Towards an articulation of the material and visual turn in organization studies." *Organization Studies* 39 (5–6): 597–616.

Guido, G. (2001). *The Salience of Marketing Stimuli: An Incongruity-salience Hypothesis on Consumer Awareness*. London: Kluwer Academic Publications.

Halliday, M.A.K. (1978). *Language as Social Semiotic*. London: Arnold.

Halliday, M.A.K. (1985) "Context of situation." In M.A.K. Halliday and R. Hasan (Eds) *Language, Context and Text: Aspects of Language in a Social-semiotic Perspective*. Geelong: Deakin University Press, 3–14.

Iedema, R. (2003). "Multimodality, resemiotization: Extending the analysis of discourse to multimodal semiotic practices." *Visual Communication* 2(10): 29–57.

Quattrone, P., M. Ronzani, D. Jancsary, and M. A. Höllerer. (2021). "Beyond the visible, the material and the performative: Shifting perspectives on the visual in organization studies." *Organization Studies* 42(8): 1197–1218.

Weber, M. (1921/1972). *Wirtschaft und Gesellschaft: Grundriß der verstehenden Soziologie*. 5th edition. Tübingen, Germany: J.C.B. Mohr.

Index

Aboriginal and Torres Strait Islander(s) 54, 57, 59, 62–63
Aboriginal art 60, 63, 66
affect: and working life 100; definition of 102, 103; as modelled identity 110; multimodal construction of 99; performative aspect of 102; as positive collaboration format 106–107; research 100, 118; sociality of 102; as social practice 103
affect-driven civil servant 100, 102, 116, 236
affective: aspects of organizations 100; civil servant identities 116; civil servants 114; identities 100, 103–104, 111, 115–118; potentials 101–102, 106, 109, 114, 117; practices 99–101, 103, 110, 111, 115, 117–118; professional practices 103–104, 115
affective affordance(s) 100, 103–107, 111–112, 114–117; analysis of 105; and civil servants 107; concept of 104; multimodal 100, 105, 108, 109, 116; in platform of values 104
affects: critical analysis of 103; representation(s) of 102–103
affinity categories 172; ideational affinities 172; interpersonal affinities 172; textual affinities 172
affinity mechanisms 172–173
affordance(s): and multimodality 104; centralisation of technological 92; material 37; multimodal 108; and multimodal communication 38; of technology 77; of "textuarisation" 17
Agency 155–156, **160**
Allied Hands Breaking Swastika (Henri Kay Henrion) 108
alphabetical search 177–178
ambience format 107
anthropomorphic illustrations 110
appraisal framework (Martin and White's) 103
artefact(s): semiotic 168, 170; linguistic 101; multimodal 30, 37, 40, 101–102, 105

balanced scorecard 38
becoming (Guattari's concept) 101
benevolent gaze 16
binding 147, 157–158, **160**
bonding 147, 157, 160
brand colour as representational meaning 85; building designs and employee interactions 143
built environment(s): and framing 148; as a communicative text 145; configuration of 122; design of 148; and interactional meanings 146–147, 156–157; modes and media 144; and navigation 148; and promenade 158; and representational meaning 145; semiotic approach to 143; and social values of institutions 162; at UNSW 144

CALD *see* culturally and linguistically diverse
CCO *see* communication constitutes organization
Center 148, 158, **160**
cervical screening (test) 56, 59–62, 66
City in History: Its Origins Its Transformations and Its Prospects (Mumford) 73
civil servants: as as emotional subjects 100; desired affective properties

of 109; as public authority representatives 119
committed subjects 114
commodification: and sexualisation 222; of knowledge 75; of objects and identities 216; of women 222
communication: and social action 126; brand 73; practices 4, 212, 232; products of 10, 29; sites of 29; spatial-visual 170; visual 7, 55, 60, 131, 168, 214
communication constitutes organization (CCO) 166
communication practices: corporate 35; external 232; internal 232; standardized 212; study of 71
communicative: artefacts 37; communicative practices 3, 15, 17, 32, 167, 236; functions 7, 73, 78
compositional meaning(s): and identity and solidarity 137; function of 147; impact of interactional meaning on 158; and key questions 146; and spatial design 157–158
context: conceptualisation of 14; of culture 5, 6, 14; interpretation 214; of situation(al) 5, 167, 185
contraception, emergency 59, 64
Control 147, 156–157
corporate: culture 216; identity 76, 80, 92, 154
corporate social responsibility 27; Austrian 16
corporate visual identity (CVI) elements 80, 82, 87, 91
courage 108, 116
covert: classification 69; taxonomies 88
COVID-19 and spatial design 136
critical: consulting 44; multimodal discourse studies 102
cross-fertilisation 16, 25, 28
cultural: barriers 57; cachet 217; context 236; legitimacy 10, 25
culturally and linguistically diverse (CALD) 54, 59; communities 57, 60; people 61
CVI *see* corporate visual identity (CVI) elements

data collection in organizations 40, 43, 45
DCGCA *see* Director of Communications Government and Community Affairs

decentralised autonomous organizations 238
deictic expressions 79
design: and workplace relations 138; choices and function 84; functional 26, 89; identity 212–213; organizational identity 74–75, 78, 92, 212–214, 217, 225; practice of Fortune 500 84
design changes: and relational meaning 160; at UNSW 162
dialogicity 105
Director of Communications Government and Community Affairs (DCGCA) 59
discourse: organizational discourse 15; marketisation of 35; strategic use of 101
discursive identities 114
dynamic rank scale 172–173

effectuated semiotic sequences 91; employee-assisted search 179–180
entextualisation: agents of 196; process of 190
ethics of enthusiasm 116
ethnographic fieldwork 190

Family Planning New South Wales (FPNSW) 54–60, 62, 65–66, 68, 70; and emergency contraception 59, 64
Fayol, Henri 28
feedback: importance of 43, 44; in multimodal configurations 209
female reproductive organs 66–67, 69
femvertising 222
fertilisation 66–67
formalisation 9, 31, 231, 237
form and function: shifts in 82–83; of design elements 76
FPNSW *see* Family Planning New South Wales
framing 147–148, 157–158; of corporate decisions 37; devices 131, 157, 170; and meaning 170; permeability in 131; of the space 130; strong 132–133; weak 132–133

gaze(s) 7, 16, 202; benevolent 16; clinical gaze 191; partner-like 16; scrutinising 16; Weber's gaze 28
genre and multimodality model 77
Getty Images: and legitimacy work 223; and politicized language 223

'Given-New' 174, 178, 181
Global North and organizations 30
grammatical metaphor 106
graphic communication design 215

Halliday's concepts: field 14–15; logical metafunction 145, 159; metafunctions 6–7, 74, 128; mode 14–15; segmentation of verbal language 172; systemic functional linguistics 168; tenor 14–15
health: information resources 56, 59; literacy 54, 70; promotion campaign 57; promotion team 56–59, 235, 236; sexual and reproductive 17, 27, 54, 66
health promotion: materials 54; practices 33, 54; resources 54–55; services 27, 54; work 33, 54
heterosexual relationships 63
hierarchical power relations 106
higher education commercialisation 93
HIV/AIDS campaign in Africa 60
homophobia 66
human papillomavirus 62
hybridisation 146
hyper-regulation of language 216
hypertext(uality) 75
hypotactic relations 148, **160**

'Ideal-Real' 174, 178, 181
identification types 76
image(s): function of 86; and low literacy levels 57
imagined audience 75
informal outdoor learning (spaces) 144, 150, 234
information: addition of 69; architecture 74–75; deletion of 68; density of a website 78; rearrangement of 69; transformation of 69
innovation: in social semiotics 27
institutional legitimacy 82
instructional drawings 66
intellectual property 43
interactional meaning systems 145; control 147; power 147
inter-organizational interaction 33
interpersonal grammatical metaphor 105–106 interpretative position 104, 114
intertextual chains 192
intra-organizational relationship 237
isomorphic adaptation 31

Know Your Health: Cervical Screening Test (brochure/campaign) 60–61, 67–68

language: definition of (in Malinowski) 5–6
language barriers 57
layout: and office functions and meanings 235; of a website 78
layout unit(s) 75, 78–79, 84, 87, 90–92; representational logic of 75; sequencing of 91
locality and authenticity 222
look of a webpage 75
Low Down (booklet for CALD people) 60, 63, 65, 66–69

Malinowski, Bronislaw 5, 6, 27
Malinowski's concepts: context of culture 5–6, 14–15; context of situation 5
management: as semiotic practice 18; discourse and verbal interaction 133
management of emotion 101
managerial: control forms 32; work as semiotic work 46
Margins 148, 158
Marketing and Semiotics-New Directions in the Study of Signs for Sale (Umiker-Sebeok) 5
Marketing Semiotics (Oswald) 5
marketisation: and organizations 73; of discourse 35
materiality 26, 218, 222; in institutions 166; of organizations 37; texture and 213–214; at UNSW 162; of a visual sign 78
material space 122; and meaning 126; use of 126
meaning(s) 7, 18, 25–26, 32–33, 54, 68, 74, 78, 93, 124, 137–138, 213; affective 99–100, 106; brand 91, 93; compositional 126–127, 130, 135–136, 145–**146**, 157–159; cultural 31; experiential 212, 222; functional 25; interactional 126–127, 130–132, 134, 146, 156–158; interpersonal 7; layers of 7; organizational-level 13; relational 145–146, 148, 154, 159–160; representational 126, 128, 130–132, 137–138, 145, 146, 154–155, 159; social 13, 26, 32; and social context 126; societal 31;

Index 243

symbolic 25; textual 78; ways of changing 68–69
meaning-making: activities of organizations 15; within a cultural community 167; discursive 102; organizational 186; practices of 31; processes of 101; resources 73, 76; resources for interpersonal 7; resources of 183; semiotic 166; and society and culture 2
Meaning of Meaning (Ogden and Richards) 6
metafunction(s) (Halliday) 6–7, 91, 128, 130, 145, 148, 172; analytical questions for **146**, 148; compositional 128; ideational 168; interactional 128; interpersonal 74, 168; representational 74, 128; textual 74, 168
metafunctional analysis 34, 154, 162; terminology *145*
Michels, Robert 28
Microsoft SmartArt 26
MMSS *see* multimodal social semiotic(s)
modelled: format 107; identities diagram 110
monomodal verbal text 237
multimodal: communication 11–12, 15–18, 34, 38–39, 167, 185, 231–233, 237, 239; conversation analysis 10, 16, 39, 106, 110, 114, 118, 134, 234; discourse analysis 93, 102, 143; literacy 40; research 11, 29–30, 40–42; *text in use* 167
multimodality: and accounting and accountability 38; implicit 4; and management 37, 38; and management of organizations 46; and meaning 18, 37; meaning 57; of meaning-making (in organizations) 2, 238; and operating theatre 190; and organizational researchers 11; rise of 4; social semiotic research on 25; and visual communication 213; and websites 76
multimodal social semiotic(s) (MMSS) 3, 8, 12, 30, 166–168, 183; analysis 169, 185; approach 185; in shopping situations 167; and social actions 186; theoretical framework 185; theory of 74
multimodal texts 14, 26, 36, 39, 54, 100, 114, 166, 168, 219; organizational 186; visual 172

narrative: drawings 66; images 66; multimodal 37; process type 146; visual(s) 66–67
navigation support of a website 78
non-modalised *statements* 105
nonverbal communication 27
Nordic Resistance Movement 104
normative isomorphism 17, 39

office space(s): and functions 127; architecture 37; designs 122; open-plan 125
open-plan: area 125, 128, 131, 134; designs 122, 130, 134; workspace 130
open-plan office(s) 122–125, 127, 131, 133, 135, 136, 155; advantages of 123; and avoiding distractions 136; communication 122; design of 123; rise of 123; and social distancing 122
optimisation 31, 74; efficiency 35
organization: and hierarchy 2; definition of 1, 8; design 37; institutional definition of 8–9; instrumental definition of 9; semiotic principles of 74; social aspects of 122; societally legitimate 33; visual aspects of 29
organizational: collaboration 33; culture(s) 1, 138, 154, 237; environments 31, 35; forms 8–9, 13, 31, 33, 233, 235, 238; goals 33, 40, 234; institutionalism 25; legitimation 29; research 12, 14, 26, 28, 36, 106, 116; roles 3, 32; semiotics 3, 12–14, 25, 32, 46, 68–69, 186; semiotics and diagrams 8; settings 40, 43, 45; space and physical environment 166; texts 184; texts and multimodality 101; theory 13
organizational communication 25, 33, 35, 123, 137, 234; complexities of 123; functions of 3; multimodal 40; multimodal genres of 26; practice 4
organizational identity 29, 34, 73–74, 76–78, 82, 86, 90–92, 115, 144, 213, 225–226; communication 93; corporate 213; and societal values 212; of UNSW 91
organizational practices 10, 12, 35, 39, 68, 216, 235; multimodality of 32
organizational semiotics 232; benefits of 39, 40; core assumptions of 13; cornerstones of 12; opportunities

for 32; practical value of 34; as a research program 45; and resemiotisation 68
organizations: as meaning-making practices 1; formal 30; platform 9; as products of communication 10; as semiotic entities 1; semiotic nature of 2, 3; as sites of communication 10; as sites of social semiotics research 45; societal environment of 3, 32; standard processes in 43; study of 10, 28; as tri-functional entities 12
organization studies and social semiotics 232
organization theory 29, 36; field of 28; visual turn in 30
overt taxonomies (OT) 88; on UNSW homepage 88

Panzani pasta advertisement 4
paractic relations 148, **160**
paradox of technology 93
Paris School 4
partner-like gaze 16
period hygiene 62
permeability 131, 133, 148
physical environment and venting 134
physical settings and behaviour 166
platform of values (*värdegrund*) 99–104; and affective identities 118; in collaborative organizations 109–110; genre 100, 106; and the Riksbank *111*; strategies 234; and the Swedish Geotechnical Institute *113*; texts 105–106, 112, 115–117
pluri-disciplinarity (Novotny's idea) 14
poetic language in advertising 4
post-bureaucratic: organizations 114; turn in organizations 15
Power 147, 155–157, 159–**160**, 235
PowerPoint as marketing act 26
Prague School 4
prioritisation of information 89
privacy and confidentiality 43
process(es): classificational 87, 90; conceptual 146; narrative 108, 146; non-transactional 146, 154–155; transactional 146, 154–155
production site 76
profit maximisation 31, 35
promenade 158
public administration: rule-based 100

public authorities: as bureaucratic organizations 106; professional practices of 104, 106, 115, 118
public authority: and affective situations 103; rules of 118

rank *173*; components *173*; figures *173*; groupings *173*; scale *173*; structure 184; text wholes *173*
rank scale zoom 172
rationalisation 9; of society 28
rationality: objectivity and 100; technical 26; and transparency 118
rational myths 26
recontextualisation 6; in social semiotics 27
register 16, 34representational changes 84
research: and giving back 44; on affect 101; collaboration(s) 44–45; ethnographic 55, 110; partnership 42
resemiotisation 55, 132; and assessing 192; and clinical and health promotion 27; and clinical information 69; of a health facility 27; idea of 27; objectives 56; and organization semiotics 68; practices 70; study of 15

salience: hierarchy 169, 170, **171**, 176; perceivable 184; in spatial texts *169*; in web texts *169*
salience types **171**; anti-primed salience **171**; idiosyncratic salience **171**; perceptual salience **171**; preferred idiosyncratic salience **171**; primed salience **171**; self-primed 176; self-primed idiosyncratic salience **171**; semiotic salience **171**
Saussure, Ferdinand de 5–6
search: by salience 177; dynamic eye scroll 182, 183; employee-assisted 179; goal-oriented 175; resting eye scroll 182; self-primed affinity 175; zooming in and out 182
search strategy: goal-oriented self-primed verbal search 180; online 180–182; self-primed idiosyncratic and affinity 176, 180; title word 181
semiotic: analysis 16, 55, 60, 105; design 167; diversity 54, 155; literature 4; text analysis 185

semiotic practices: and products 6; multimodal 4, 8
semiotic resources 13, 117; analyses of multiple 15; co-presence of 4; organizational 153; study of multimodal 28; understanding of 15
semiotics: definition of 1–2; commercial applications of 5; definition of 1; digital 35; structuralist 5
sequencing messages 92
sexual health 65; area of 33; confidentiality and 57; information 56–57, 60, 65, 234; issues 57; literacy 38
sexually transmittable infections (STIs) 57–60, 63
sexual relationships: diversity 64; and unintended pregnancy 59
shared service center (SSC) 124–125, 127–128, 131; employees of 132; management of 132
shop layouts and search strategies 174–177
social: and spatial realities 124; collectives 8–9, 32, 36; distance and contact 128; geometry 130, 156; meaning externalisations 3; media platform integration 86
sociality 2
social practices: and contextual variables 135; and meaning-making 126; and meanings 138
social semiotic(s) 5, 7, 24–28, 34, 45, 102, 122, 190–191, 210; actions 186; and advertising 7; and affective meanings 106; aim of 2; benefits of 39–40; and built environment 143; consulting effects of 40; and (con) texts 232; critical discourse analysis 35; definition of 2–3; difference from structuralist semiotics 5; educating effects of 39; elucidating effects of social semiotics 39; frame 190; in health care organizations 210; and linguistics 232; and meaning-making 76; and meaning-making in organizations 210; multimodal 3, 8, 12, 30, 74, 167; and multimodality 14, 167–168; and organization/management studies 238; and organization studies 25–27, 36; and practical feasibility of research 46; and practice 6, 77; practice 76, 92;

and Spatial Discourse Analysis 143; and texture 213, 214; toolbox of 34; tools of 118; as a way of studying meaning 2; of work environment 126
social semioticians and organization researchers 25
societal values 31, 33
society of organizations 1, 30
sociomateriality 2, 161
space: and organizational communication 122; and power relations 157; representational function of 146
space and interaction 122
spatial arrangements 2, 27, 88, 235
spatial design 146; and compositional meanings 157; field 126–128; genre 126; and interactional meaning 156; mode 126–127; and relational meaning 159; and representational meaning 154–155; social context 127; and social practice 126; tenor 126–128
Spatial Discourse Analysis 143–144, 148
spatial text(s): analysis of 146; contextual location 145; size of frame 145
spatiotemporal contexts 190
speech aspects 6
spoken language 27, 58, 68
SSC office layout 125
SSC *see* shared service center
stages of health resource production 58
standardisation 31, 215–216, 226, 234, 237
Starbucks: and brand identity 217; logo and new store design 218–220; logo stylization 220
statements: declarative 106; prescriptive 106
STI prevention 64
STIs *see* sexually transmittable infections
stratification of language 6
structural meaning of the layout 168
stylisation 213, 215–217, 219, 221; and cleansing 216; as identity cleansing 226; and identity loss 219
sustainability 33, 35, 112
Swedish Board of Agriculture 112
Swedish Geotechnical Institute 112, 114

246 *Index*

Swedish National Road and Transport Research Institute (VTI) 107–109, 114; and platform of values 109; signs of good employeeship 109
Systemic Functional Linguistics 126

Taylor, Frederick 28
technical demands as semiotic work 208
technical efficiency 10, 25
text-oriented affective analysis 106
textual layout 170, 183
textual systems: cohesion 168–169, 171–172; information structure 168–169, 173–176; thematic structure 168–169
textural traits of the body 223
texture(s): and capitalist demands 212; and cultural expectations 215; definition of 213, 214; and Getty Images 222; and legitimacy work 217; and materiality 213; in organizational identity 226; and regularity 214, 215; as semiotic resource 212–214, 225; and standardisation 212; and Starbucks logo 221; and texturisation in Starbucks 217; visual and material 222, 226, 227; visual-material 218; visual representation of 214
texturisation: and conveying authenticity 17; and digital technologies 227; implications of 225; as legitimacy work 215; and multimodality 215; in stock images 224
theme-rheme structure 174
transphobia 66

University of New South Wales in Sydney Australia (UNSW) 143–144, 149, 161; external circulation spaces 151; structural details of 149–150
UNSW *see* University of New South Wales in Sydney Australia
use of: colour and brand recognisability 85; images and affective meanings 104

value statements 38, 110
value words (*värdeord*) 99, 109–112; commitment 99, 108–109, 116; courage 99; openness 99, 108–109; respect 99, 108–109
verbal mode 11
viewer positioning 60; in *Yarning about Girls Business* 63
viewer positioning elements: attitude 61; contact 61; proximity 61
virtual artefact(s) 55, 76–78, 93; site of 76
visual: design and medical information 59; identification 76; mode 11; representation of clinical information 70; semiotic modalities 91; text 173
visual analysis tools: modality 60; narration and analysis 60; viewer positioning 60
visuals: and meaning-making 70; and sexual and reproductive health 17
VTI *see* Swedish National Road and Transport Research Institute (VTI)

WBA form 190, 192–194, 198, 200, 208–209
WBA *see* workplace-based assessment (WBA)
Weber, Max 28, 236
Weberian bureaucracy 236
webpage(s) 4, 75, *80–81*
website(s): Getty Images 222–225; FPNSW's 70; identity 87; infrastructure 93; of public authorities 99–100, 149, 157; university 34, 74, 88, 235, 237
workplace-based assessment (WBA): as opportunity for learning 210; form 190, 192; proforma 204, 208; purposes of 193–194
workspace and personalization 132
workspaces: and human interaction 162; material aspects of 124

Yarning about Girls Business 60, 62–67

zooming 176, 182–184, 220